JACKSON **LANZING**   COLLIN **KELLY**   MARCUS **TO**   IRMA **KNIIVILA**

JOYRIDE ™

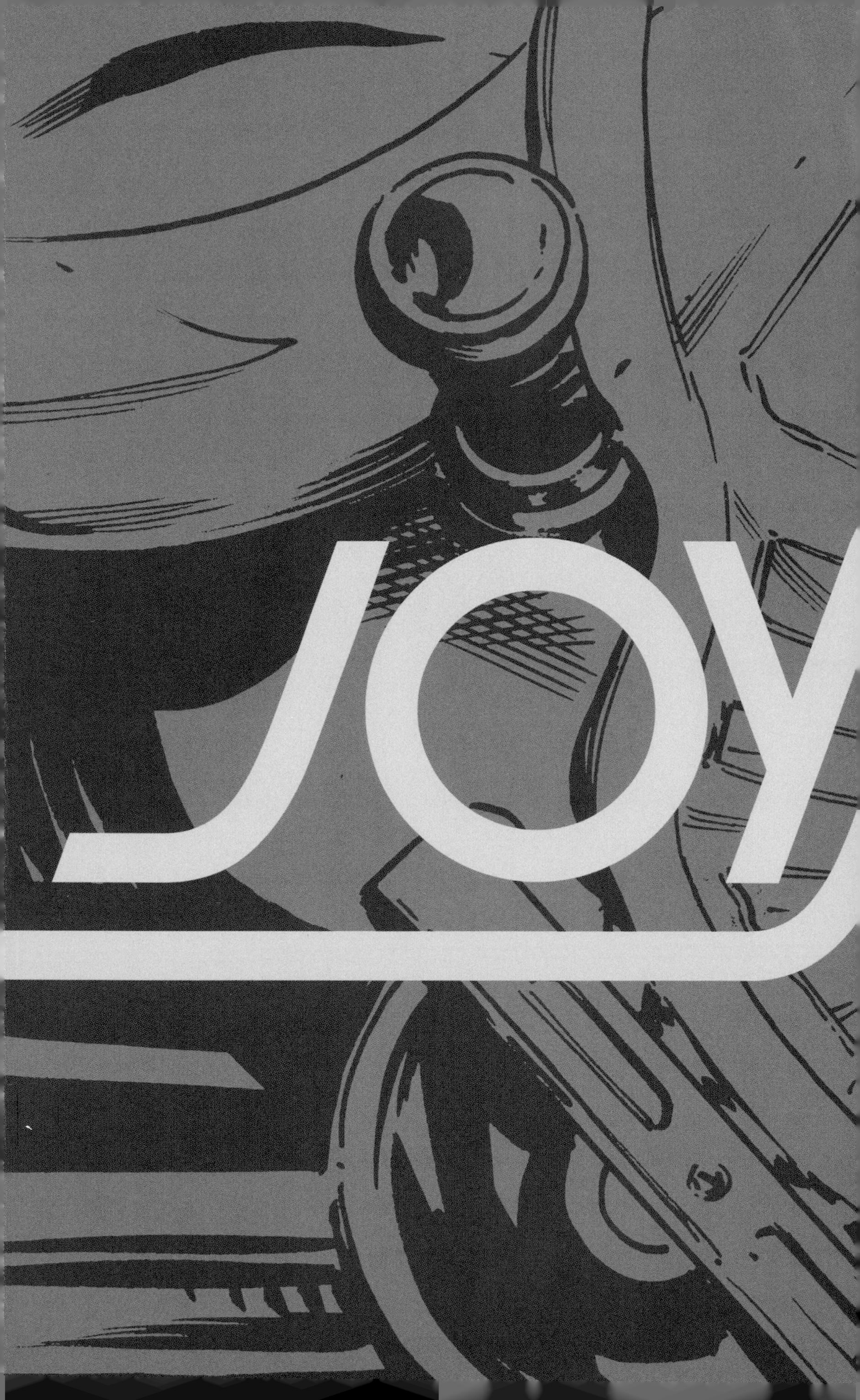
JOY

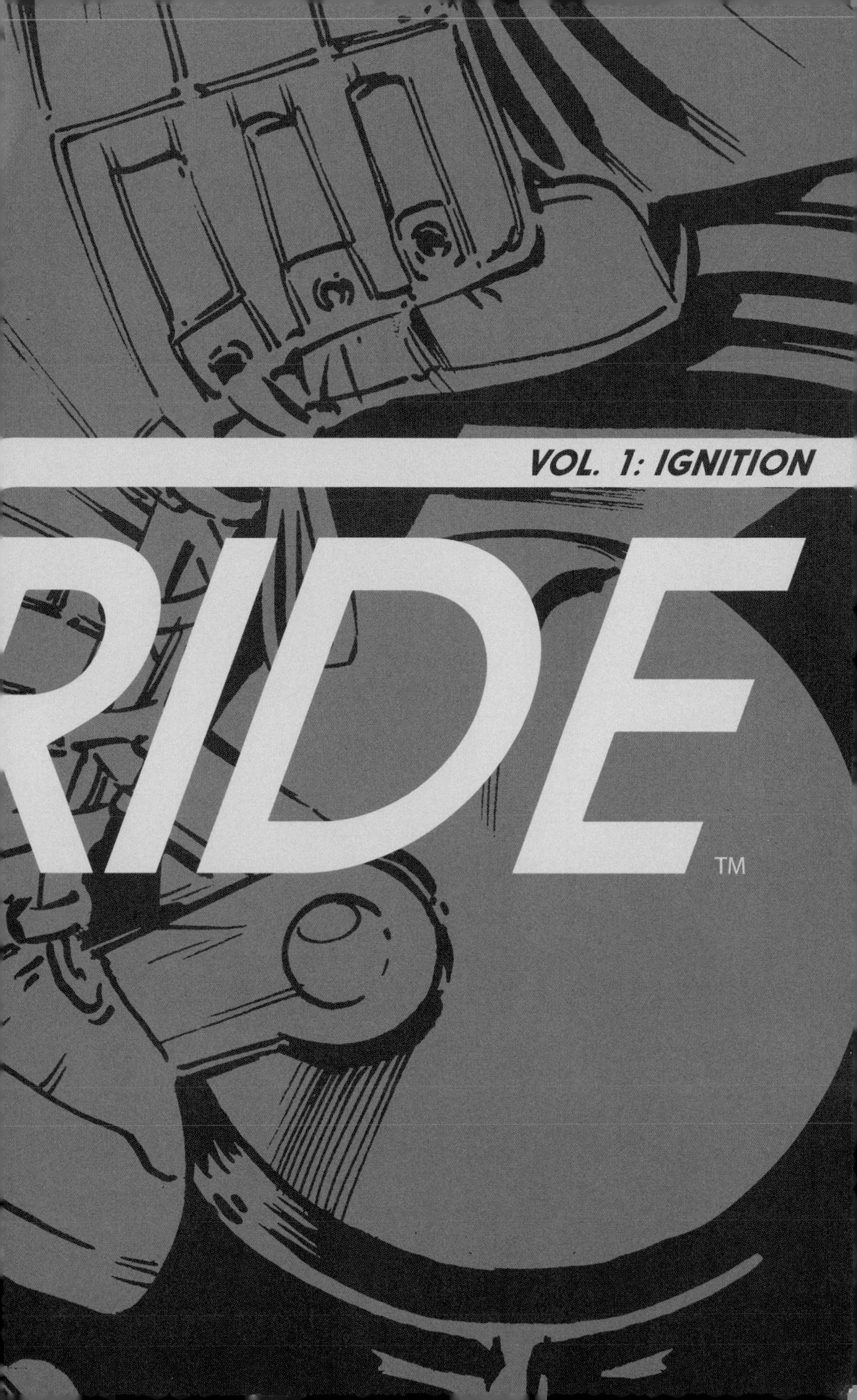

VOL. 1: IGNITION

RIDE™

Planet No. **18534261-BP**
Classification: **Beta-Prime**
Marker: **5-981-289-19822**

Planet No. **978326111-SP**
Classification: **Sigma-Prime**
Marker: **5-981-297-19744**

Planet No. **26448016**
Classification: **Gamma-Pri**
Marker: **5-981-291-16648**

Moon No. **18534261-BM1**
Classification: **Beta-Minor One**
Marker: **5-981-289-95782**

Moon No. **26448016-GM1**
Classification: **Gamma-Minor One**
Marker: **5-981-289-168741**

ROSS RICHIE CEO & Founder
MATT GAGNON Editor-in-Chief
FILIP SABLIK President of Publishing & Marketing
STEPHEN CHRISTY President of Development
LANCE KREITER VP of Licensing & Merchandising
PHIL BARBARO VP of Finance
BRYCE CARLSON Managing Editor
MEL CAYLO Marketing Manager
SCOTT NEWMAN Production Design Manager
IRENE BRADISH Operations Manager
SIERRA HAHN Senior Editor
DAFNA PLEBAN Editor, Talent Development
SHANNON WATTERS Editor
ERIC HARBURN Editor
WHITNEY LEOPARD Associate Editor
JASMINE AMIRI Associate Editor
CHRIS ROSA Associate Editor
ALEX GALER Associate Editor
CAMERON CHITTOCK Associate Editor
MARY GUMPORT Assistant Editor
MATTHEW LEVINE Assistant Editor
KELSEY DIETERICH Production Designer
JILLIAN CRAB Production Designer
MICHELLE ANKLEY Production Designer
GRACE PARK Production Design Assistant
AARON FERRARA Operations Coordinator
ELIZABETH LOUGHRIDGE Accounting Coordinator
STEPHANIE HOCUTT Social Media Coordinator
JOSÉ MEZA Sales Assistant
JAMES ARRIOLA Mailroom Assistant
HOLLY AITCHISON Operations Assistant
SAM KUSEK Direct Market Representative
AMBER PARKER Administrative Assistant

VISUAL RESEARCH ASSISTANT
DANI V

DESIGNER
SCOTT NEWMAN

ASSOCIATE EDITOR
CAMERON CHITTOCK

EDITOR
DAFNA PLEBAN

BOOM!
STUDIOS

JOYRIDE Volume One,
September 2016. Published
by BOOM! Studios, a division
of Boom Entertainment, Inc.
Joyride is ™ & © 2016 Jackson
Lanzing, Collin Kelly & Marcus To. Originally published
in single magazine form as JOYRIDE No. 1-4. ™ & © 2016
Jackson Lanzing, Collin Kelly & Marcus To. All Rights
Reserved. BOOM! Studios™ and the BOOM! Studios logo
are trademarks of Boom Entertainment, Inc., registered in
various countries and categories. All characters, events,
and institutions depicted herein are fictional. Any similarity
between any of the names, characters, persons, events,
and/or institutions in this publication to actual names,
characters, and persons, whether living or dead, events,
and/or institutions is unintended and purely coincidental.
BOOM! Studios does not read or accept unsolicited
submissions of ideas, stories, or artwork.

A catalog record of this book is available from OCLC and
from the BOOM! Studios website, www.boom-studios.com,
on the Librarians Page.

BOOM! Studios, 5670 Wilshire Boulevard, Suite 450,
Los Angeles, CA 90036-5679. Printed in Canada. First Printing.

ISBN: 978-1-60886-951-0, eISBN: 978-1-61398-622-6

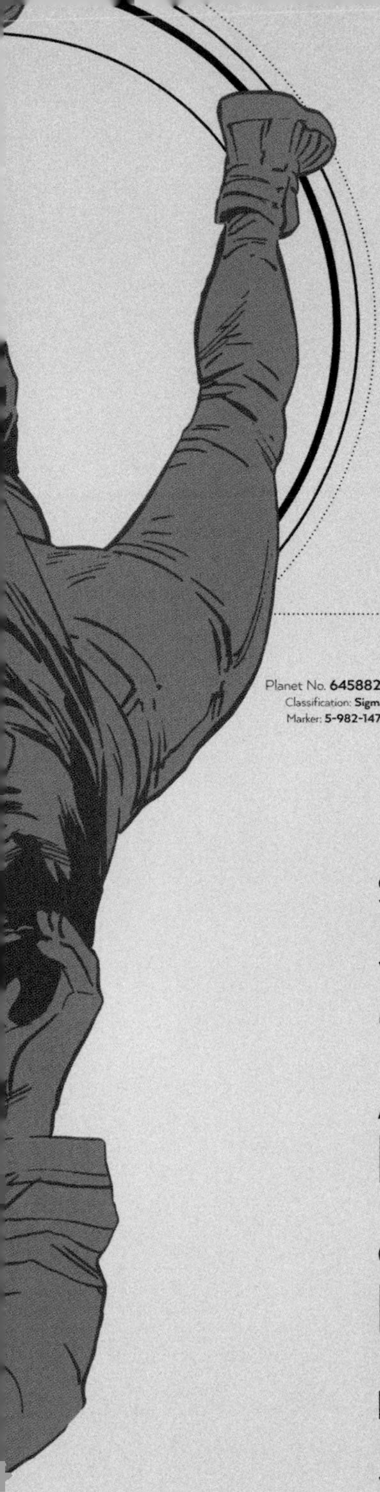

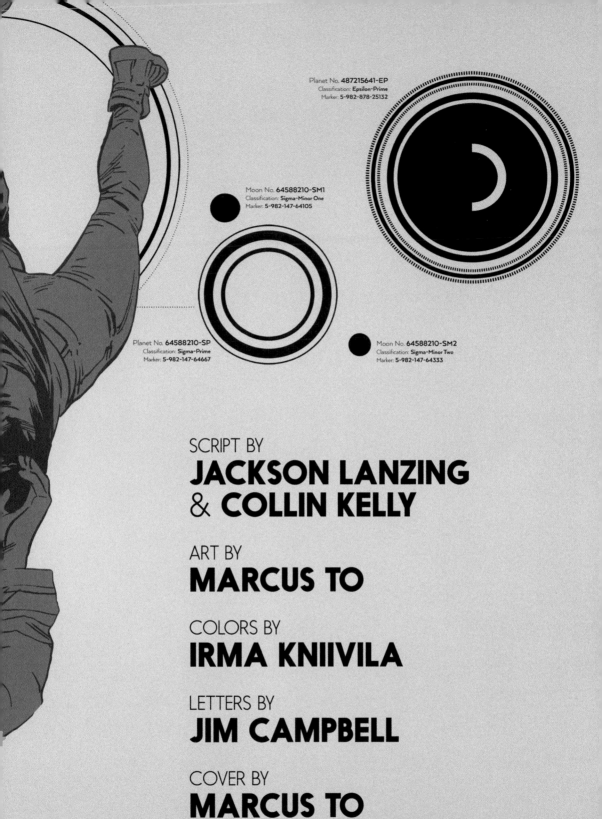

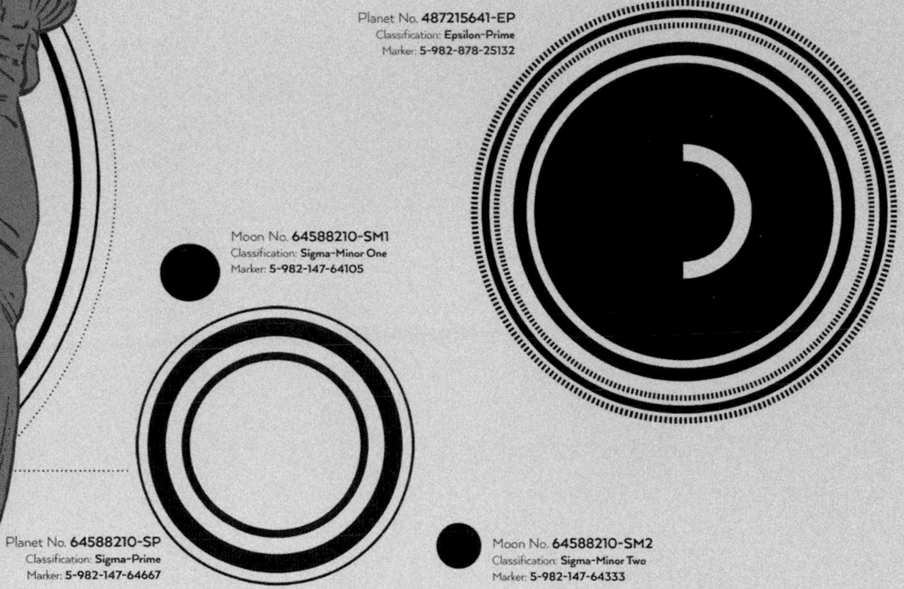
Planet No. 487215641-EP
Classification: Epsilon-Prime
Marker: 5-982-878-25132
Moon No. 64588210-SM1
Classification: Sigma-Minor One
Marker: 5-982-147-64105
Planet No. 64588210-SP
Classification: Sigma-Prime
Marker: 5-982-147-64667
Moon No. 64588210-SM2
Classification: Sigma-Minor Two
Marker: 5-982-147-64333

SCRIPT BY
JACKSON LANZING & COLLIN KELLY

ART BY
MARCUS TO

COLORS BY
IRMA KNIIVILA

LETTERS BY
JIM CAMPBELL

COVER BY
MARCUS TO
WITH COLORS BY **IRMA KNIIVILA**

CREATED BY
MARCUS TO, JACKSON LANZING & COLLIN KELLY

CHAPTER **ONE**

GRAND THEFT STARSHIP

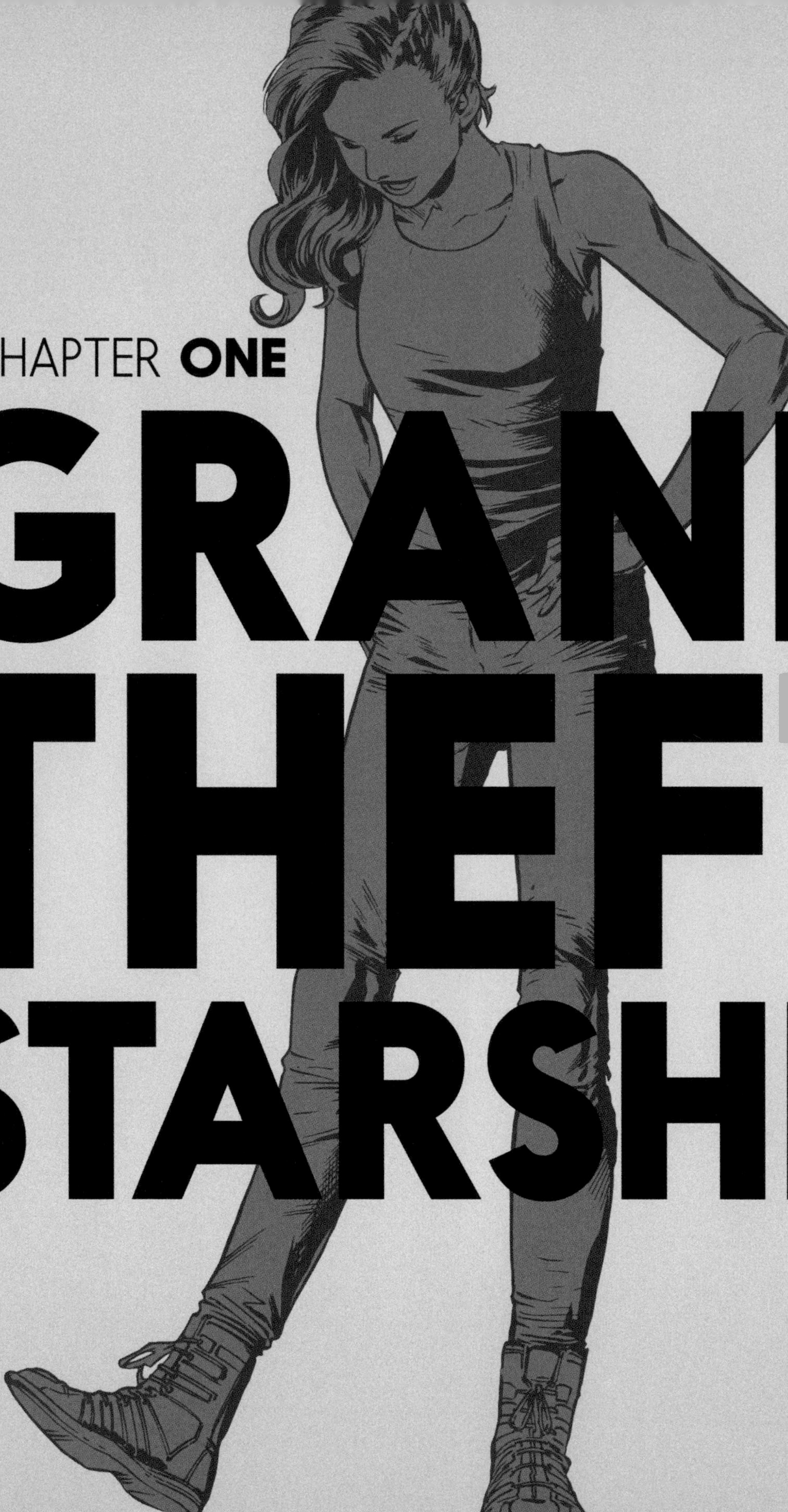

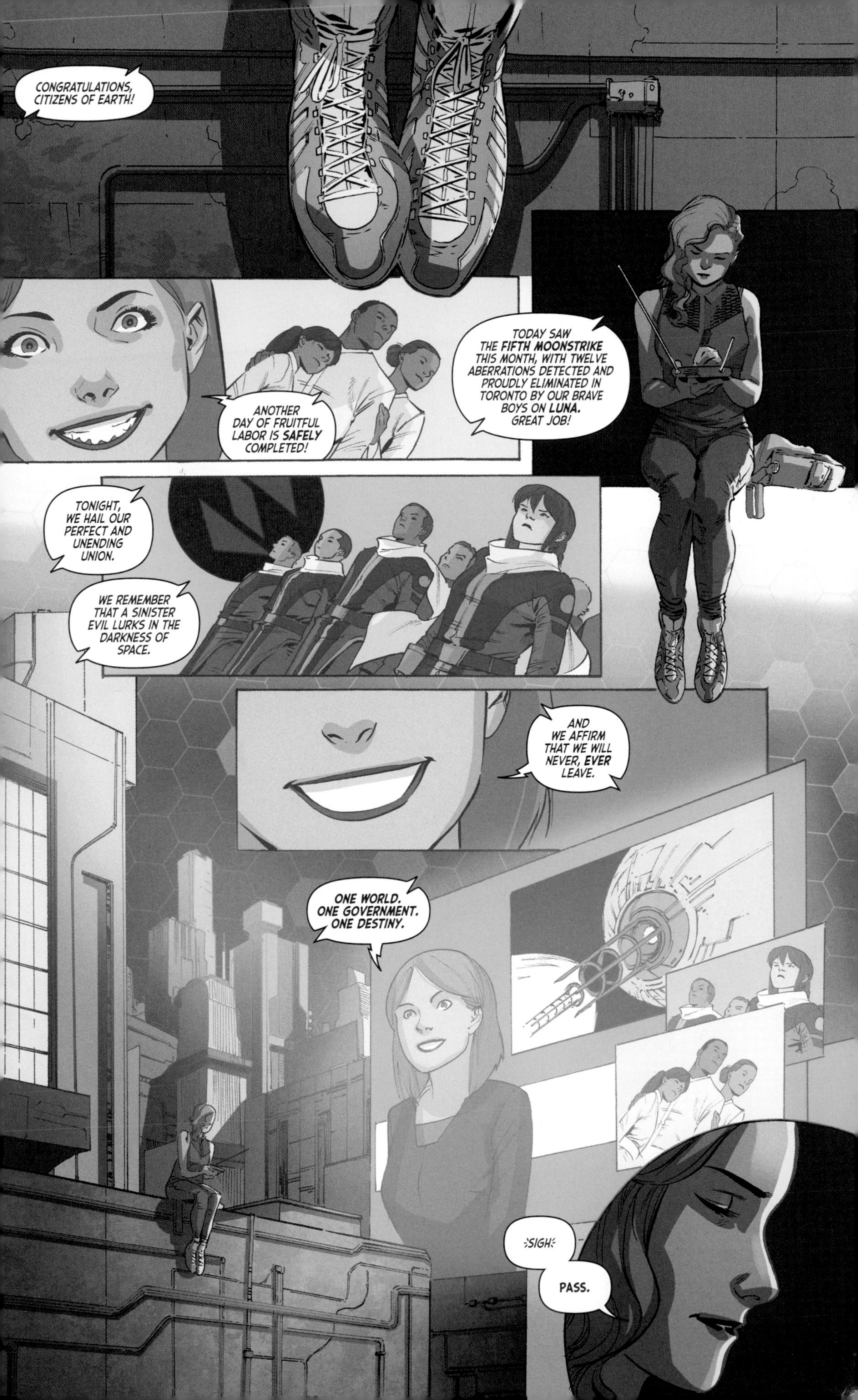
CONGRATULATIONS, CITIZENS OF EARTH!
ANOTHER DAY OF FRUITFUL LABOR IS SAFELY COMPLETED!
TODAY SAW THE FIFTH MOONSTRIKE THIS MONTH, WITH TWELVE ABERRATIONS DETECTED AND PROUDLY ELIMINATED IN TORONTO BY OUR BRAVE BOYS ON LUNA. GREAT JOB!
TONIGHT, WE HAIL OUR PERFECT AND UNENDING UNION.
WE REMEMBER THAT A SINISTER EVIL LURKS IN THE DARKNESS OF SPACE.
AND WE AFFIRM THAT WE WILL NEVER, EVER LEAVE.
ONE WORLD. ONE GOVERNMENT. ONE DESTINY.
SIGH
PASS.

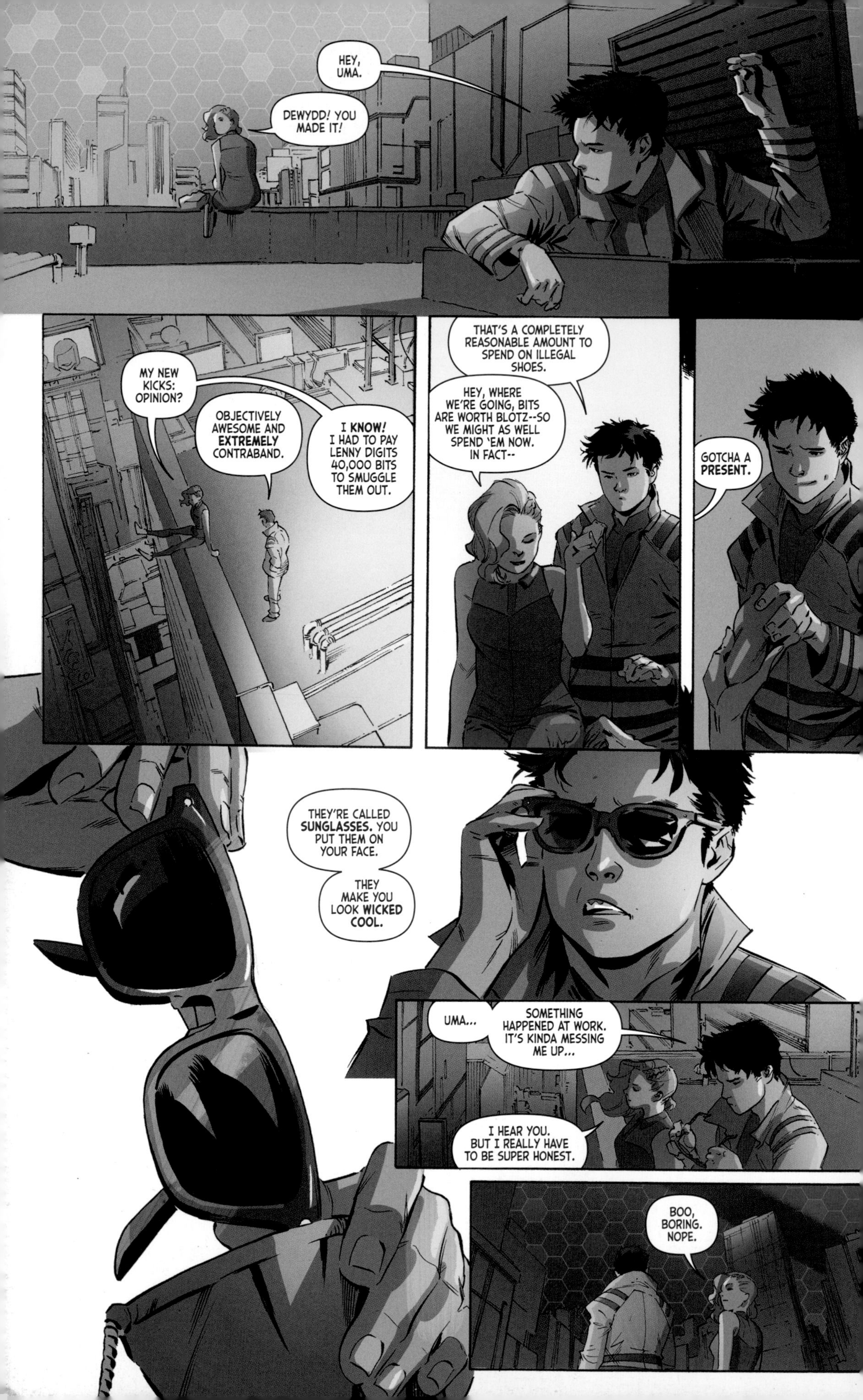
HEY, UMA.
DEWYDD! YOU MADE IT!
MY NEW KICKS: OPINION?
OBJECTIVELY AWESOME AND EXTREMELY CONTRABAND.
I KNOW! I HAD TO PAY LENNY DIGITS 40,000 BITS TO SMUGGLE THEM OUT.
THAT'S A COMPLETELY REASONABLE AMOUNT TO SPEND ON ILLEGAL SHOES.
HEY, WHERE WE'RE GOING, BITS ARE WORTH BLOTZ--SO WE MIGHT AS WELL SPEND 'EM NOW. IN FACT--
GOTCHA A PRESENT.
THEY'RE CALLED SUNGLASSES. YOU PUT THEM ON YOUR FACE.
THEY MAKE YOU LOOK WICKED COOL.
UMA...
SOMETHING HAPPENED AT WORK. IT'S KINDA MESSING ME UP...
I HEAR YOU. BUT I REALLY HAVE TO BE SUPER HONEST.
BOO, BORING. NOPE.

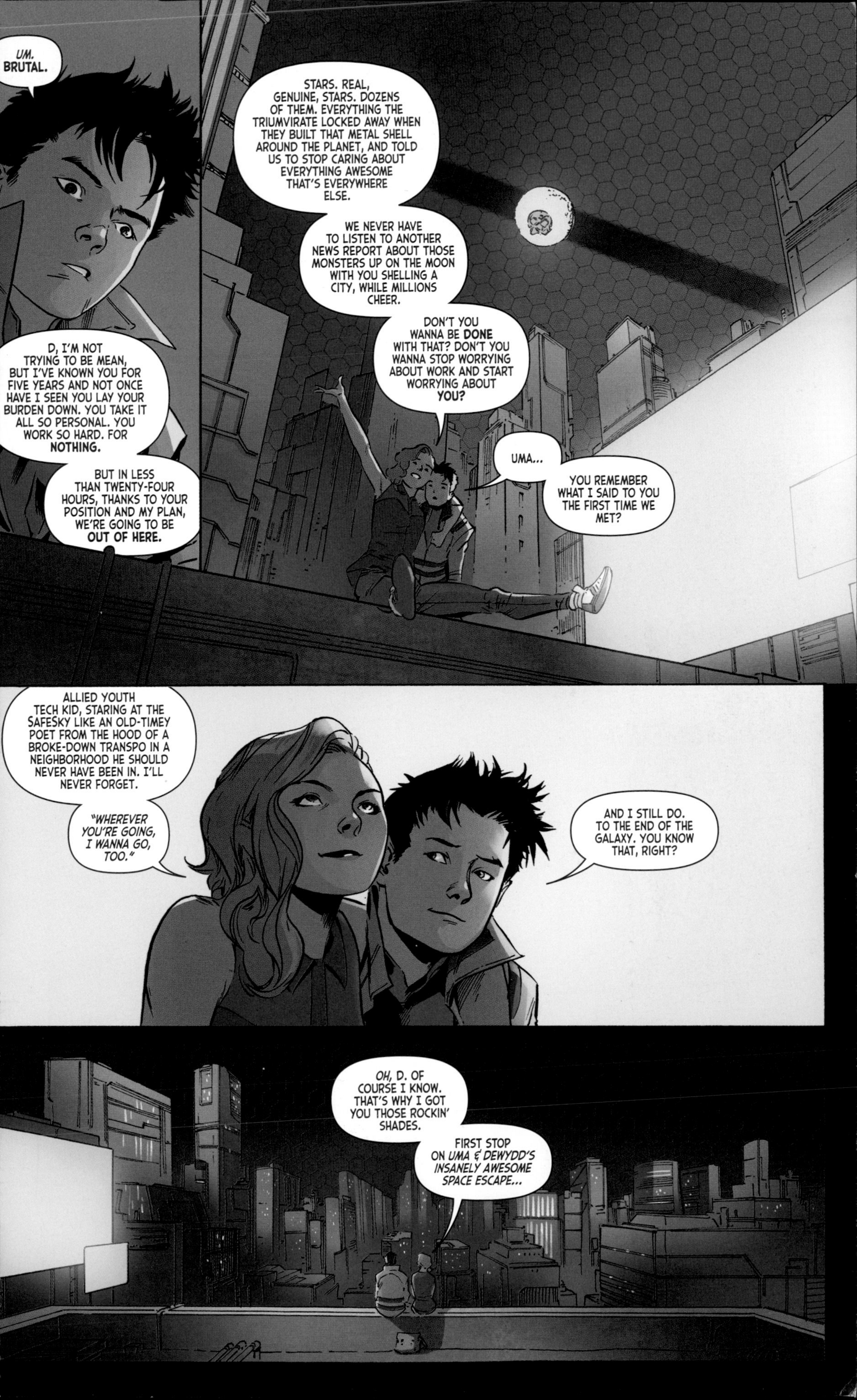
UM. BRUTAL.
STARS. REAL, GENUINE, STARS. DOZENS OF THEM. EVERYTHING THE TRIUMVIRATE LOCKED AWAY WHEN THEY BUILT THAT METAL SHELL AROUND THE PLANET, AND TOLD US TO STOP CARING ABOUT EVERYTHING AWESOME THAT'S EVERYWHERE ELSE.
WE NEVER HAVE TO LISTEN TO ANOTHER NEWS REPORT ABOUT THOSE MONSTERS UP ON THE MOON WITH YOU SHELLING A CITY, WHILE MILLIONS CHEER.
DON'T YOU WANNA BE **DONE** WITH THAT? DON'T YOU WANNA STOP WORRYING ABOUT WORK AND START WORRYING ABOUT **YOU?**
D, I'M NOT TRYING TO BE MEAN, BUT I'VE KNOWN YOU FOR FIVE YEARS AND NOT ONCE HAVE I SEEN YOU LAY YOUR BURDEN DOWN. YOU TAKE IT ALL SO PERSONAL. YOU WORK SO HARD. FOR **NOTHING.**
BUT IN LESS THAN TWENTY-FOUR HOURS, THANKS TO YOUR POSITION AND MY PLAN, WE'RE GOING TO BE **OUT OF HERE.**
UMA...
YOU REMEMBER WHAT I SAID TO YOU THE FIRST TIME WE MET?
ALLIED YOUTH TECH KID, STARING AT THE SAFESKY LIKE AN OLD-TIMEY POET FROM THE HOOD OF A BROKE-DOWN TRANSPO IN A NEIGHBORHOOD HE SHOULD NEVER HAVE BEEN IN. I'LL NEVER FORGET.
"WHEREVER YOU'RE GOING, I WANNA GO, TOO."
AND I STILL DO. TO THE END OF THE GALAXY. YOU KNOW THAT, RIGHT?
OH, D. OF COURSE I KNOW. THAT'S WHY I GOT YOU THOSE ROCKIN' SHADES.
FIRST STOP ON *UMA & DEWYDD'S INSANELY AWESOME SPACE ESCAPE...*

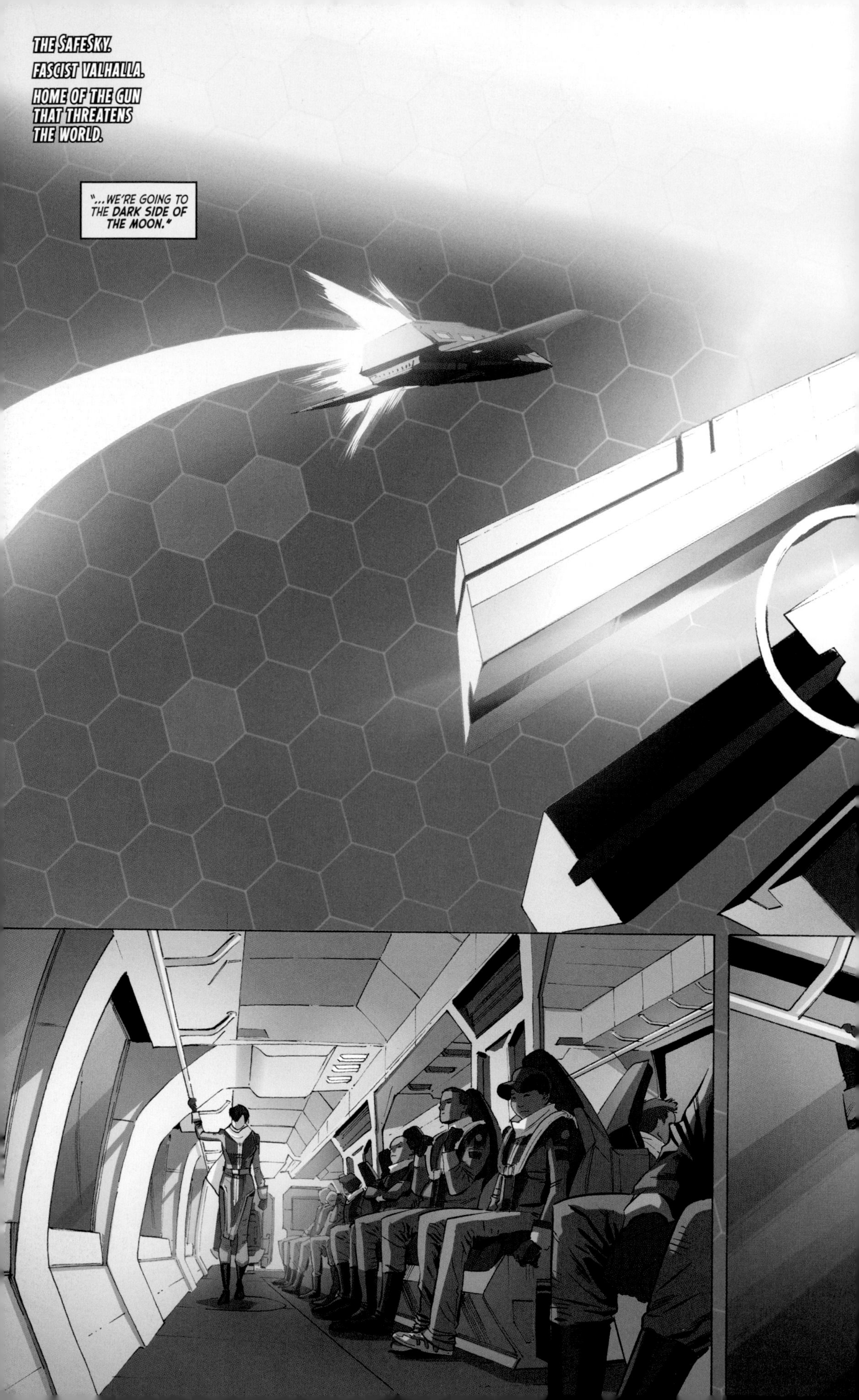
THE SAFESKY.
FASCIST VALHALLA.
HOME OF THE GUN THAT THREATENS THE WORLD.
"...WE'RE GOING TO THE DARK SIDE OF THE MOON."

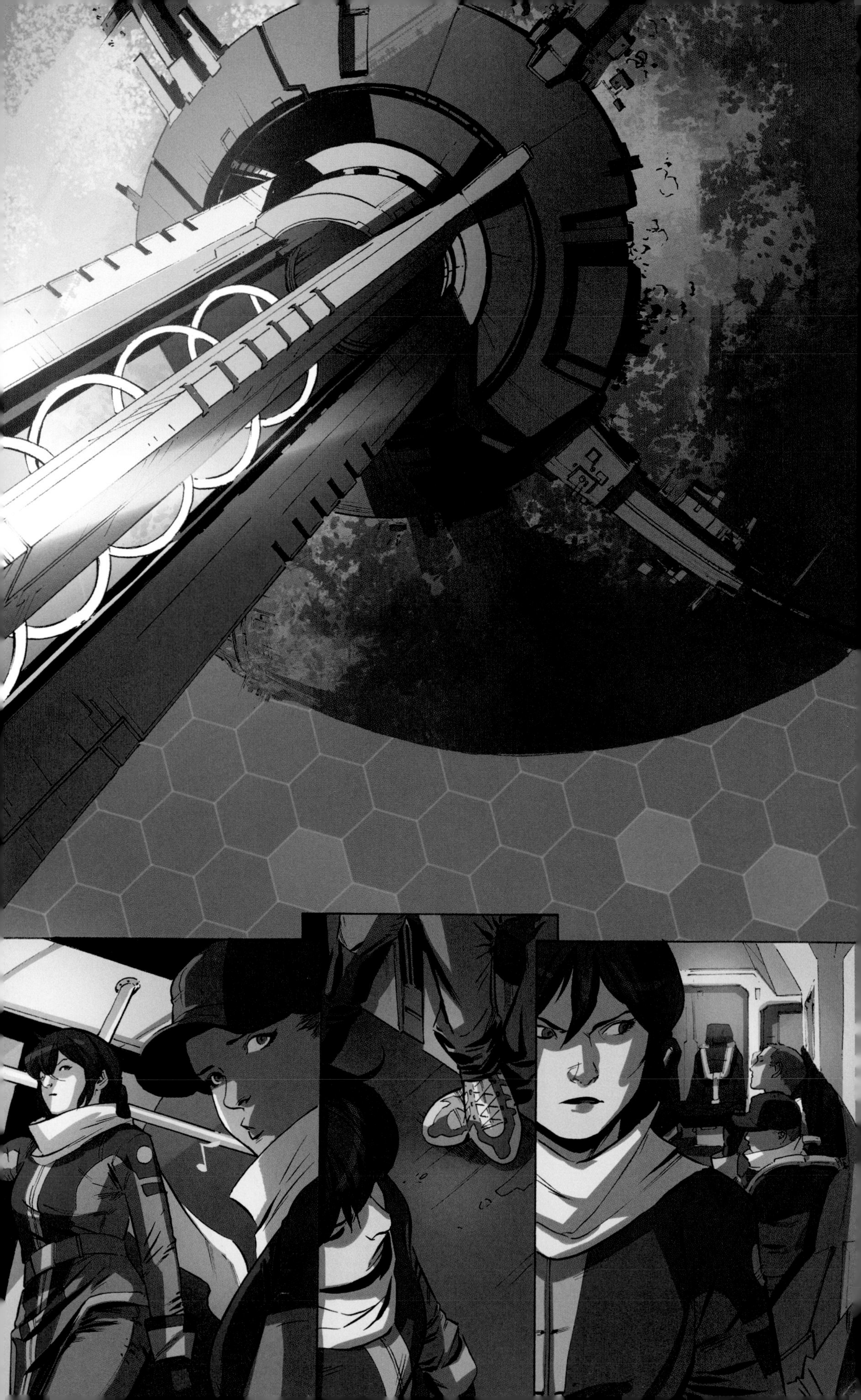

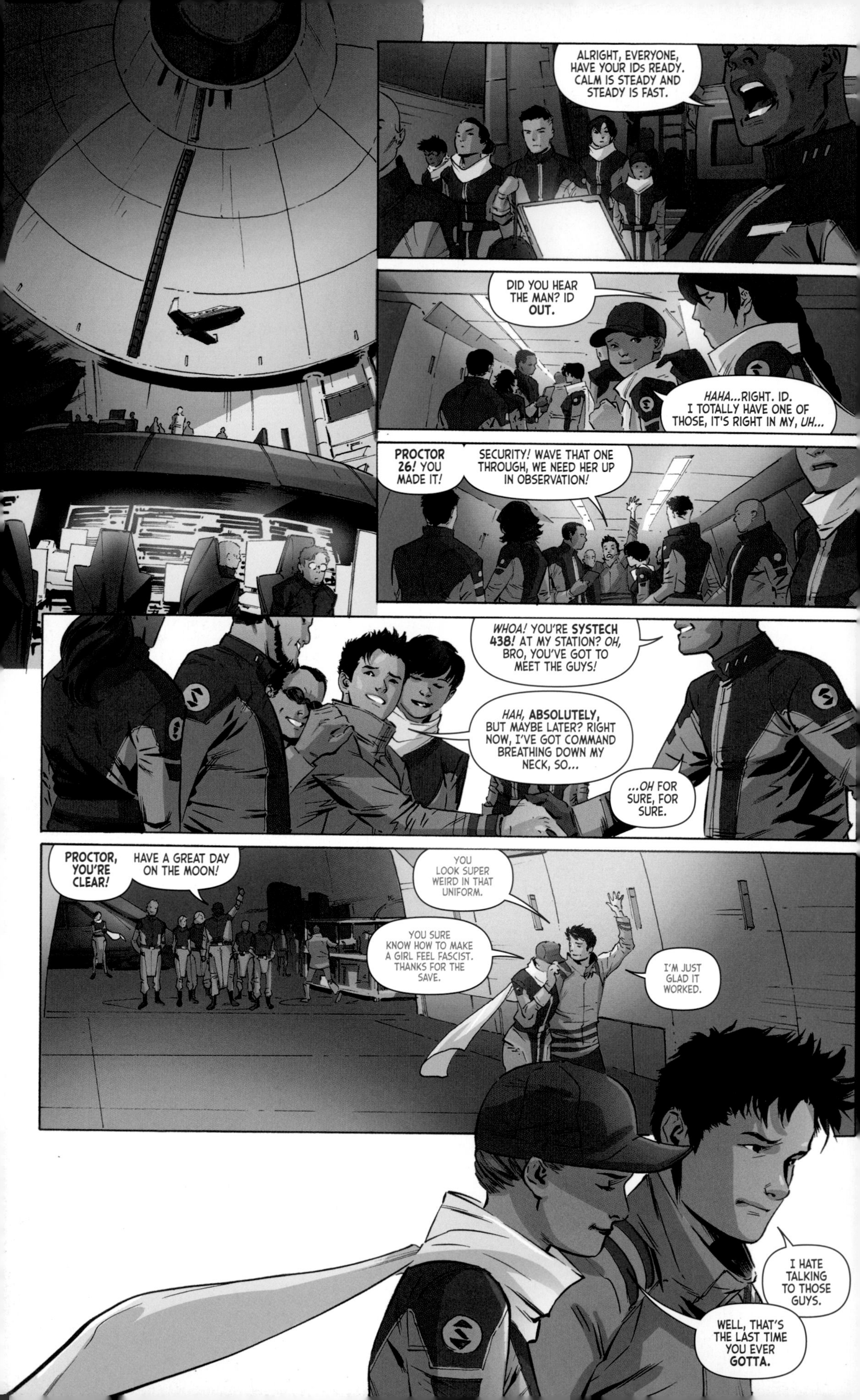
ALRIGHT, EVERYONE, HAVE YOUR IDs READY. CALM IS STEADY AND STEADY IS FAST.
DID YOU HEAR THE MAN? ID **OUT.**
*HAHA...*RIGHT. ID. I TOTALLY HAVE ONE OF THOSE, IT'S RIGHT IN MY, *UH...*
PROCTOR 26! YOU MADE IT!
SECURITY! WAVE THAT ONE THROUGH, WE NEED HER UP IN OBSERVATION!
WHOA! YOU'RE **SYSTECH 438!** AT MY STATION? *OH,* BRO, YOU'VE GOT TO MEET THE GUYS!
HAH, **ABSOLUTELY,** BUT MAYBE LATER? RIGHT NOW, I'VE GOT COMMAND BREATHING DOWN MY NECK, SO...
...OH FOR SURE, FOR SURE.
PROCTOR, YOU'RE CLEAR!
HAVE A GREAT DAY ON THE MOON!
YOU LOOK SUPER WEIRD IN THAT UNIFORM.
YOU SURE KNOW HOW TO MAKE A GIRL FEEL FASCIST. THANKS FOR THE SAVE.
I'M JUST GLAD IT WORKED.
I HATE TALKING TO THOSE GUYS.
WELL, THAT'S THE LAST TIME YOU EVER **GOTTA.**

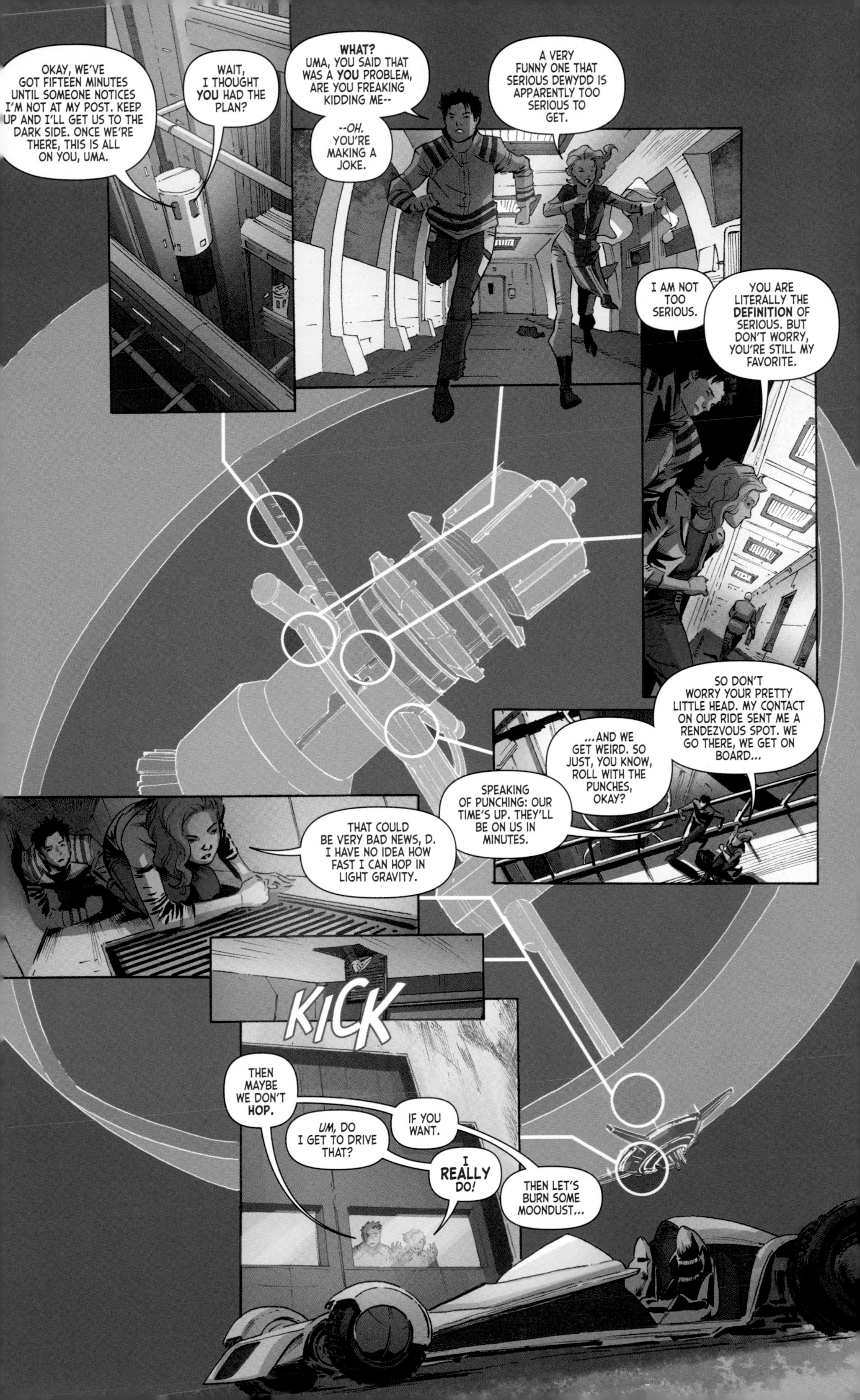
OKAY, WE'VE GOT FIFTEEN MINUTES UNTIL SOMEONE NOTICES I'M NOT AT MY POST. KEEP UP AND I'LL GET US TO THE DARK SIDE. ONCE WE'RE THERE, THIS IS ALL ON YOU, UMA.
WAIT, I THOUGHT **YOU** HAD THE PLAN?
WHAT? UMA, YOU SAID THAT WAS A **YOU** PROBLEM, ARE YOU FREAKING KIDDING ME--
--*OH.* YOU'RE MAKING A JOKE.
A VERY FUNNY ONE THAT SERIOUS DEWYDD IS APPARENTLY TOO SERIOUS TO GET.
I AM NOT TOO SERIOUS.
YOU ARE LITERALLY THE **DEFINITION** OF SERIOUS. BUT DON'T WORRY, YOU'RE STILL MY FAVORITE.
SO DON'T WORRY YOUR PRETTY LITTLE HEAD. MY CONTACT ON OUR RIDE SENT ME A RENDEZVOUS SPOT. WE GO THERE, WE GET ON BOARD...
...AND WE GET WEIRD. SO JUST, YOU KNOW, ROLL WITH THE PUNCHES, OKAY?
SPEAKING OF PUNCHING: OUR TIME'S UP. THEY'LL BE ON US IN MINUTES.
THAT COULD BE VERY BAD NEWS, D. I HAVE NO IDEA HOW FAST I CAN HOP IN LIGHT GRAVITY.
KICK
THEN MAYBE WE DON'T **HOP.**
UM, DO I GET TO DRIVE THAT?
IF YOU WANT.
I **REALLY** *DO!*
THEN LET'S BURN SOME MOONDUST...

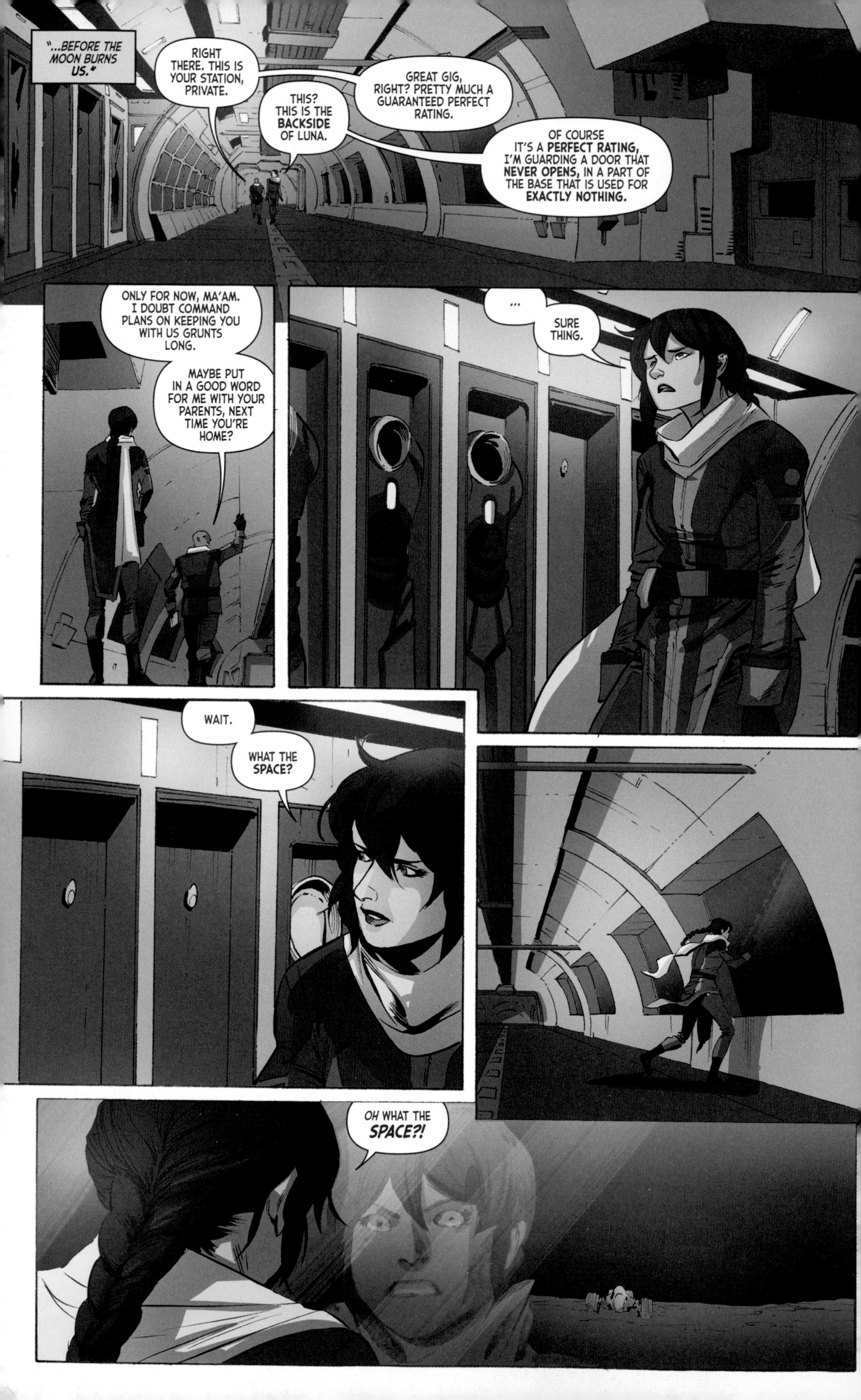
"...BEFORE THE MOON BURNS US."
RIGHT THERE. THIS IS YOUR STATION, PRIVATE.
THIS? THIS IS THE BACKSIDE OF LUNA.
GREAT GIG, RIGHT? PRETTY MUCH A GUARANTEED PERFECT RATING.
OF COURSE IT'S A PERFECT RATING, I'M GUARDING A DOOR THAT NEVER OPENS, IN A PART OF THE BASE THAT IS USED FOR EXACTLY NOTHING.
ONLY FOR NOW, MA'AM. I DOUBT COMMAND PLANS ON KEEPING YOU WITH US GRUNTS LONG.
MAYBE PUT IN A GOOD WORD FOR ME WITH YOUR PARENTS, NEXT TIME YOU'RE HOME?
...
SURE THING.
WAIT.
WHAT THE SPACE?
OH WHAT THE SPACE?!

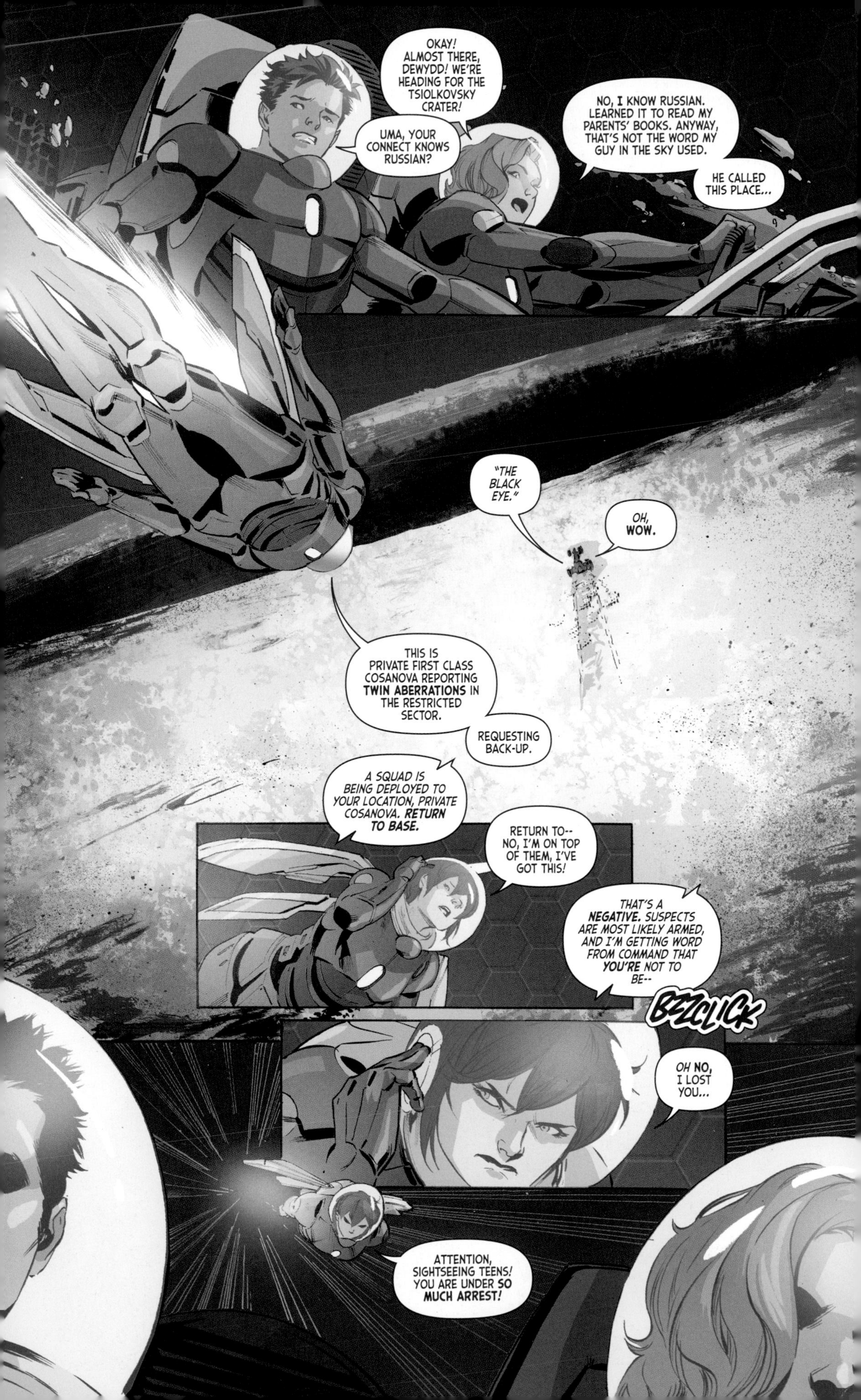
OKAY! ALMOST THERE, DEWYDD! WE'RE HEADING FOR THE TSIOLKOVSKY CRATER!
UMA, YOUR CONNECT KNOWS RUSSIAN?
NO, I KNOW RUSSIAN. LEARNED IT TO READ MY PARENTS' BOOKS. ANYWAY, THAT'S NOT THE WORD MY GUY IN THE SKY USED.
HE CALLED THIS PLACE...
"THE BLACK EYE."
OH, WOW.
THIS IS PRIVATE FIRST CLASS COSANOVA REPORTING TWIN ABERRATIONS IN THE RESTRICTED SECTOR.
REQUESTING BACK-UP.
A SQUAD IS BEING DEPLOYED TO YOUR LOCATION, PRIVATE COSANOVA. RETURN TO BASE.
RETURN TO-- NO, I'M ON TOP OF THEM, I'VE GOT THIS!
THAT'S A NEGATIVE. SUSPECTS ARE MOST LIKELY ARMED, AND I'M GETTING WORD FROM COMMAND THAT YOU'RE NOT TO BE--
BZZCLICK
OH NO, I LOST YOU...
ATTENTION, SIGHTSEEING TEENS! YOU ARE UNDER SO MUCH ARREST!

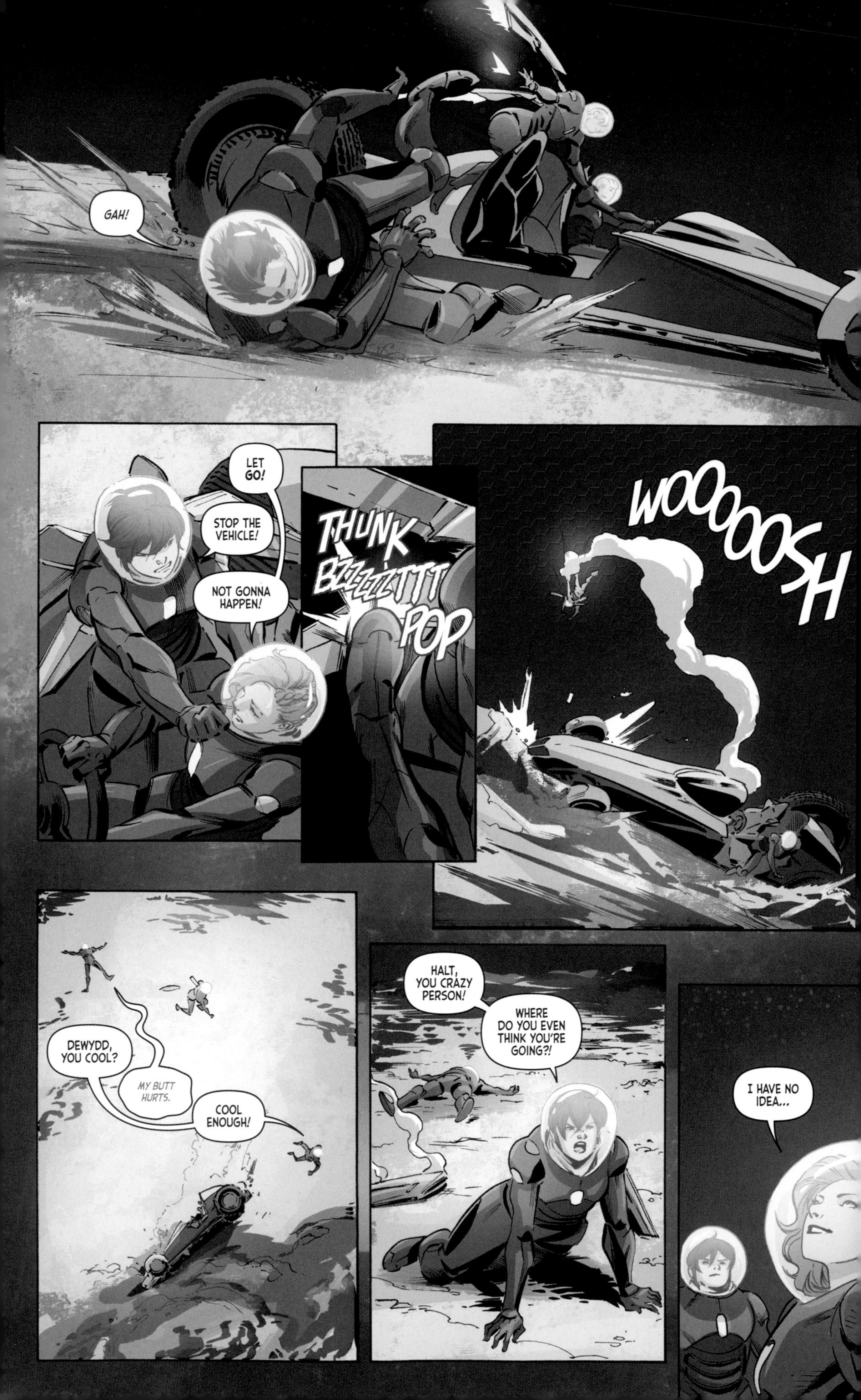
GAH!
LET GO!
STOP THE VEHICLE!
NOT GONNA HAPPEN!
THUNK
BZZZZZTTTT
POP
WOOOOOOSH
DEWYDD, YOU COOL?
MY BUTT HURTS.
COOL ENOUGH!
HALT, YOU CRAZY PERSON!
WHERE DO YOU EVEN THINK YOU'RE GOING?!
I HAVE NO IDEA...

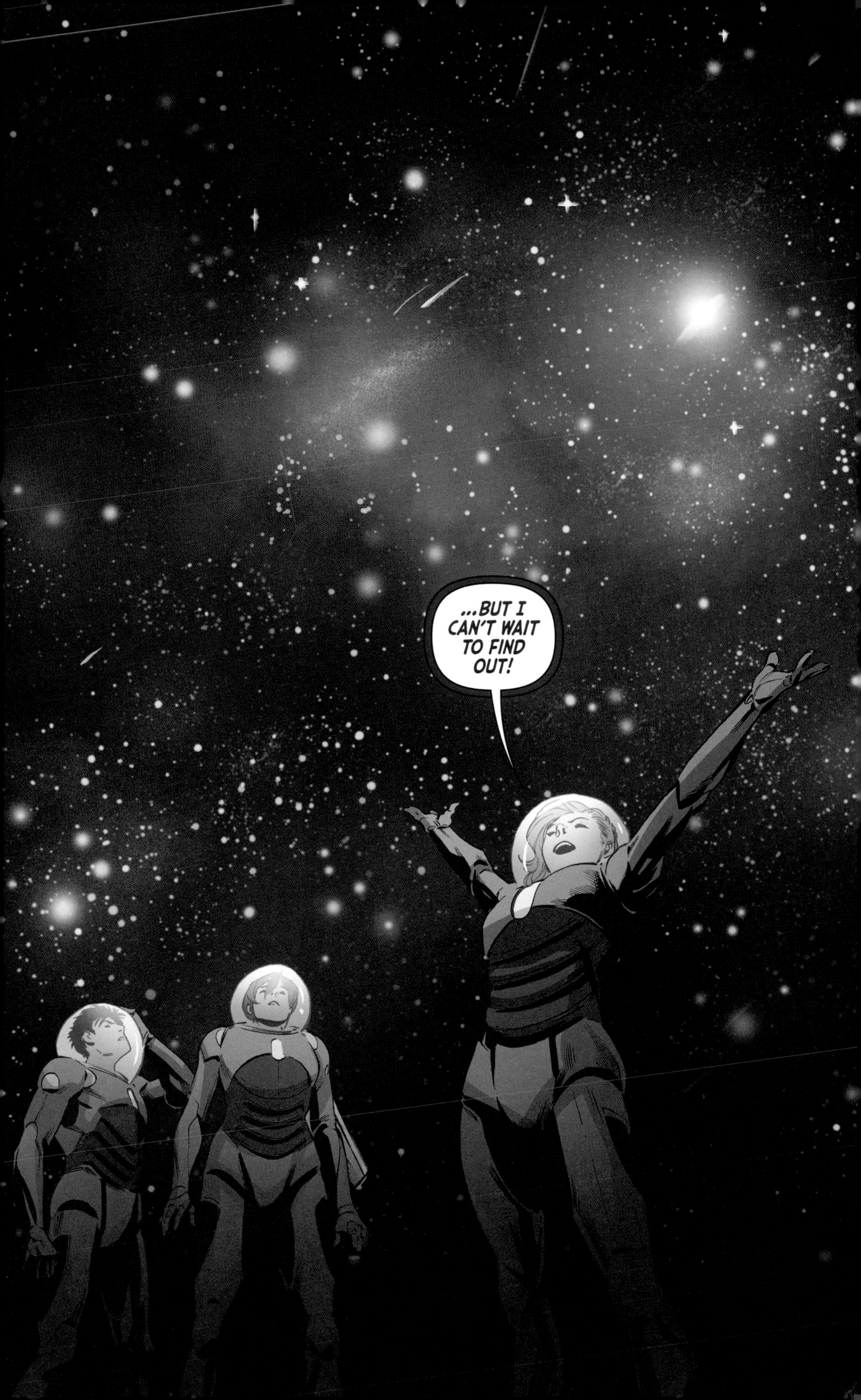
...BUT I CAN'T WAIT TO FIND OUT!

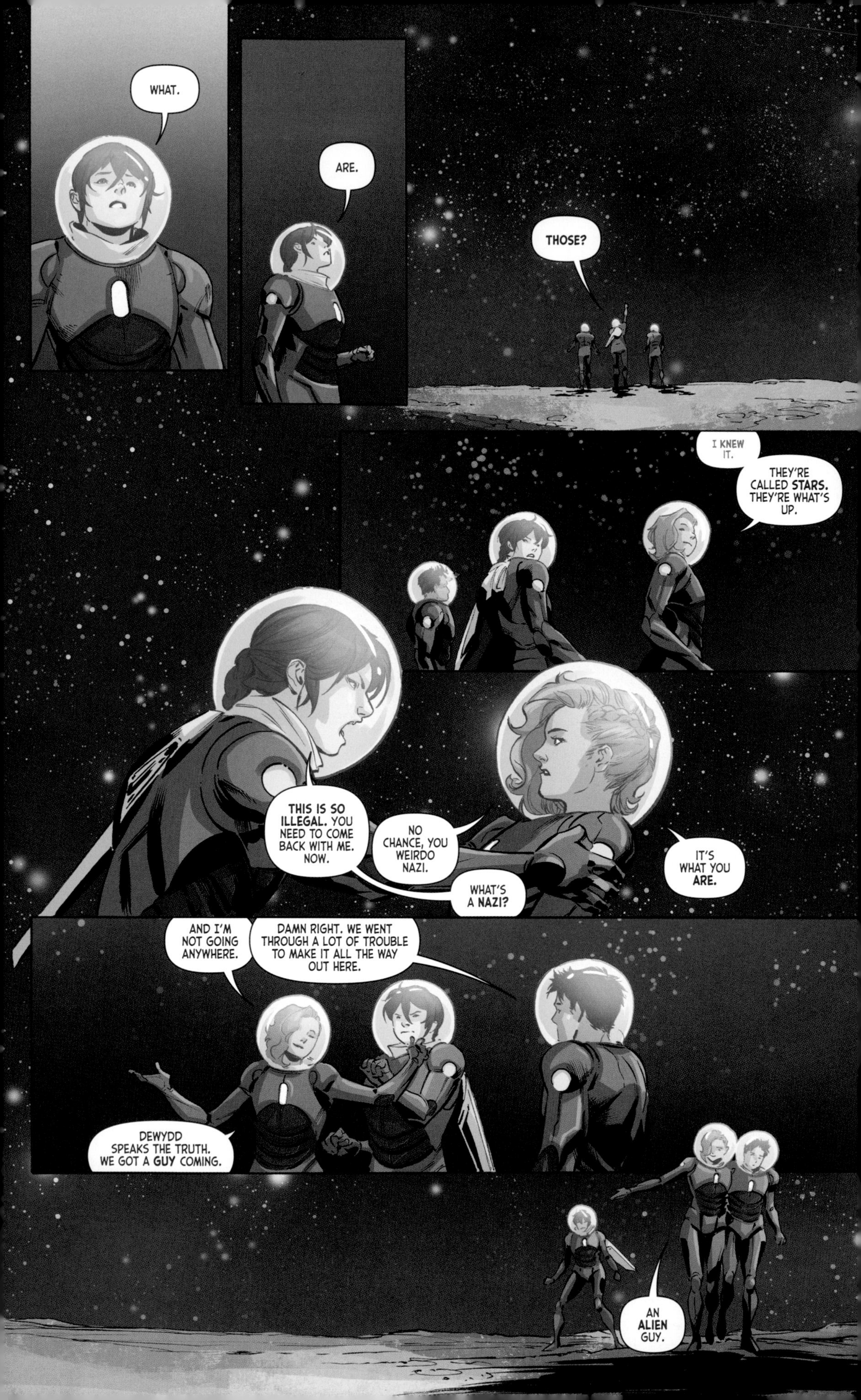
WHAT.
ARE.
THOSE?
I KNEW IT.
THEY'RE CALLED STARS. THEY'RE WHAT'S UP.
THIS IS SO ILLEGAL. YOU NEED TO COME BACK WITH ME. NOW.
NO CHANCE, YOU WEIRDO NAZI.
WHAT'S A NAZI?
IT'S WHAT YOU ARE.
AND I'M NOT GOING ANYWHERE.
DAMN RIGHT. WE WENT THROUGH A LOT OF TROUBLE TO MAKE IT ALL THE WAY OUT HERE.
DEWYDD SPEAKS THE TRUTH. WE GOT A GUY COMING.
AN ALIEN GUY.

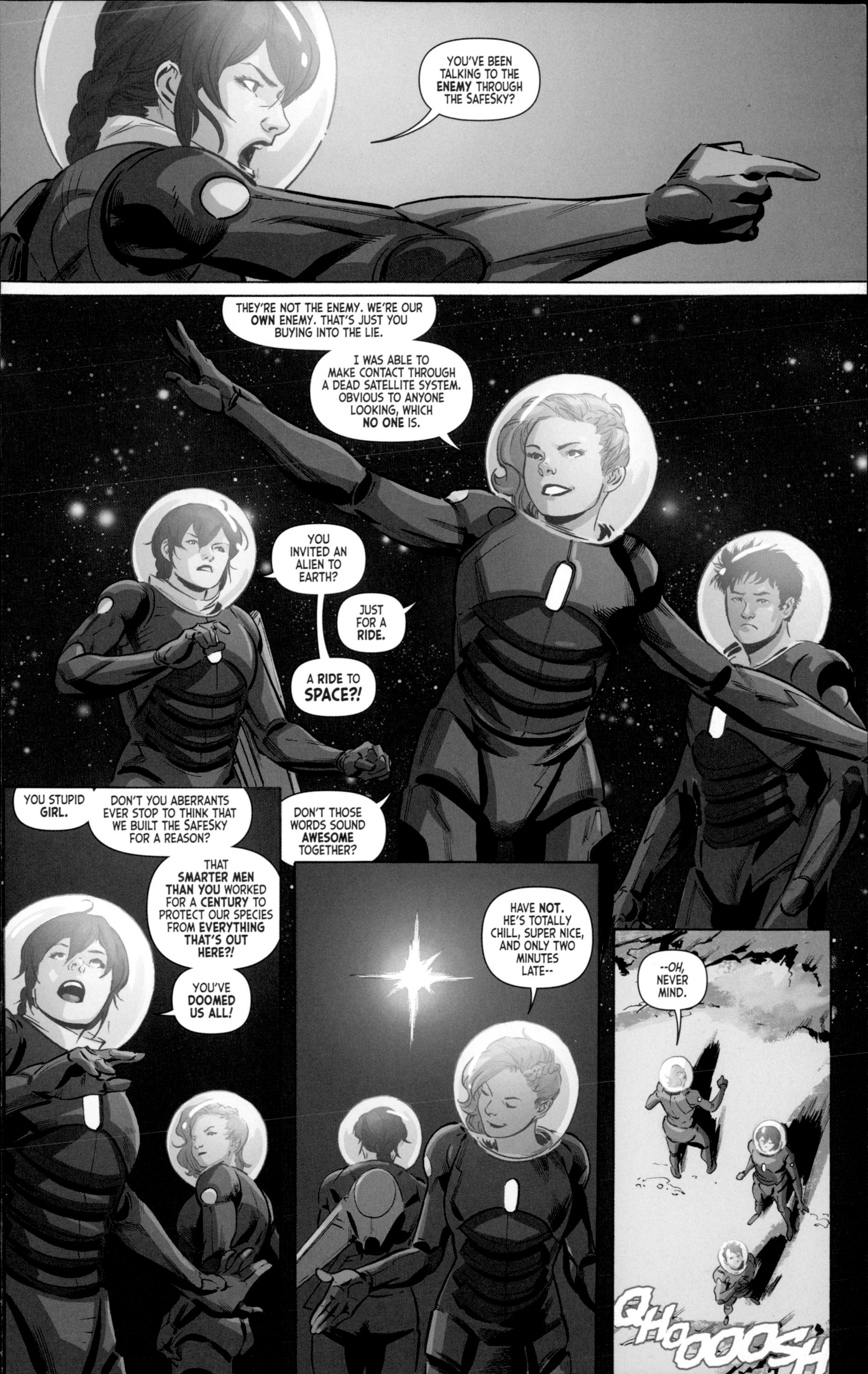

YOU'VE BEEN TALKING TO THE **ENEMY** THROUGH THE SAFESKY?
THEY'RE NOT THE ENEMY. WE'RE OUR **OWN** ENEMY. THAT'S JUST YOU BUYING INTO THE LIE.
I WAS ABLE TO MAKE CONTACT THROUGH A DEAD SATELLITE SYSTEM. OBVIOUS TO ANYONE LOOKING, WHICH **NO ONE** IS.
YOU INVITED AN ALIEN TO EARTH?
JUST FOR A **RIDE.**
A **RIDE** TO **SPACE?!**
YOU STUPID **GIRL.**
DON'T YOU ABERRANTS EVER STOP TO THINK THAT WE BUILT THE SAFESKY FOR A REASON?
THAT **SMARTER MEN THAN YOU** WORKED FOR A **CENTURY** TO PROTECT OUR SPECIES FROM **EVERYTHING THAT'S OUT HERE?!**
YOU'VE **DOOMED US ALL!**
DON'T THOSE WORDS SOUND **AWESOME** TOGETHER?
HAVE **NOT.** HE'S TOTALLY CHILL, SUPER NICE, AND ONLY TWO MINUTES LATE--
--OH, NEVER MIND.
QHOOOOSH

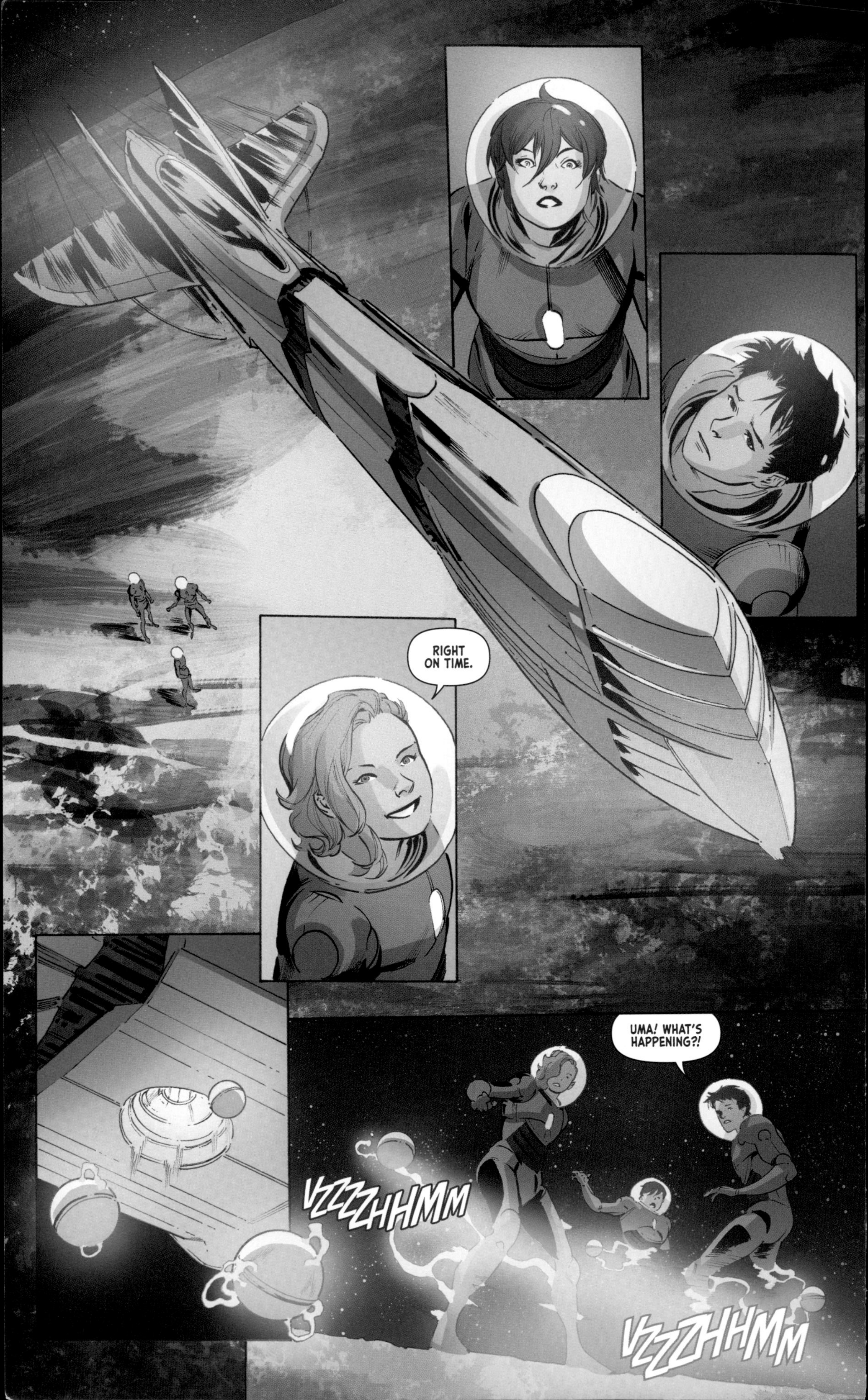
RIGHT ON TIME.
UMA! WHAT'S HAPPENING?!
VZZZZHHMMM
VZZZHHMMM

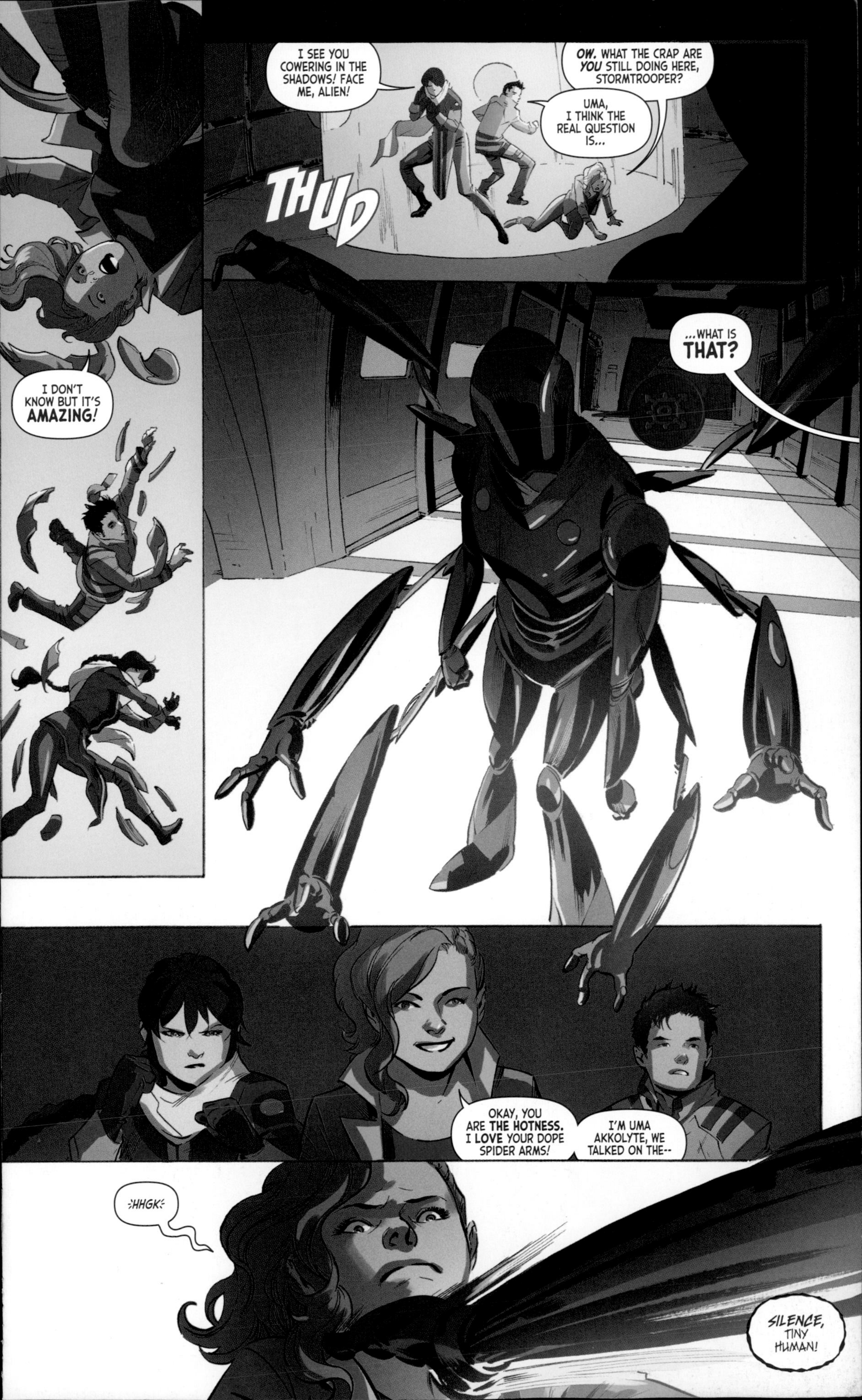
I SEE YOU COWERING IN THE SHADOWS! FACE ME, ALIEN!
OW. WHAT THE CRAP ARE YOU STILL DOING HERE, STORMTROOPER?
UMA, I THINK THE REAL QUESTION IS...
THUD
...WHAT IS THAT?
I DON'T KNOW BUT IT'S AMAZING!
OKAY, YOU ARE THE HOTNESS. I LOVE YOUR DOPE SPIDER ARMS!
I'M UMA AKKOLYTE, WE TALKED ON THE--
HHGK
SILENCE, TINY HUMAN!

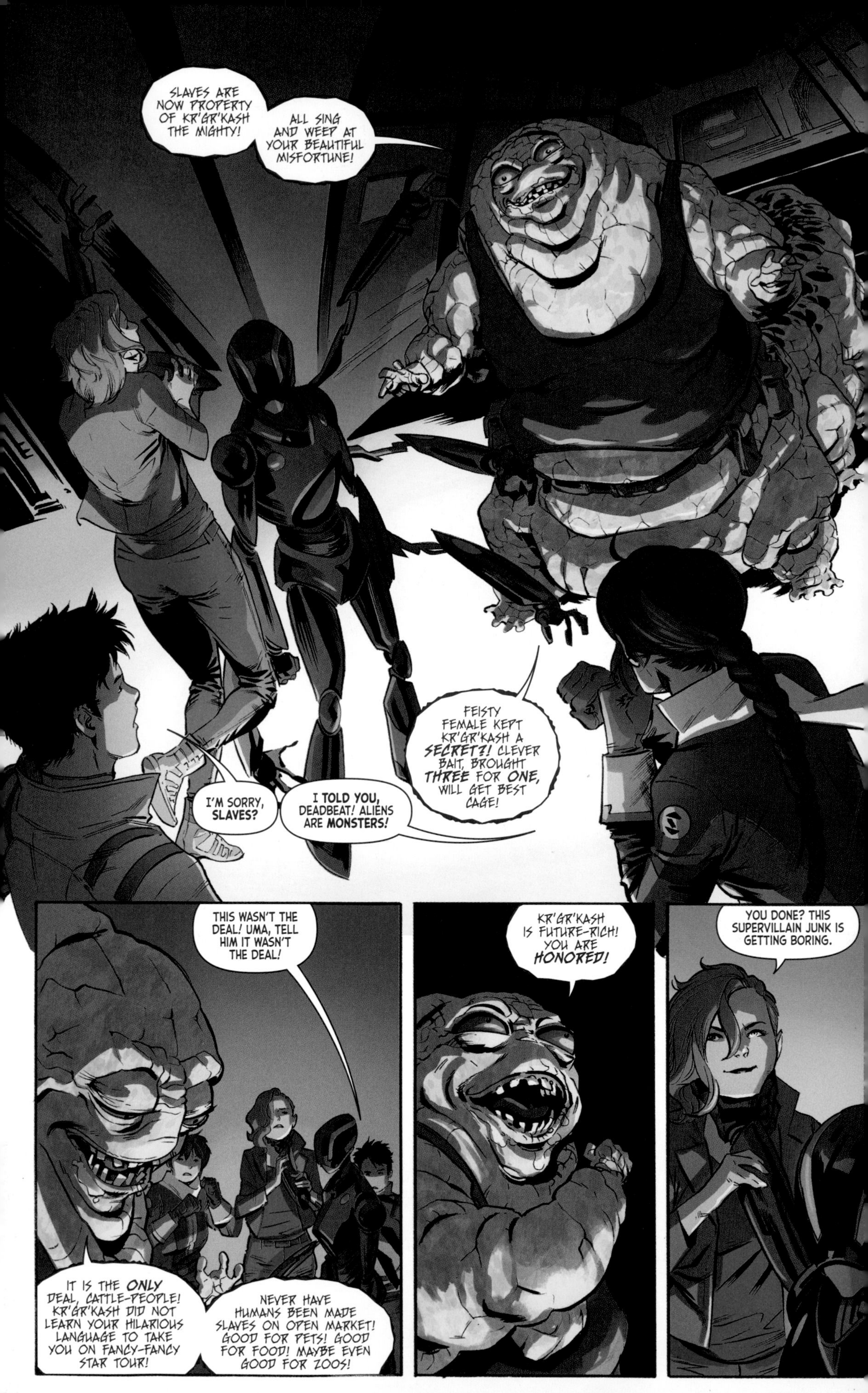
SLAVES ARE NOW PROPERTY OF KR'GR'KASH THE MIGHTY!
ALL SING AND WEEP AT YOUR BEAUTIFUL MISFORTUNE!
FEISTY FEMALE KEPT KR'GR'KASH A SECRET?! CLEVER BAIT, BROUGHT THREE FOR ONE, WILL GET BEST CAGE!
I'M SORRY, SLAVES?
I TOLD YOU, DEADBEAT! ALIENS ARE MONSTERS!
THIS WASN'T THE DEAL! UMA, TELL HIM IT WASN'T THE DEAL!
IT IS THE ONLY DEAL, CATTLE-PEOPLE! KR'GR'KASH DID NOT LEARN YOUR HILARIOUS LANGUAGE TO TAKE YOU ON FANCY-FANCY STAR TOUR!
NEVER HAVE HUMANS BEEN MADE SLAVES ON OPEN MARKET! GOOD FOR PETS! GOOD FOR FOOD! MAYBE EVEN GOOD FOR ZOOS!
KR'GR'KASH IS FUTURE-RICH! YOU ARE HONORED!
YOU DONE? THIS SUPERVILLAIN JUNK IS GETTING BORING.

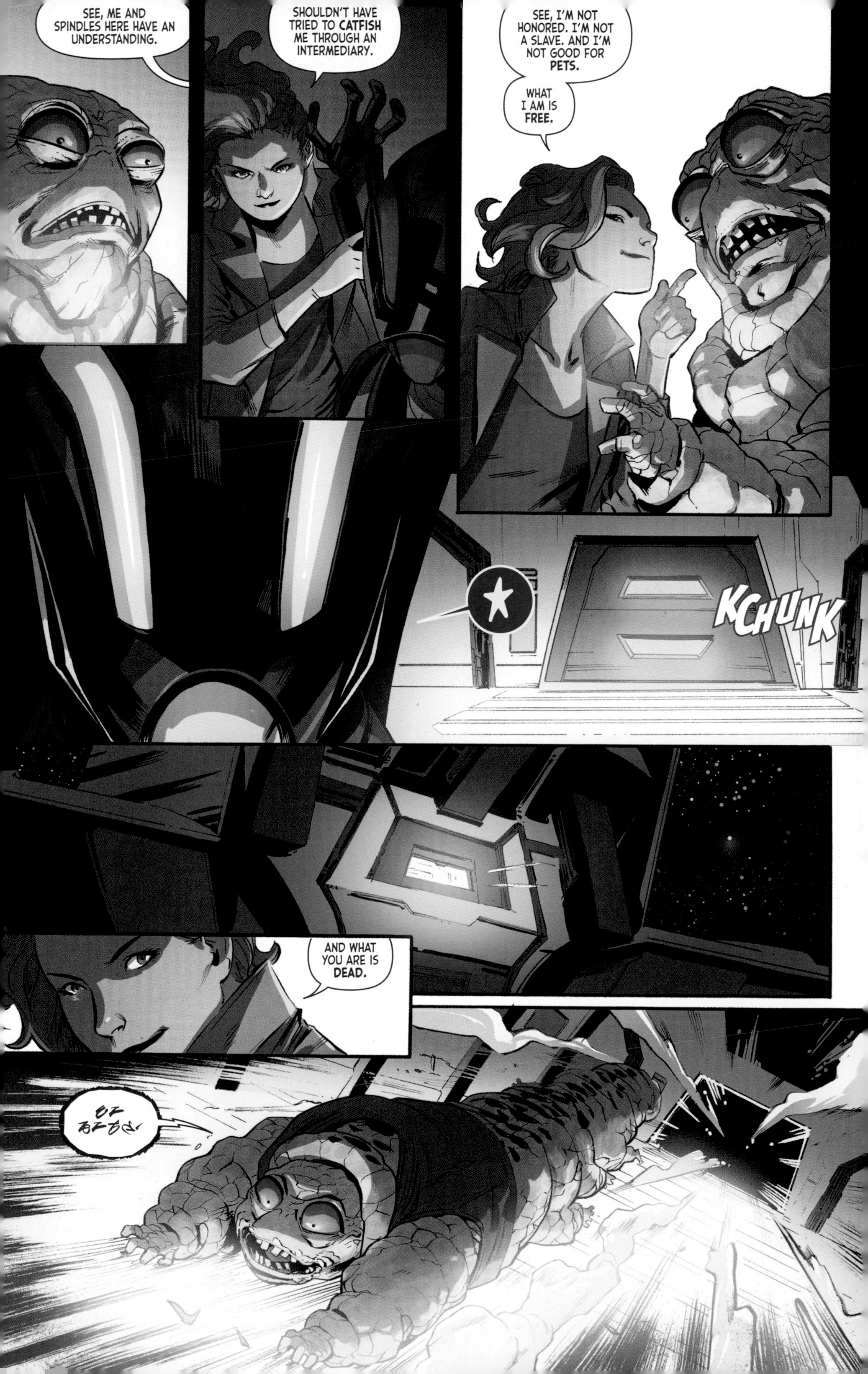
SEE, ME AND SPINDLES HERE HAVE AN UNDERSTANDING.
SHOULDN'T HAVE TRIED TO CATFISH ME THROUGH AN INTERMEDIARY.
SEE, I'M NOT HONORED. I'M NOT A SLAVE. AND I'M NOT GOOD FOR PETS.
WHAT I AM IS FREE.
KCHUNK
AND WHAT YOU ARE IS DEAD.

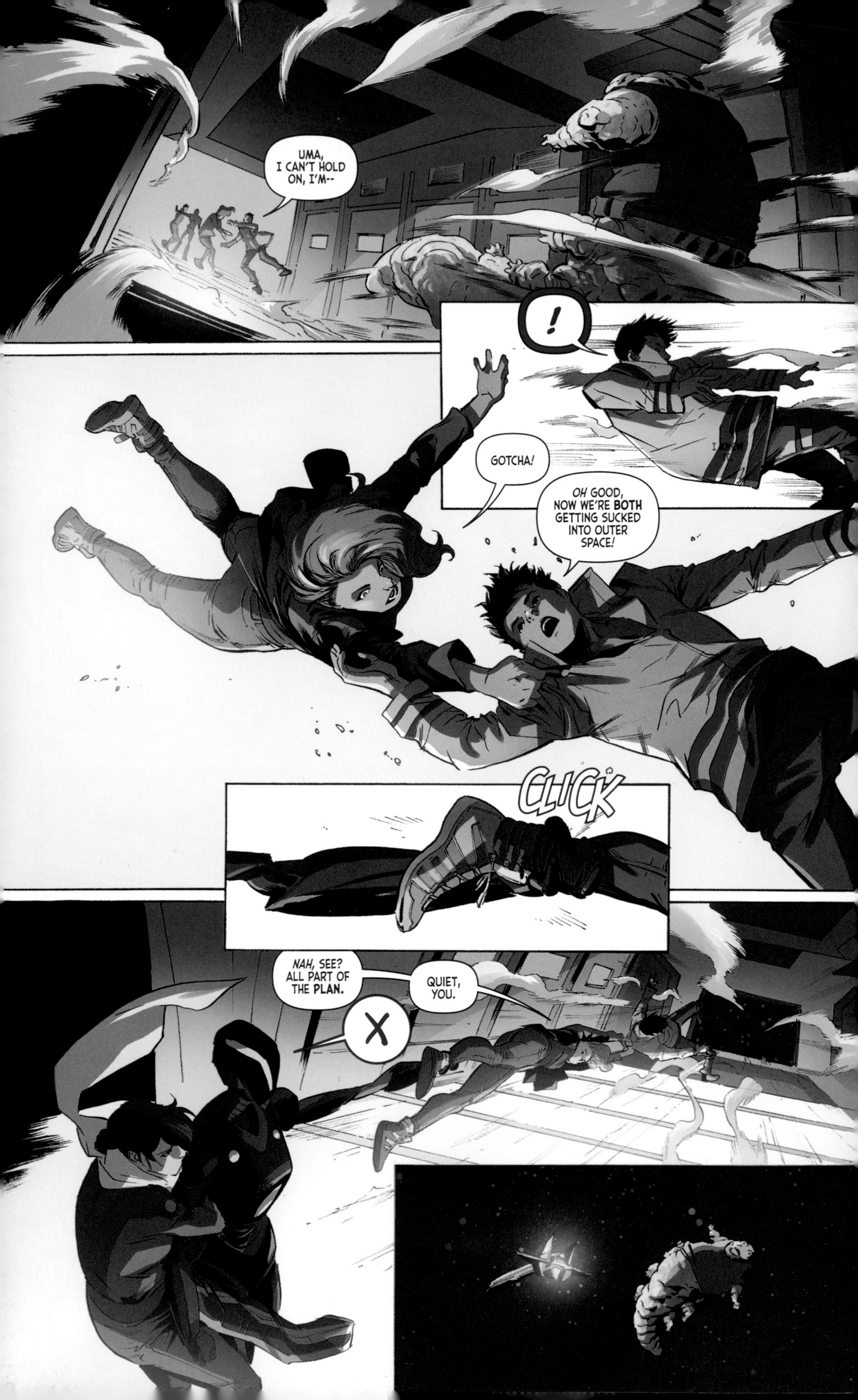
UMA, I CAN'T HOLD ON, I'M--
!
GOTCHA!
OH GOOD, NOW WE'RE BOTH GETTING SUCKED INTO OUTER SPACE!
CLICK
NAH, SEE? ALL PART OF THE PLAN.
QUIET, YOU.
X

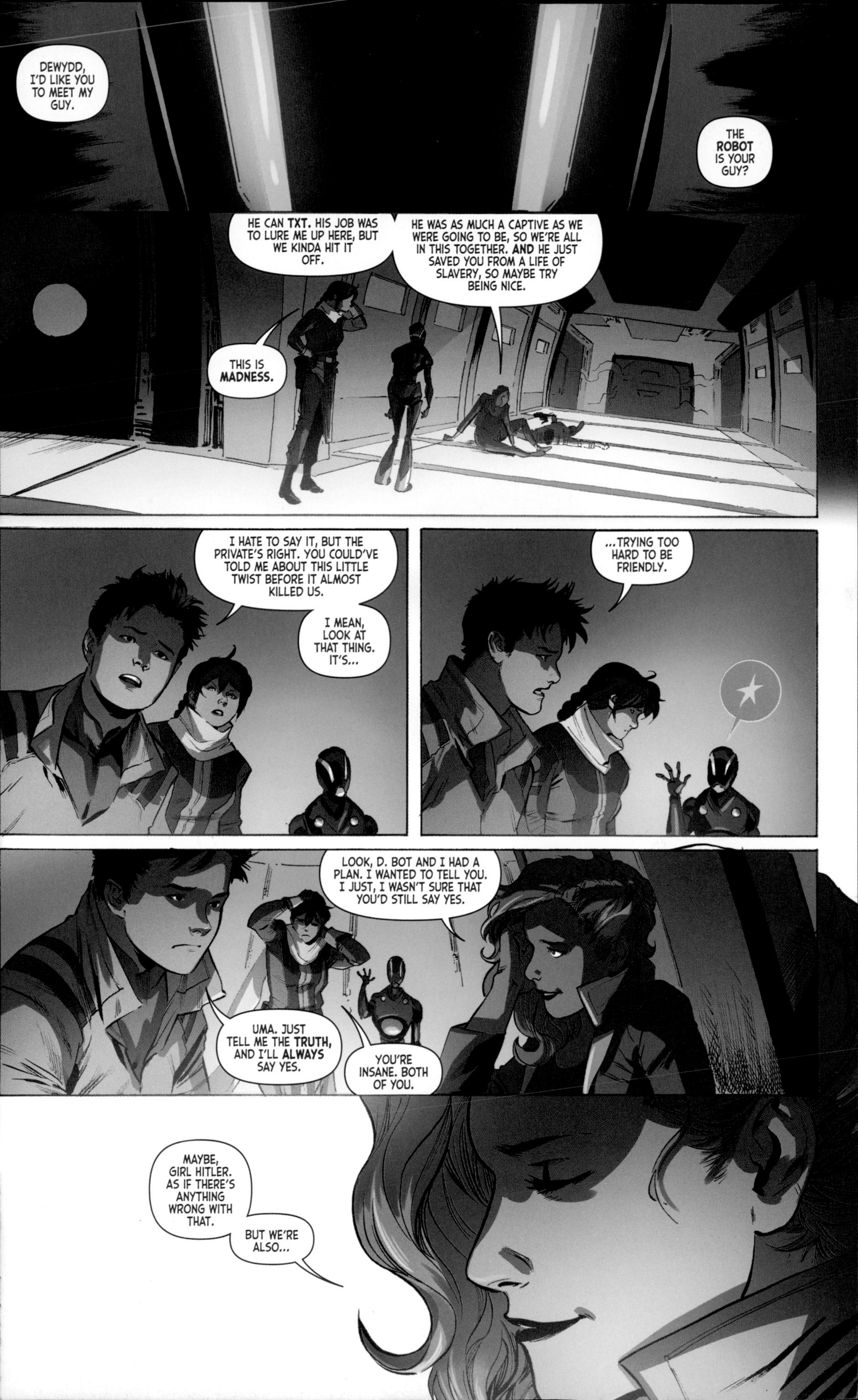
DEWYDD, I'D LIKE YOU TO MEET MY GUY.
THE ROBOT IS YOUR GUY?
HE CAN TXT. HIS JOB WAS TO LURE ME UP HERE, BUT WE KINDA HIT IT OFF.
HE WAS AS MUCH A CAPTIVE AS WE WERE GOING TO BE, SO WE'RE ALL IN THIS TOGETHER. AND HE JUST SAVED YOU FROM A LIFE OF SLAVERY, SO MAYBE TRY BEING NICE.
THIS IS MADNESS.
I HATE TO SAY IT, BUT THE PRIVATE'S RIGHT. YOU COULD'VE TOLD ME ABOUT THIS LITTLE TWIST BEFORE IT ALMOST KILLED US.
I MEAN, LOOK AT THAT THING. IT'S...
...TRYING TOO HARD TO BE FRIENDLY.
LOOK, D. BOT AND I HAD A PLAN. I WANTED TO TELL YOU. I JUST, I WASN'T SURE THAT YOU'D STILL SAY YES.
UMA. JUST TELL ME THE TRUTH, AND I'LL ALWAYS SAY YES.
YOU'RE INSANE. BOTH OF YOU.
MAYBE, GIRL HITLER. AS IF THERE'S ANYTHING WRONG WITH THAT.
BUT WE'RE ALSO...

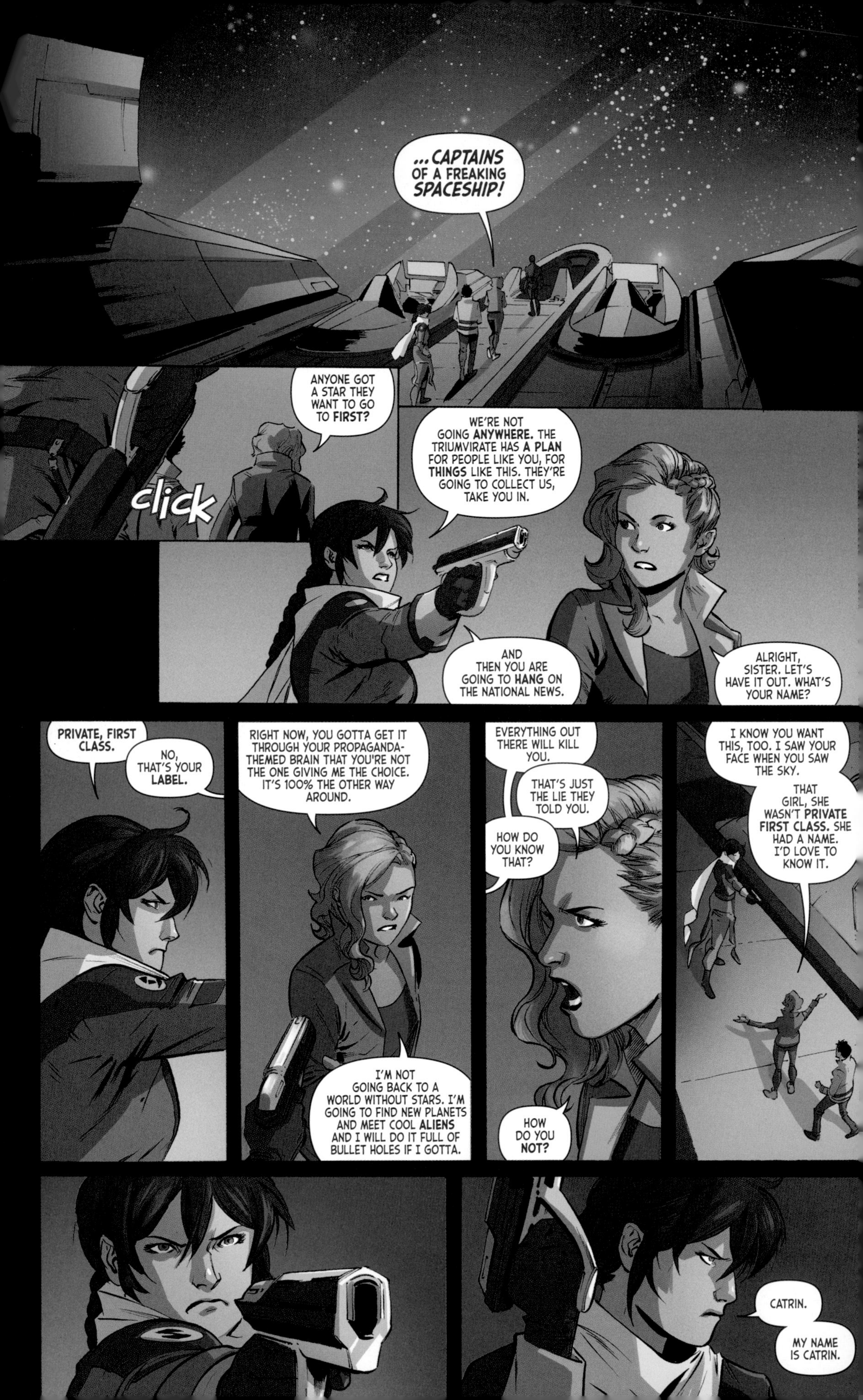
...CAPTAINS OF A FREAKING SPACESHIP!
ANYONE GOT A STAR THEY WANT TO GO TO FIRST?
CLICK
WE'RE NOT GOING ANYWHERE. THE TRIUMVIRATE HAS A PLAN FOR PEOPLE LIKE YOU, FOR THINGS LIKE THIS. THEY'RE GOING TO COLLECT US, TAKE YOU IN.
AND THEN YOU ARE GOING TO HANG ON THE NATIONAL NEWS.
ALRIGHT, SISTER. LET'S HAVE IT OUT. WHAT'S YOUR NAME?
PRIVATE, FIRST CLASS.
NO, THAT'S YOUR LABEL.
RIGHT NOW, YOU GOTTA GET IT THROUGH YOUR PROPAGANDA-THEMED BRAIN THAT YOU'RE NOT THE ONE GIVING ME THE CHOICE. IT'S 100% THE OTHER WAY AROUND.
I'M NOT GOING BACK TO A WORLD WITHOUT STARS. I'M GOING TO FIND NEW PLANETS AND MEET COOL ALIENS AND I WILL DO IT FULL OF BULLET HOLES IF I GOTTA.
EVERYTHING OUT THERE WILL KILL YOU.
THAT'S JUST THE LIE THEY TOLD YOU.
HOW DO YOU KNOW THAT?
HOW DO YOU NOT?
I KNOW YOU WANT THIS, TOO. I SAW YOUR FACE WHEN YOU SAW THE SKY.
THAT GIRL, SHE WASN'T PRIVATE FIRST CLASS. SHE HAD A NAME. I'D LOVE TO KNOW IT.
CATRIN.
MY NAME IS CATRIN.

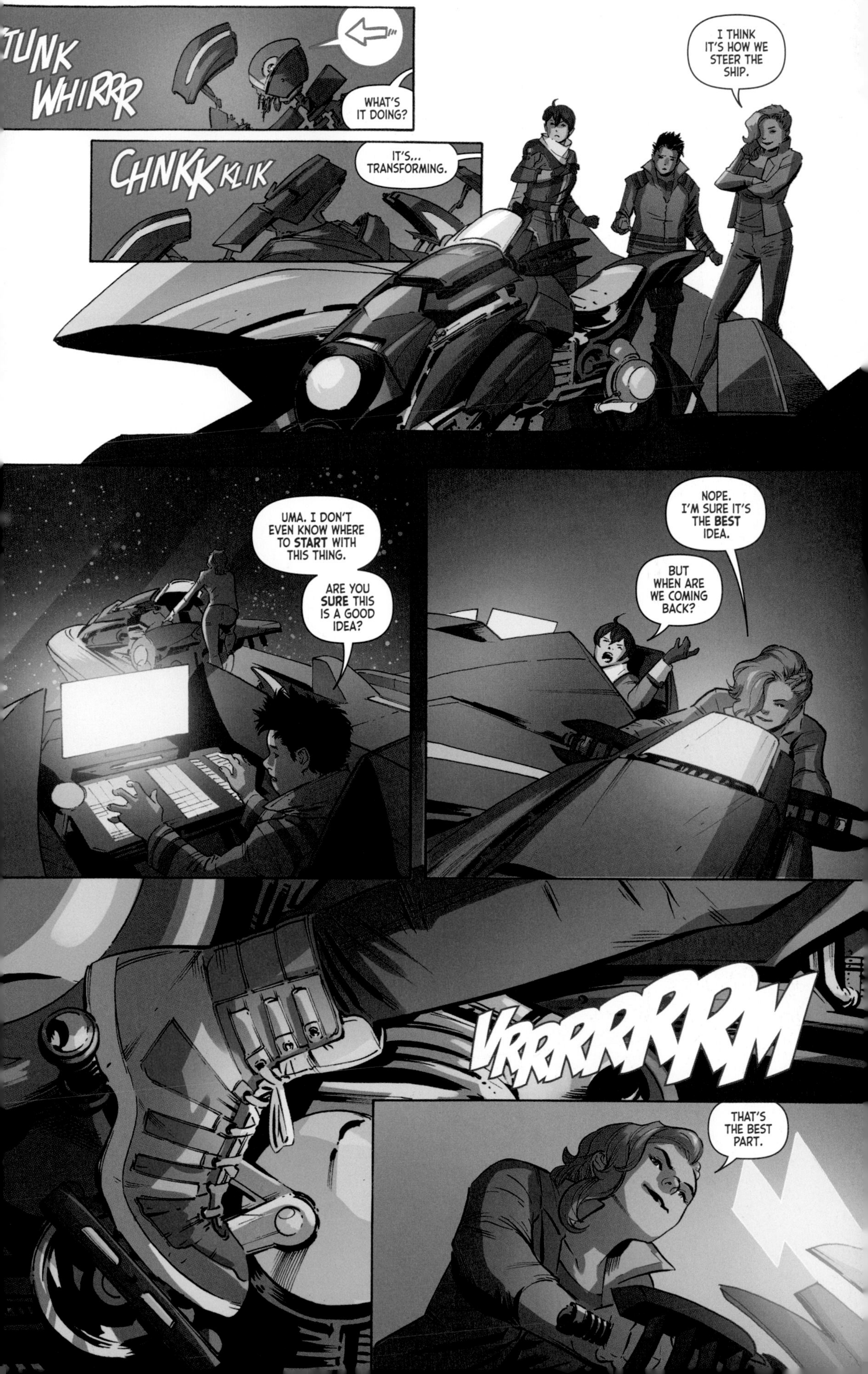
TUNK
WHIRRR
WHAT'S IT DOING?
I THINK IT'S HOW WE STEER THE SHIP.
CHNKK KLIK
IT'S... TRANSFORMING.
UMA. I DON'T EVEN KNOW WHERE TO START WITH THIS THING.
ARE YOU SURE THIS IS A GOOD IDEA?
NOPE. I'M SURE IT'S THE BEST IDEA.
BUT WHEN ARE WE COMING BACK?
VRRRRRRRM
THAT'S THE BEST PART.

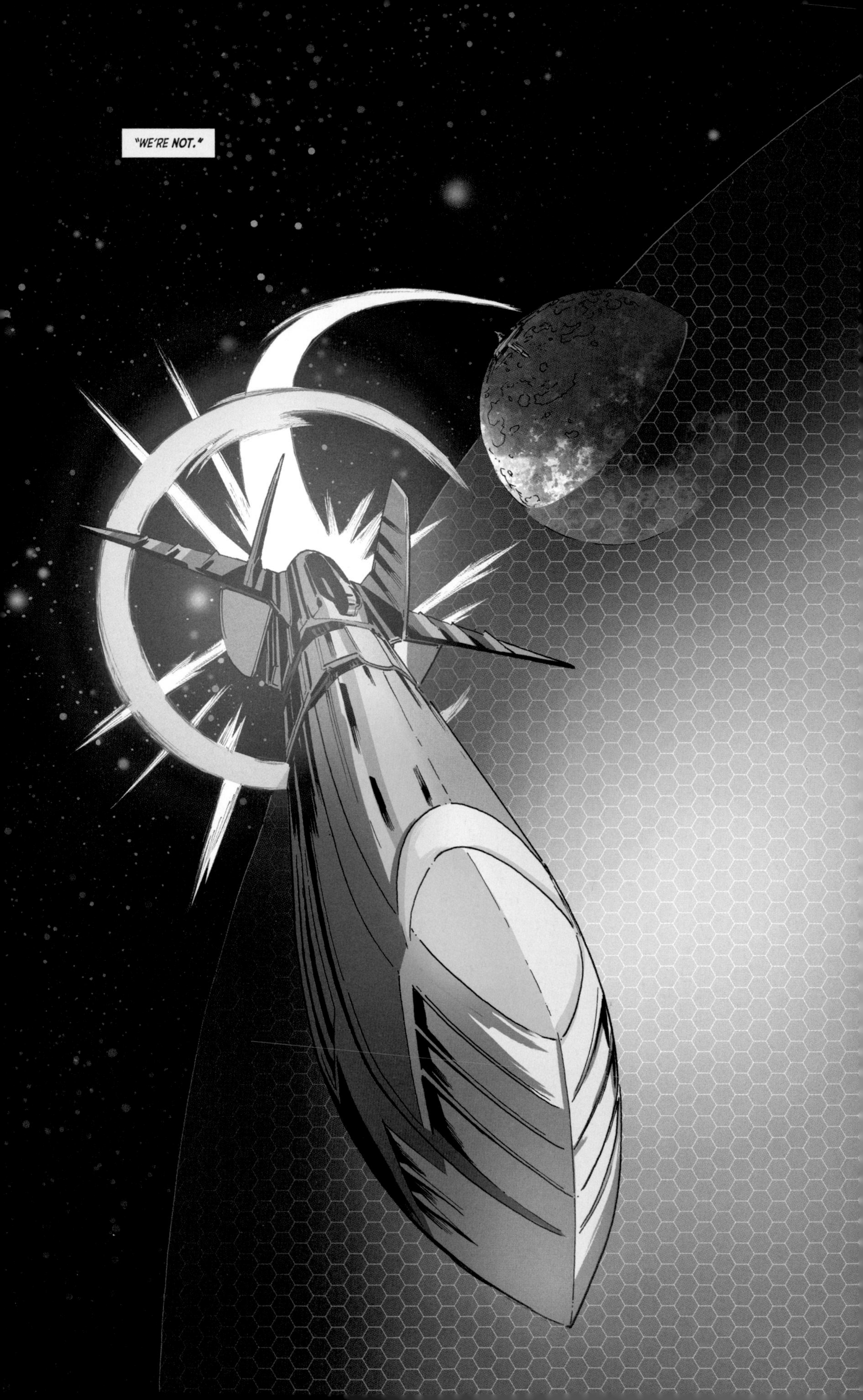
"WE'RE NOT."

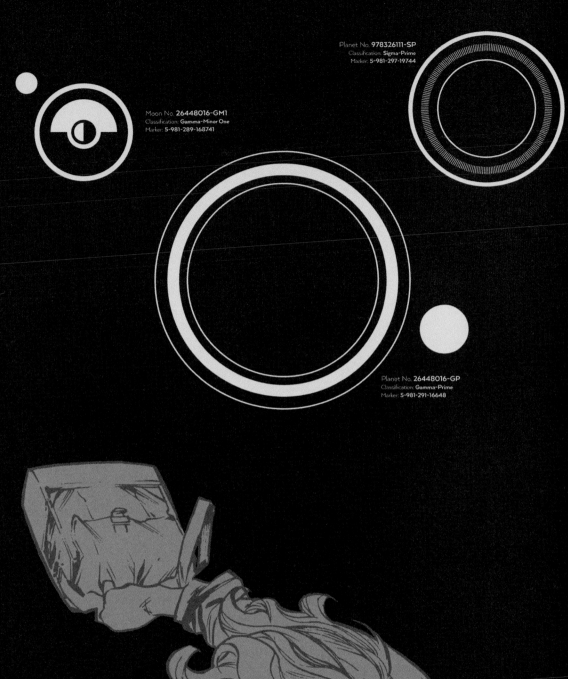

Planet No. **978326111-SP**
Classification: **Sigma-Prime**
Marker: **5-981-297-19744**

Moon No. **26448016-GM1**
Classification: **Gamma-Minor One**
Marker: **5-981-289-168741**

Planet No. **26448016-GP**
Classification: **Gamma-Prime**
Marker: **5-981-291-16648**

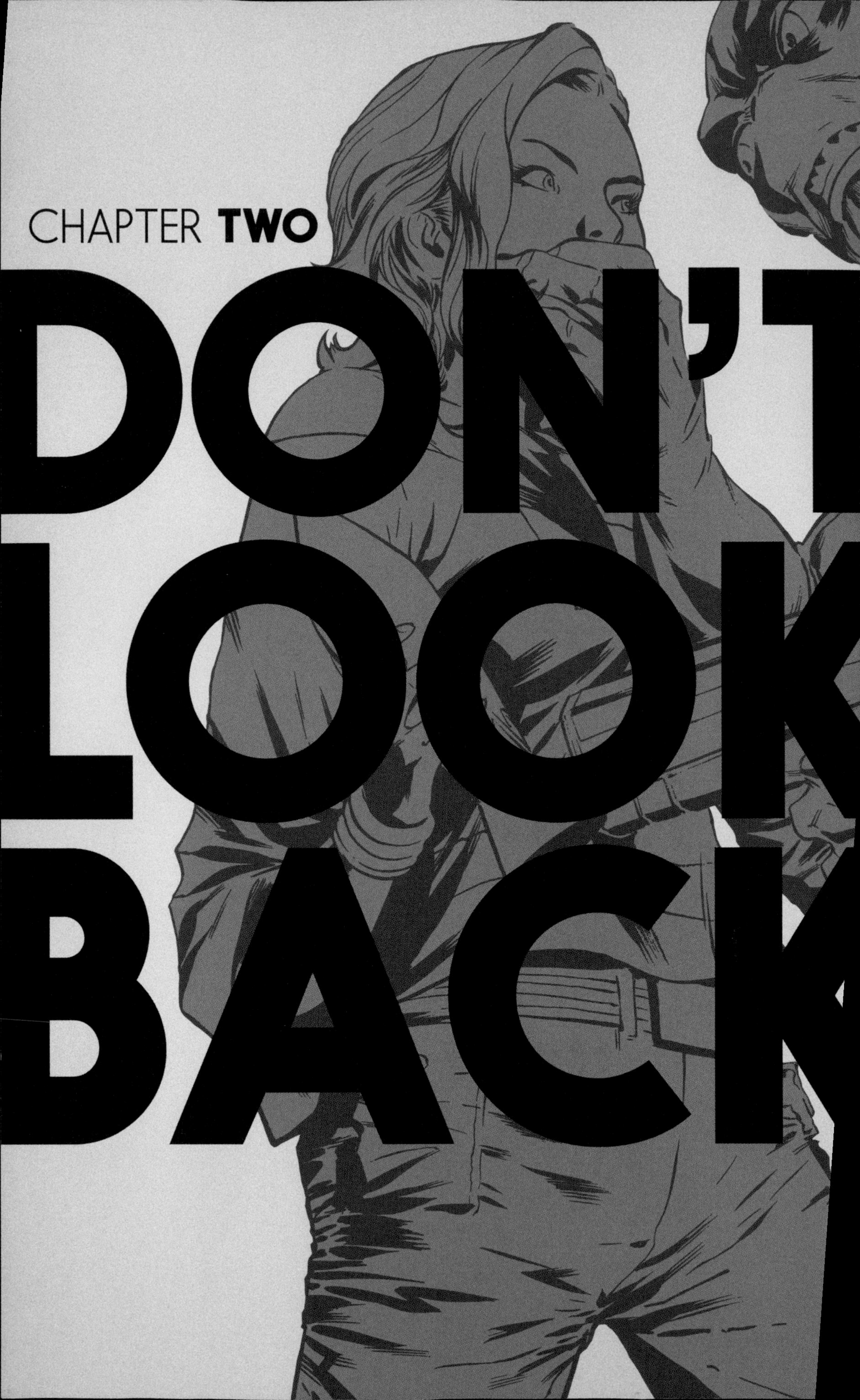
CHAPTER TWO
DON'T LOOK BACK

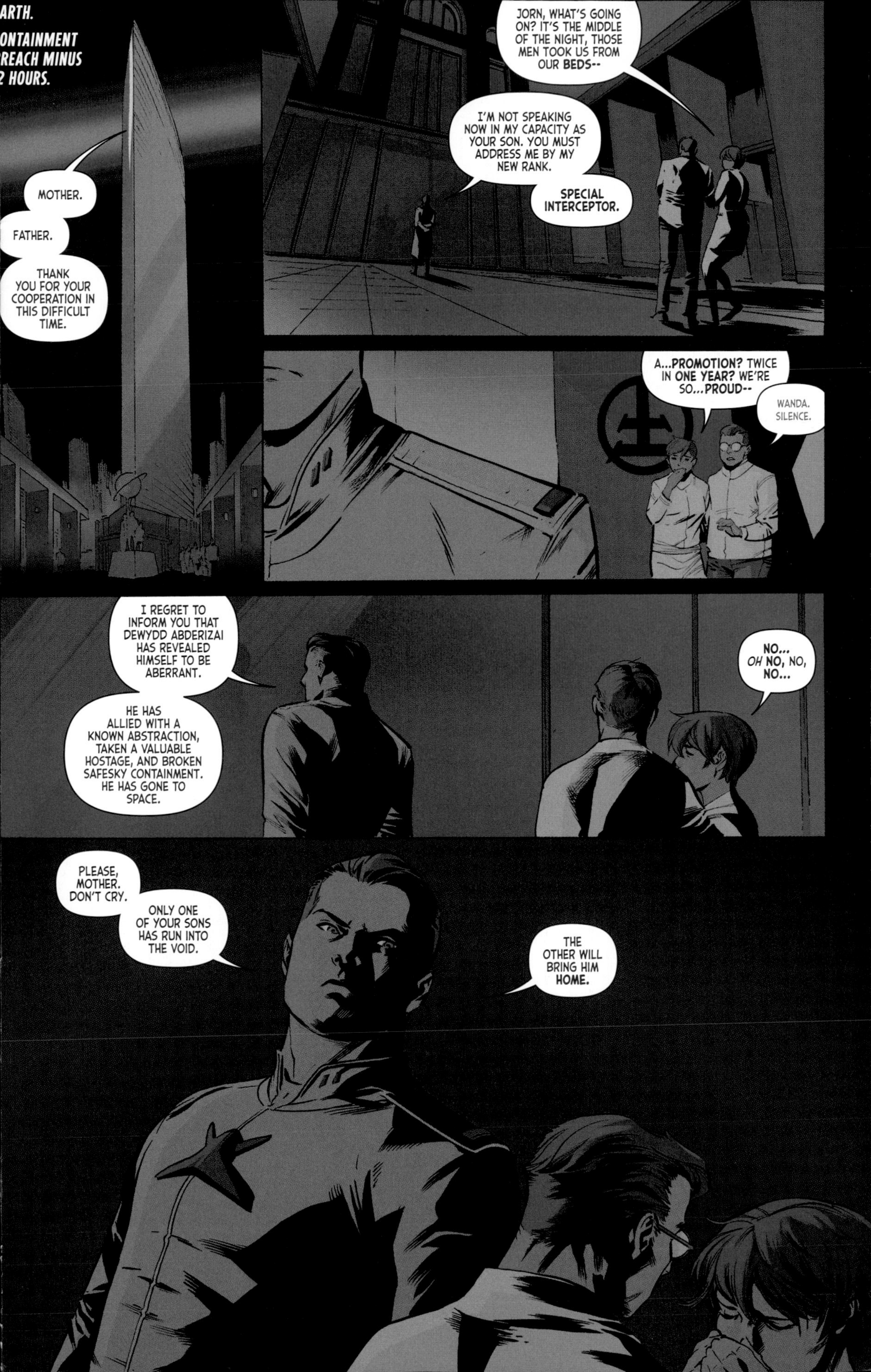
ARTH.
ONTAINMENT
REACH MINUS
2 HOURS.
MOTHER.
FATHER.
THANK YOU FOR YOUR COOPERATION IN THIS DIFFICULT TIME.
JORN, WHAT'S GOING ON? IT'S THE MIDDLE OF THE NIGHT, THOSE MEN TOOK US FROM OUR BEDS--
I'M NOT SPEAKING NOW IN MY CAPACITY AS YOUR SON. YOU MUST ADDRESS ME BY MY NEW RANK.
SPECIAL INTERCEPTOR.
A...PROMOTION? TWICE IN ONE YEAR? WE'RE SO...PROUD--
WANDA. SILENCE.
I REGRET TO INFORM YOU THAT DEWYDD ABDERIZAI HAS REVEALED HIMSELF TO BE ABERRANT.
HE HAS ALLIED WITH A KNOWN ABSTRACTION, TAKEN A VALUABLE HOSTAGE, AND BROKEN SAFESKY CONTAINMENT. HE HAS GONE TO SPACE.
NO... OH NO, NO, NO...
PLEASE, MOTHER. DON'T CRY.
ONLY ONE OF YOUR SONS HAS RUN INTO THE VOID.
THE OTHER WILL BRING HIM HOME.

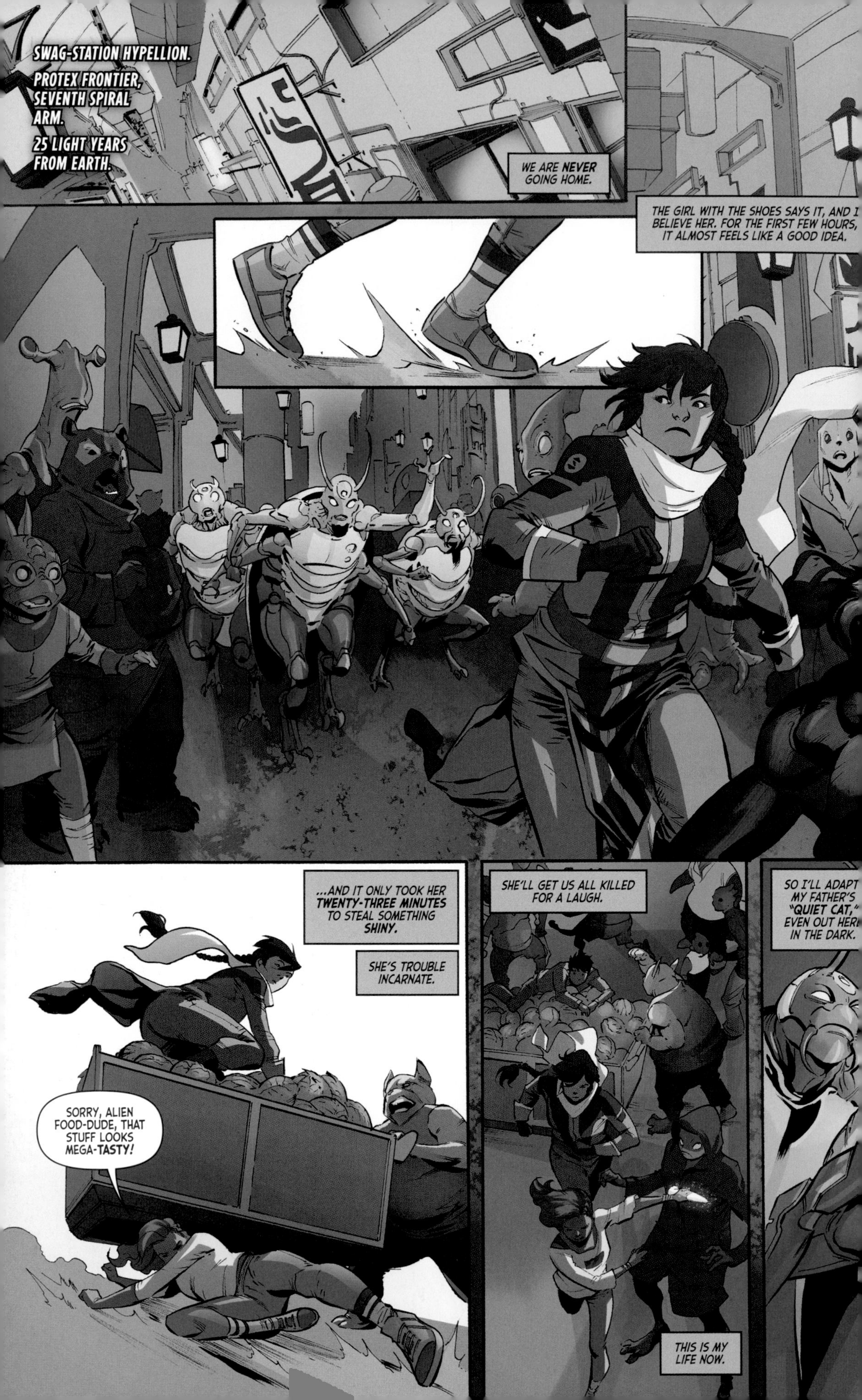
SWAG-STATION HYPELLION.
PROTEX FRONTIER, SEVENTH SPIRAL ARM.
25 LIGHT YEARS FROM EARTH.
WE ARE **NEVER** GOING HOME.
THE GIRL WITH THE SHOES SAYS IT, AND I BELIEVE HER. FOR THE FIRST FEW HOURS, IT ALMOST FEELS LIKE A GOOD IDEA.
...AND IT ONLY TOOK HER **TWENTY-THREE MINUTES** TO STEAL SOMETHING **SHINY.**
SHE'S TROUBLE INCARNATE.
SORRY, ALIEN FOOD-DUDE, THAT STUFF LOOKS MEGA-**TASTY!**
SHE'LL GET US ALL KILLED FOR A LAUGH.
THIS IS MY LIFE NOW.
SO I'LL ADAPT MY FATHER'S **"QUIET CAT,"** EVEN OUT HER IN THE DARK.

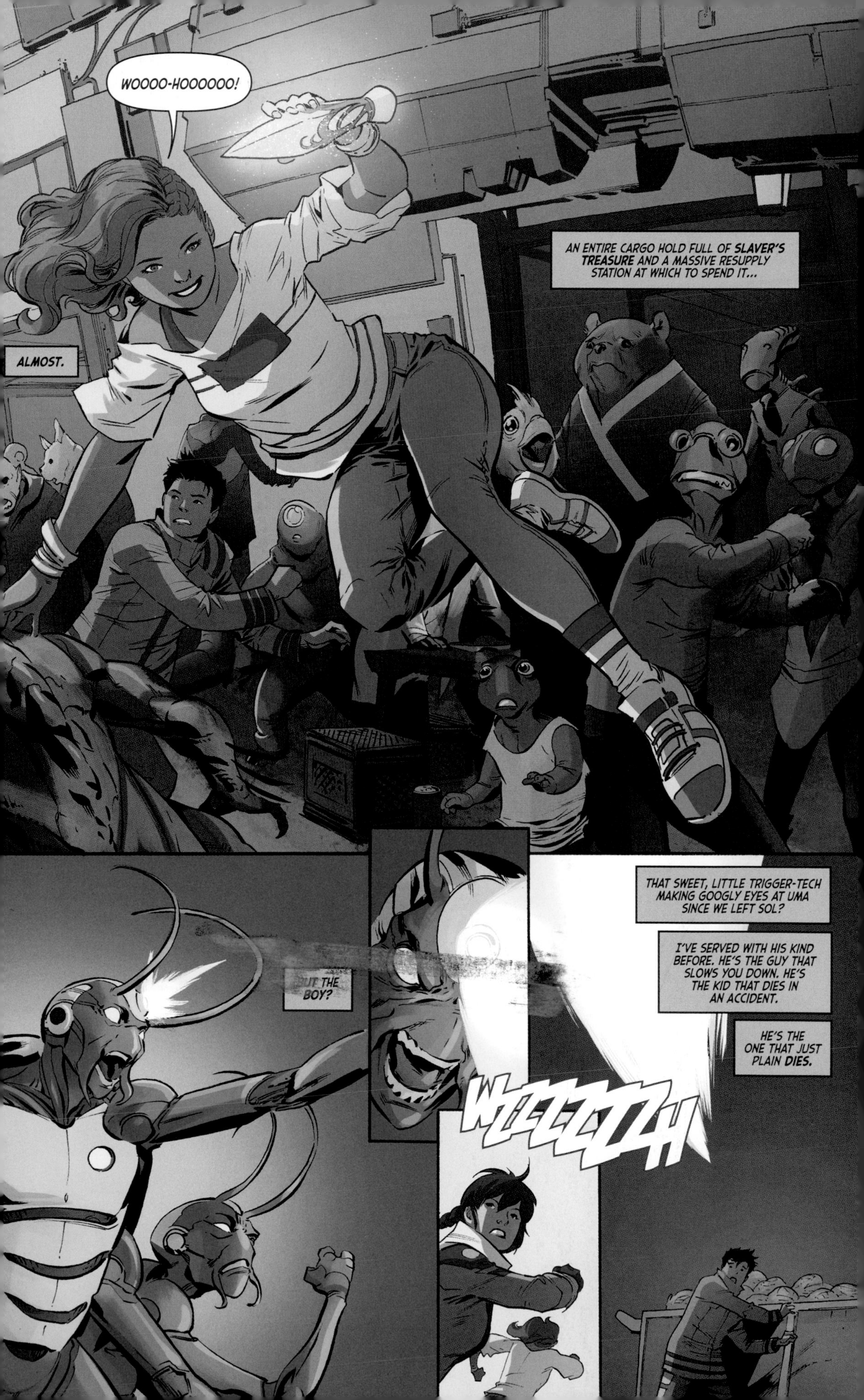
WOOOO-HOOOOOO!
AN ENTIRE CARGO HOLD FULL OF SLAVER'S TREASURE AND A MASSIVE RESUPPLY STATION AT WHICH TO SPEND IT...
ALMOST.
THAT SWEET, LITTLE TRIGGER-TECH MAKING GOOGLY EYES AT UMA SINCE WE LEFT SOL?
BUT THE BOY?
I'VE SERVED WITH HIS KIND BEFORE. HE'S THE GUY THAT SLOWS YOU DOWN. HE'S THE KID THAT DIES IN AN ACCIDENT.
HE'S THE ONE THAT JUST PLAIN DIES.
WZZZZZH

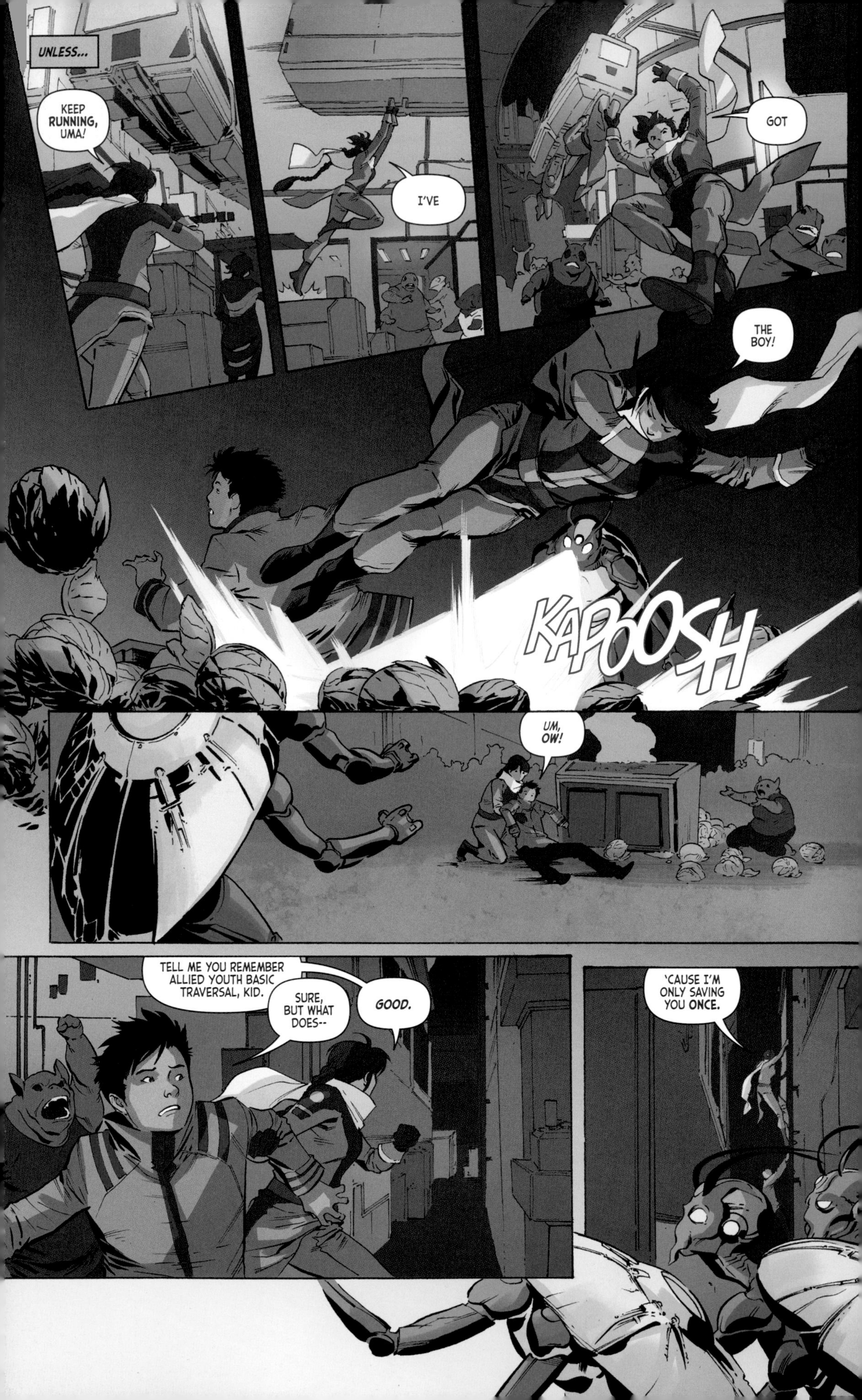
UNLESS...
KEEP RUNNING, UMA!
I'VE
GOT
THE BOY!
KAPOOSH
UM, OW!
TELL ME YOU REMEMBER ALLIED YOUTH BASIC TRAVERSAL, KID.
SURE, BUT WHAT DOES--
GOOD.
'CAUSE I'M ONLY SAVING YOU ONCE.

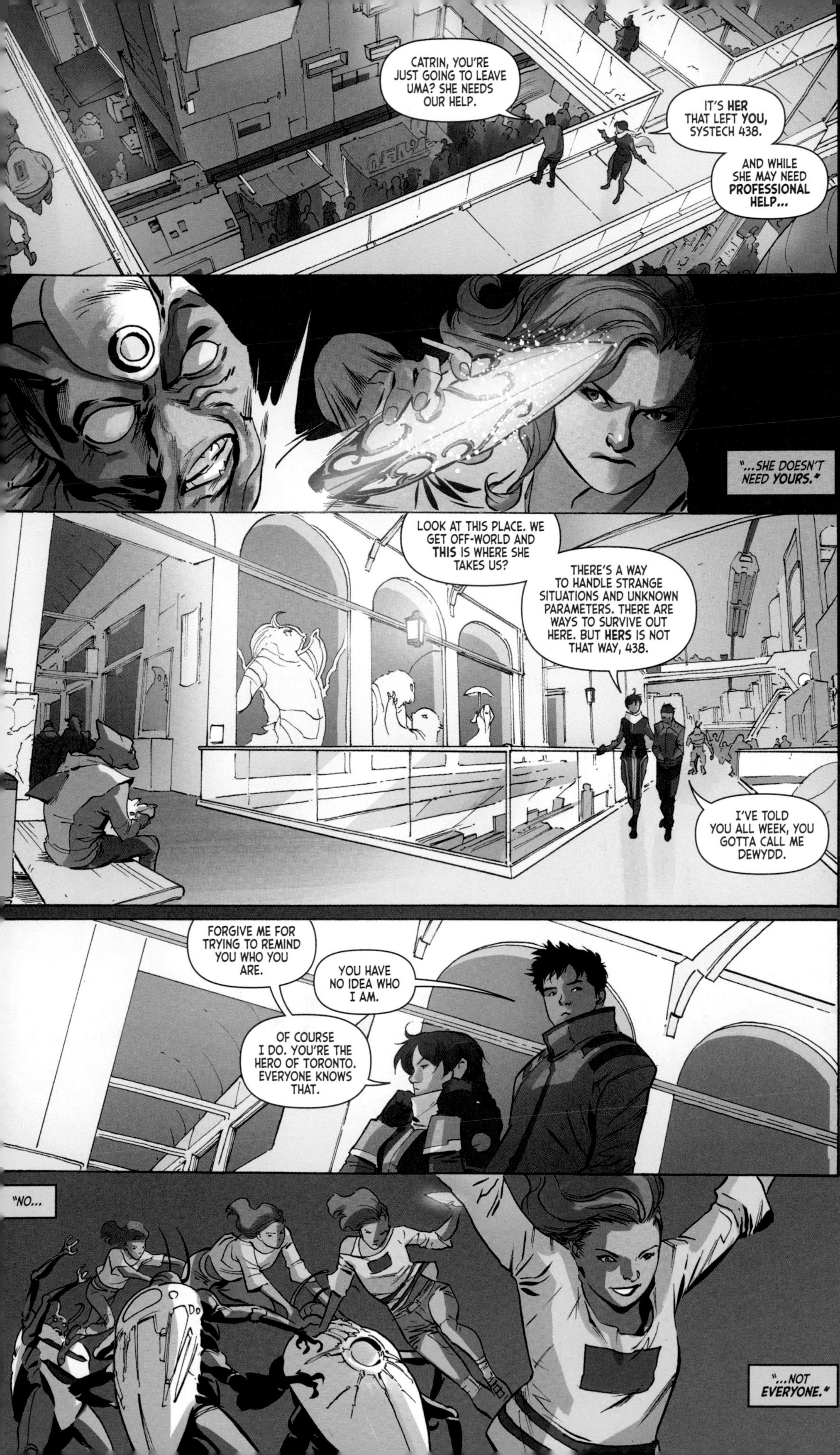
CATRIN, YOU'RE JUST GOING TO LEAVE UMA? SHE NEEDS OUR HELP.
IT'S **HER** THAT LEFT **YOU**, SYSTECH 438.
AND WHILE SHE MAY NEED **PROFESSIONAL HELP...**
"...SHE DOESN'T NEED **YOURS.**"
LOOK AT THIS PLACE. WE GET OFF-WORLD AND **THIS** IS WHERE SHE TAKES US?
THERE'S A WAY TO HANDLE STRANGE SITUATIONS AND UNKNOWN PARAMETERS. THERE ARE WAYS TO SURVIVE OUT HERE. BUT **HERS** IS NOT THAT WAY, 438.
I'VE TOLD YOU ALL WEEK, YOU GOTTA CALL ME DEWYDD.
FORGIVE ME FOR TRYING TO REMIND YOU WHO YOU ARE.
YOU HAVE NO IDEA WHO I AM.
OF COURSE I DO. YOU'RE THE HERO OF TORONTO. EVERYONE KNOWS THAT.
"NO...
"...NOT **EVERYONE.**"

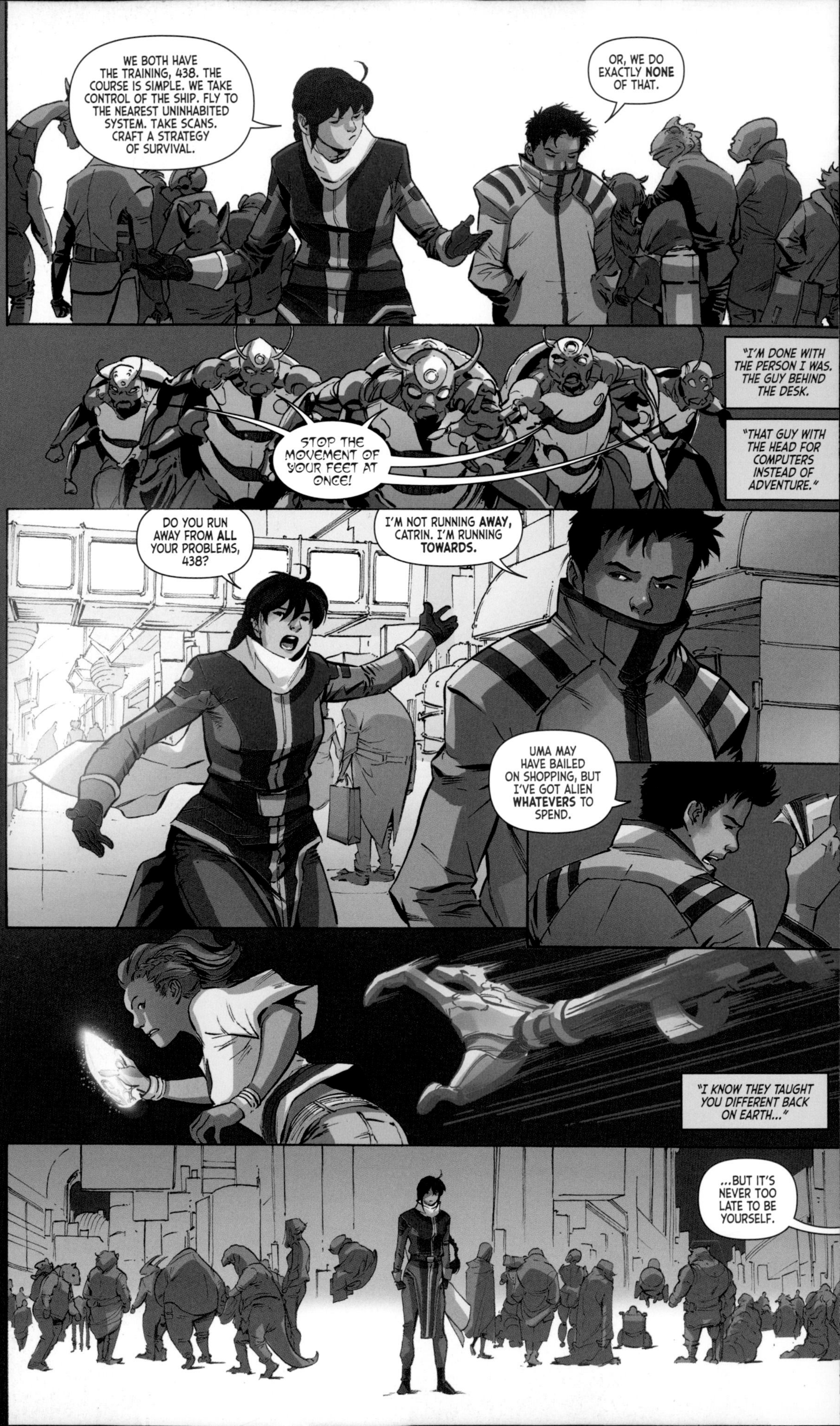
WE BOTH HAVE THE TRAINING, 438. THE COURSE IS SIMPLE. WE TAKE CONTROL OF THE SHIP. FLY TO THE NEAREST UNINHABITED SYSTEM. TAKE SCANS. CRAFT A STRATEGY OF SURVIVAL.
OR, WE DO EXACTLY NONE OF THAT.
STOP THE MOVEMENT OF YOUR FEET AT ONCE!
"I'M DONE WITH THE PERSON I WAS. THE GUY BEHIND THE DESK.
"THAT GUY WITH THE HEAD FOR COMPUTERS INSTEAD OF ADVENTURE."
DO YOU RUN AWAY FROM ALL YOUR PROBLEMS, 438?
I'M NOT RUNNING AWAY, CATRIN. I'M RUNNING TOWARDS.
UMA MAY HAVE BAILED ON SHOPPING, BUT I'VE GOT ALIEN WHATEVERS TO SPEND.
"I KNOW THEY TAUGHT YOU DIFFERENT BACK ON EARTH..."
...BUT IT'S NEVER TOO LATE TO BE YOURSELF.

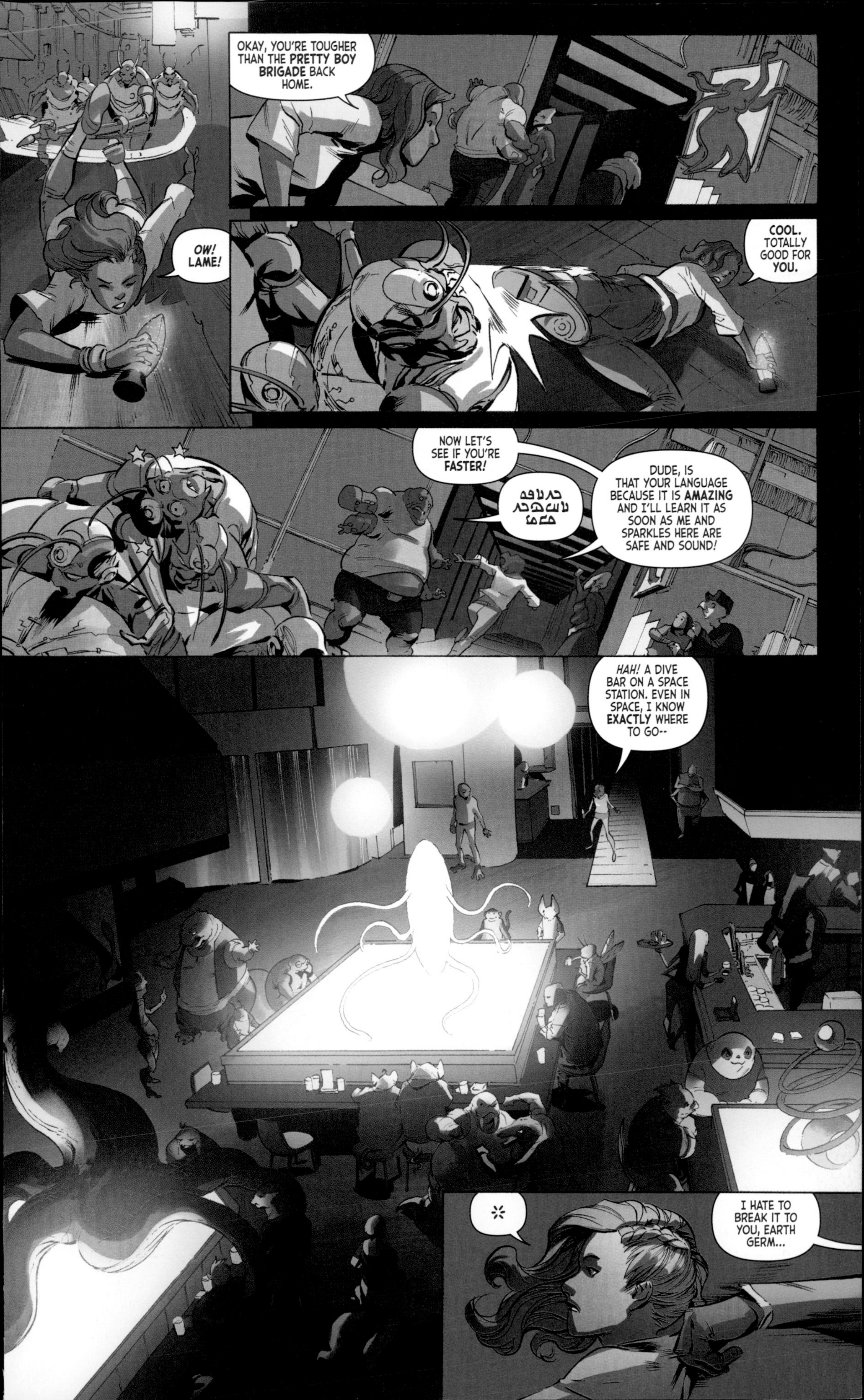
OKAY, YOU'RE TOUGHER THAN THE PRETTY BOY BRIGADE BACK HOME.
OW! LAME!
COOL. TOTALLY GOOD FOR YOU.
NOW LET'S SEE IF YOU'RE FASTER!
DUDE, IS THAT YOUR LANGUAGE BECAUSE IT IS AMAZING AND I'LL LEARN IT AS SOON AS ME AND SPARKLES HERE ARE SAFE AND SOUND!
HAH! A DIVE BAR ON A SPACE STATION. EVEN IN SPACE, I KNOW EXACTLY WHERE TO GO--
I HATE TO BREAK IT TO YOU, EARTH GERM...

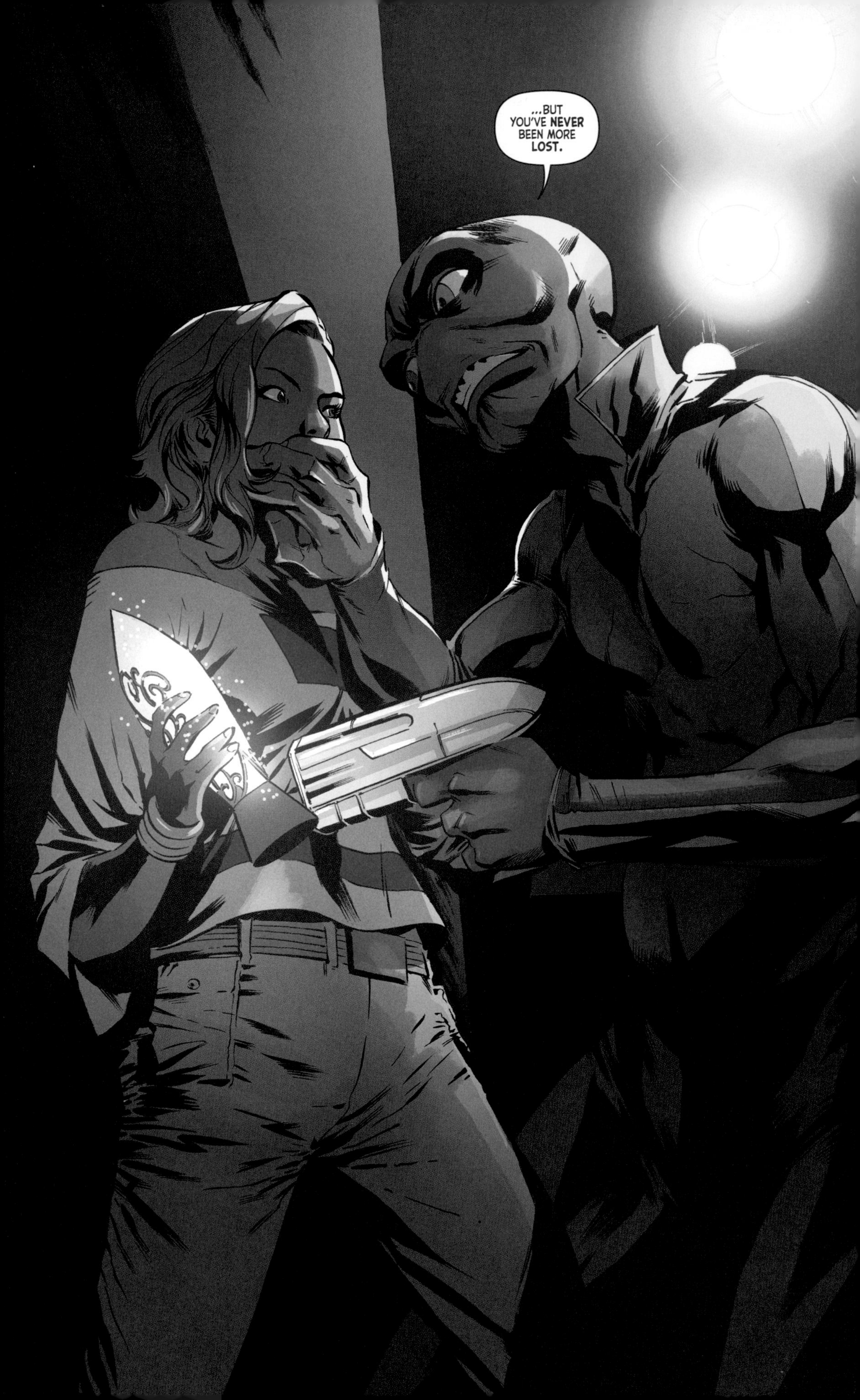
...BUT YOU'VE NEVER BEEN MORE LOST.

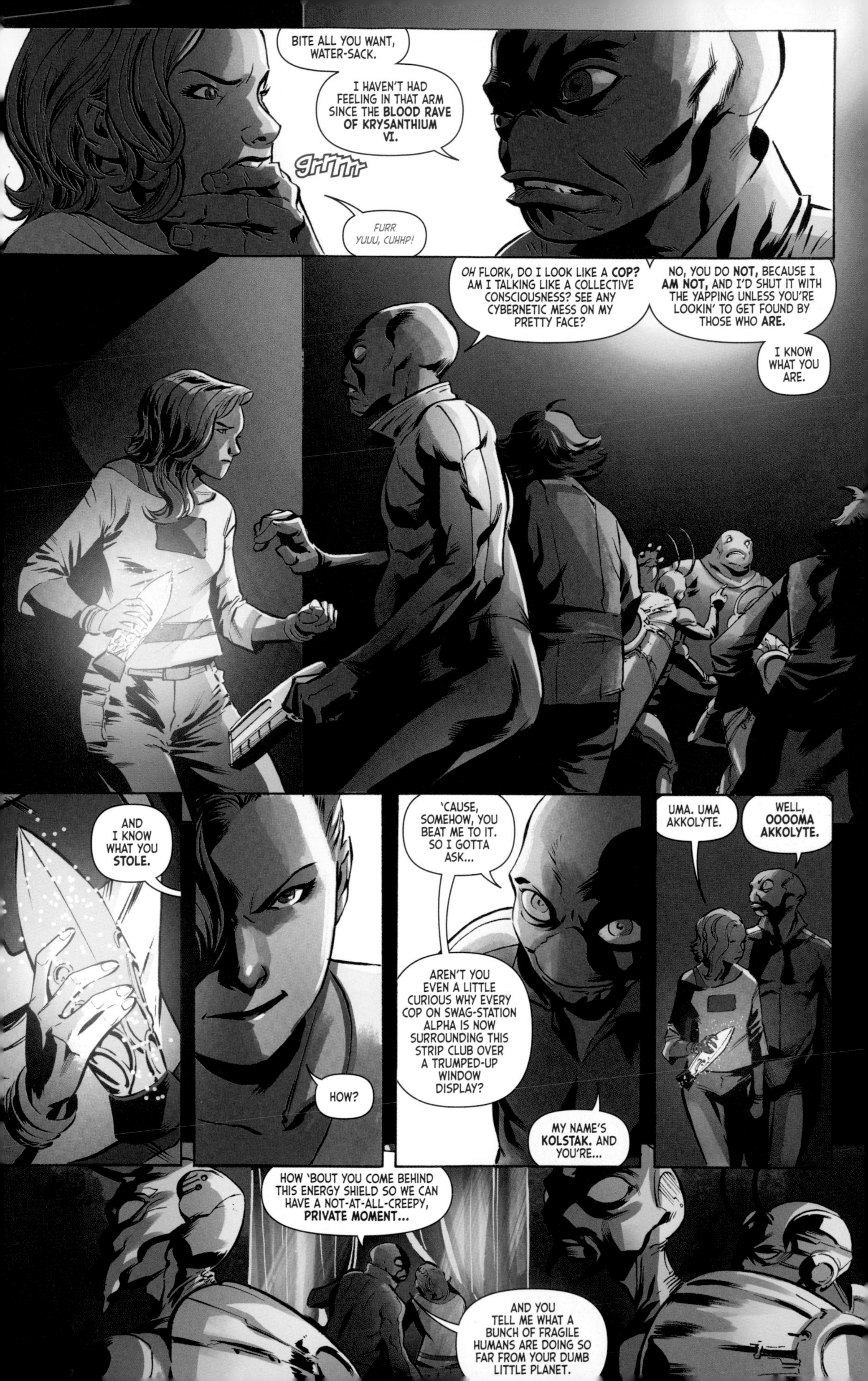
BITE ALL YOU WANT, WATER-SACK.
I HAVEN'T HAD FEELING IN THAT ARM SINCE THE **BLOOD RAVE OF KRYSANTHIUM VI.**
GRRRR
FURR YUUU, CUHHP!
OH FLORK, DO I LOOK LIKE A **COP?** AM I TALKING LIKE A COLLECTIVE CONSCIOUSNESS? SEE ANY CYBERNETIC MESS ON MY PRETTY FACE?
NO, YOU DO **NOT,** BECAUSE I **AM NOT,** AND I'D SHUT IT WITH THE YAPPING UNLESS YOU'RE LOOKIN' TO GET FOUND BY THOSE WHO **ARE.**
I KNOW WHAT YOU ARE.
AND I KNOW WHAT YOU **STOLE.**
HOW?
'CAUSE, SOMEHOW, YOU BEAT ME TO IT. SO I GOTTA ASK...
AREN'T YOU EVEN A LITTLE CURIOUS WHY EVERY COP ON SWAG-STATION ALPHA IS NOW SURROUNDING THIS STRIP CLUB OVER A TRUMPED-UP WINDOW DISPLAY?
MY NAME'S **KOLSTAK.** AND YOU'RE...
UMA. UMA AKKOLYTE.
WELL, **OOOOMA AKKOLYTE.**
HOW 'BOUT YOU COME BEHIND THIS ENERGY SHIELD SO WE CAN HAVE A NOT-AT-ALL-CREEPY, **PRIVATE MOMENT...**
AND YOU TELL ME WHAT A BUNCH OF FRAGILE HUMANS ARE DOING SO FAR FROM YOUR DUMB LITTLE PLANET.

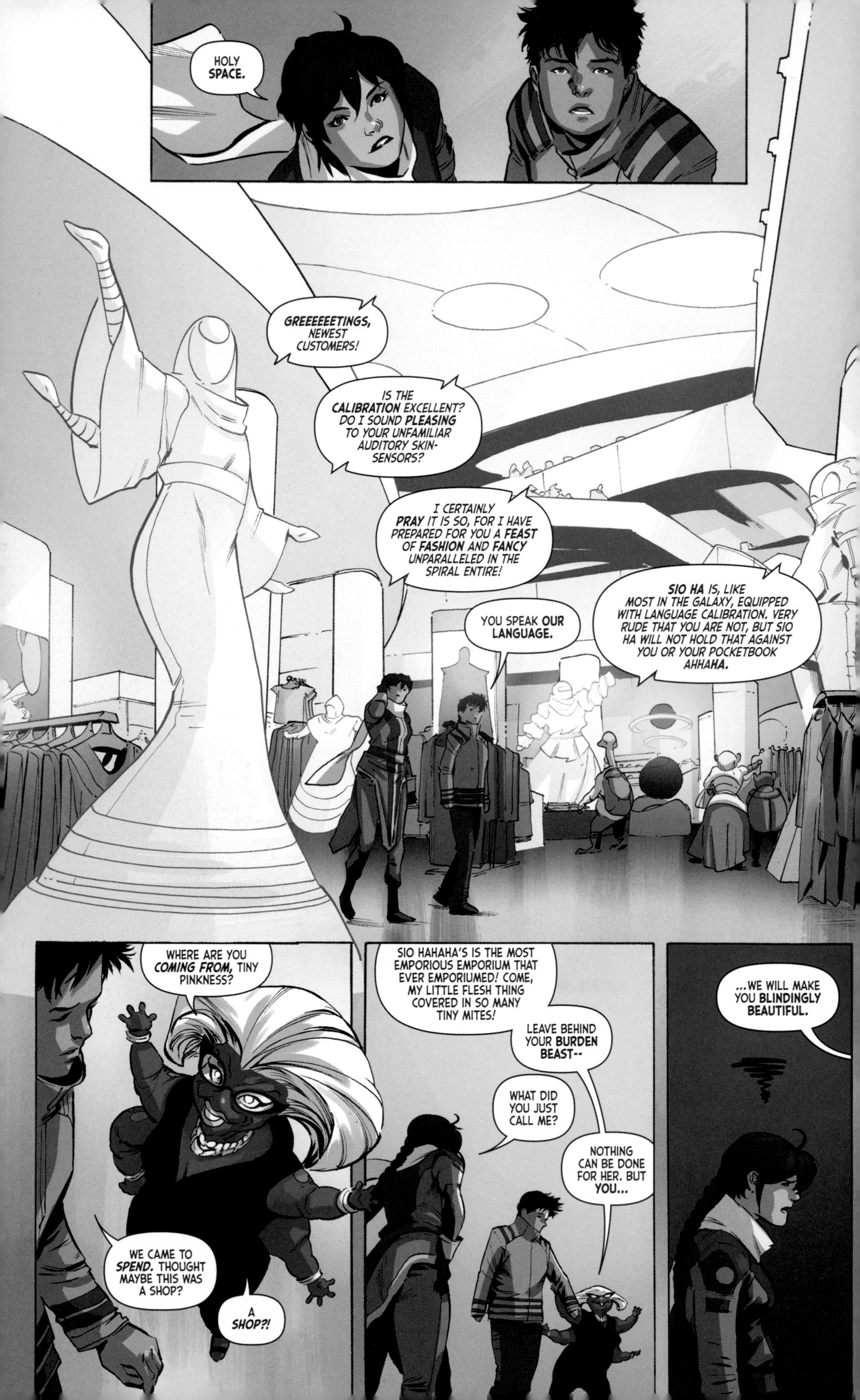
HOLY SPACE.
GREEEEEETINGS, NEWEST CUSTOMERS!
IS THE CALIBRATION EXCELLENT? DO I SOUND PLEASING TO YOUR UNFAMILIAR AUDITORY SKIN-SENSORS?
I CERTAINLY PRAY IT IS SO, FOR I HAVE PREPARED FOR YOU A FEAST OF FASHION AND FANCY UNPARALLELED IN THE SPIRAL ENTIRE!
YOU SPEAK OUR LANGUAGE.
SIO HA IS, LIKE MOST IN THE GALAXY, EQUIPPED WITH LANGUAGE CALIBRATION. VERY RUDE THAT YOU ARE NOT, BUT SIO HA WILL NOT HOLD THAT AGAINST YOU OR YOUR POCKETBOOK AHHAHA.
WHERE ARE YOU COMING FROM, TINY PINKNESS?
WE CAME TO SPEND. THOUGHT MAYBE THIS WAS A SHOP?
A SHOP?!
SIO HAHAHA'S IS THE MOST EMPORIOUS EMPORIUM THAT EVER EMPORIUMED! COME, MY LITTLE FLESH THING COVERED IN SO MANY TINY MITES!
LEAVE BEHIND YOUR BURDEN BEAST--
WHAT DID YOU JUST CALL ME?
NOTHING CAN BE DONE FOR HER. BUT YOU...
...WE WILL MAKE YOU BLINDINGLY BEAUTIFUL.

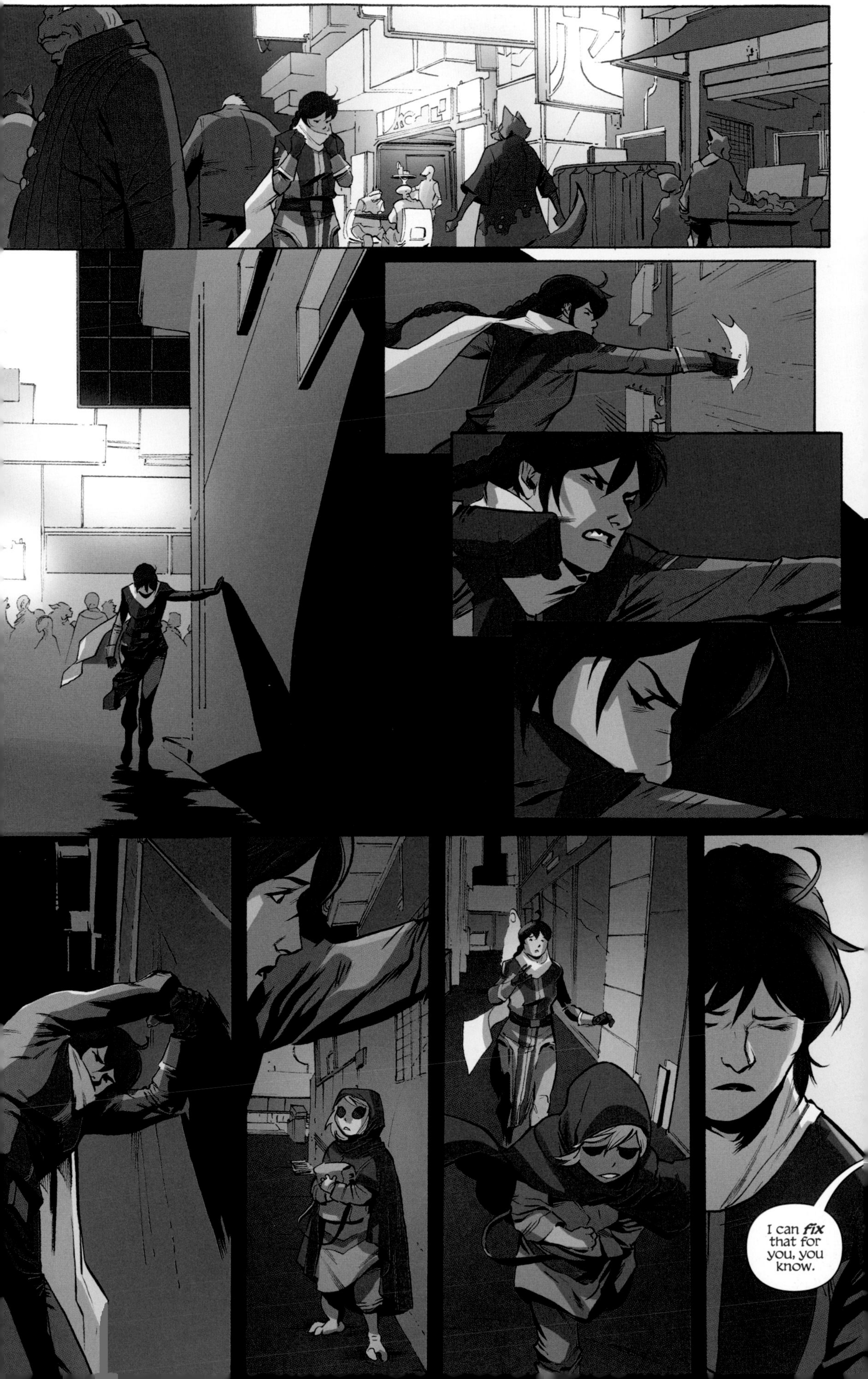
I can *fix* that for you, you know.

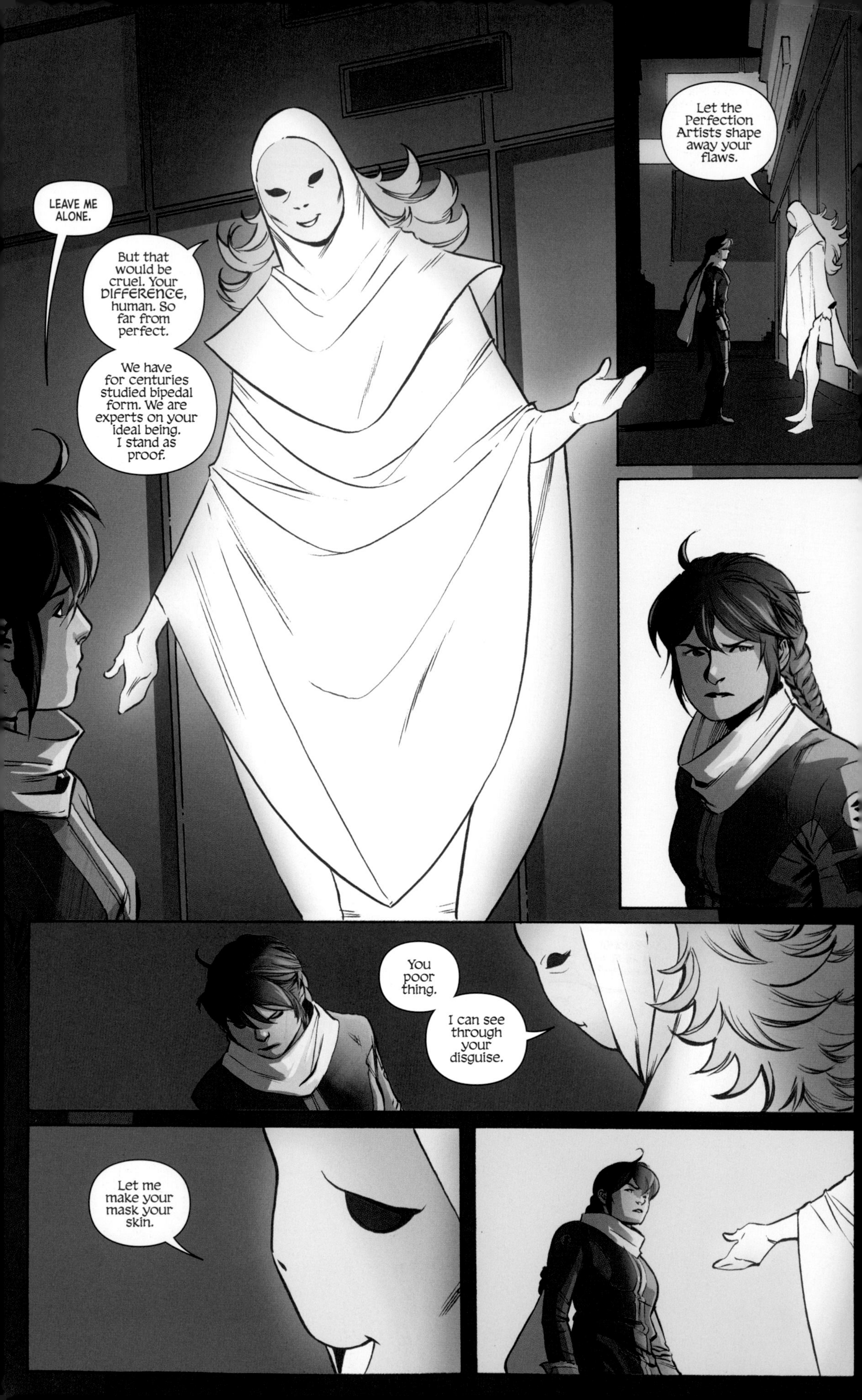

LEAVE ME ALONE.
But that would be cruel. Your DIFFERENCE, human. So far from perfect.
We have for centuries studied bipedal form. We are experts on your ideal being. I stand as proof.
Let the Perfection Artists shape away your flaws.
You poor thing.
I can see through your disguise.
Let me make your mask your skin.

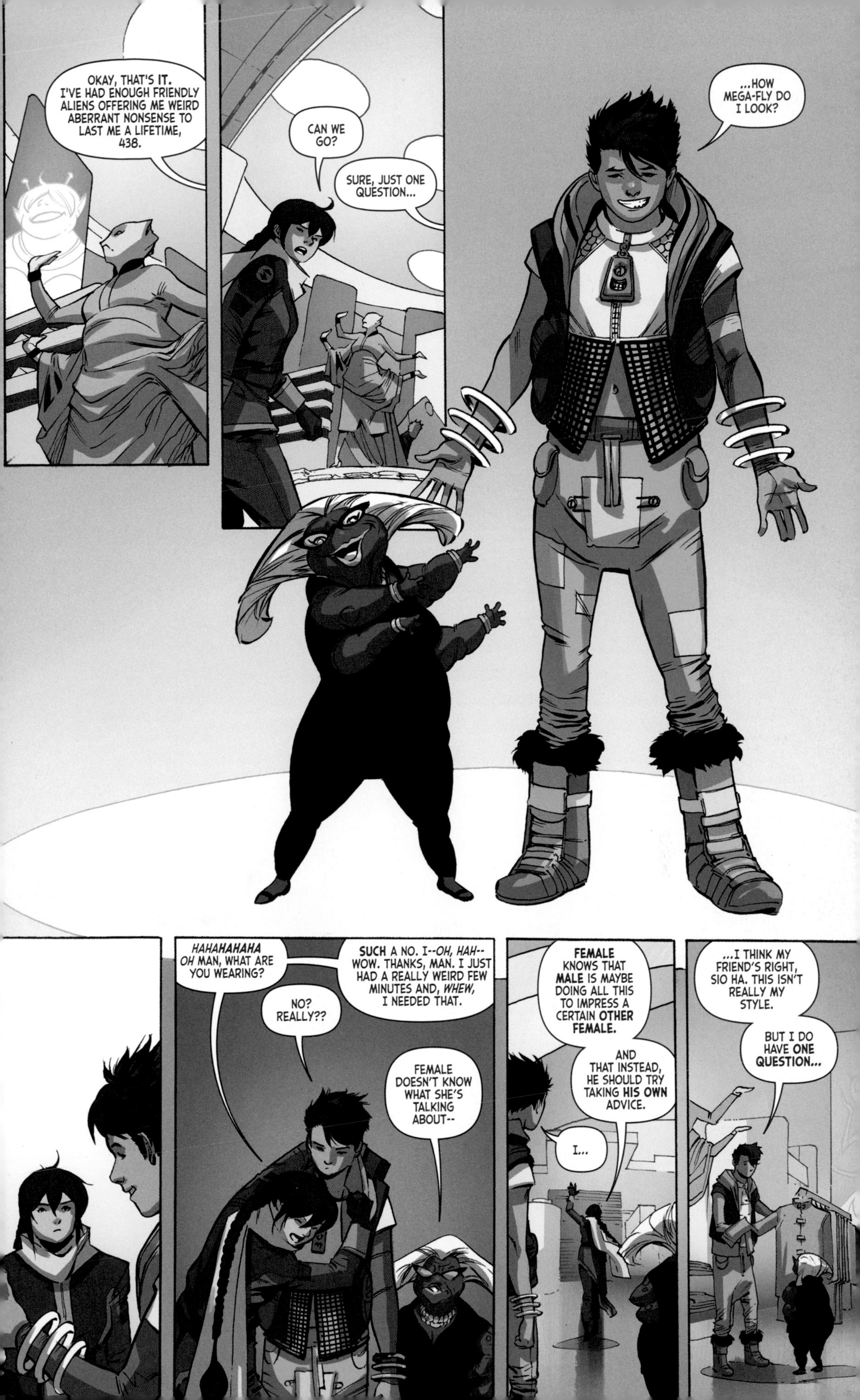

OKAY, THAT'S IT. I'VE HAD ENOUGH FRIENDLY ALIENS OFFERING ME WEIRD ABERRANT NONSENSE TO LAST ME A LIFETIME, 438.
CAN WE GO?
SURE, JUST ONE QUESTION...
...HOW MEGA-FLY DO I LOOK?
HAHAHAHAHA OH MAN, WHAT ARE YOU WEARING?
NO? REALLY??
SUCH A NO. I--OH, HAH--WOW. THANKS, MAN. I JUST HAD A REALLY WEIRD FEW MINUTES AND, WHEW, I NEEDED THAT.
FEMALE DOESN'T KNOW WHAT SHE'S TALKING ABOUT--
FEMALE KNOWS THAT MALE IS MAYBE DOING ALL THIS TO IMPRESS A CERTAIN OTHER FEMALE.
AND THAT INSTEAD, HE SHOULD TRY TAKING HIS OWN ADVICE.
I...
...I THINK MY FRIEND'S RIGHT, SIO HA. THIS ISN'T REALLY MY STYLE.
BUT I DO HAVE ONE QUESTION...

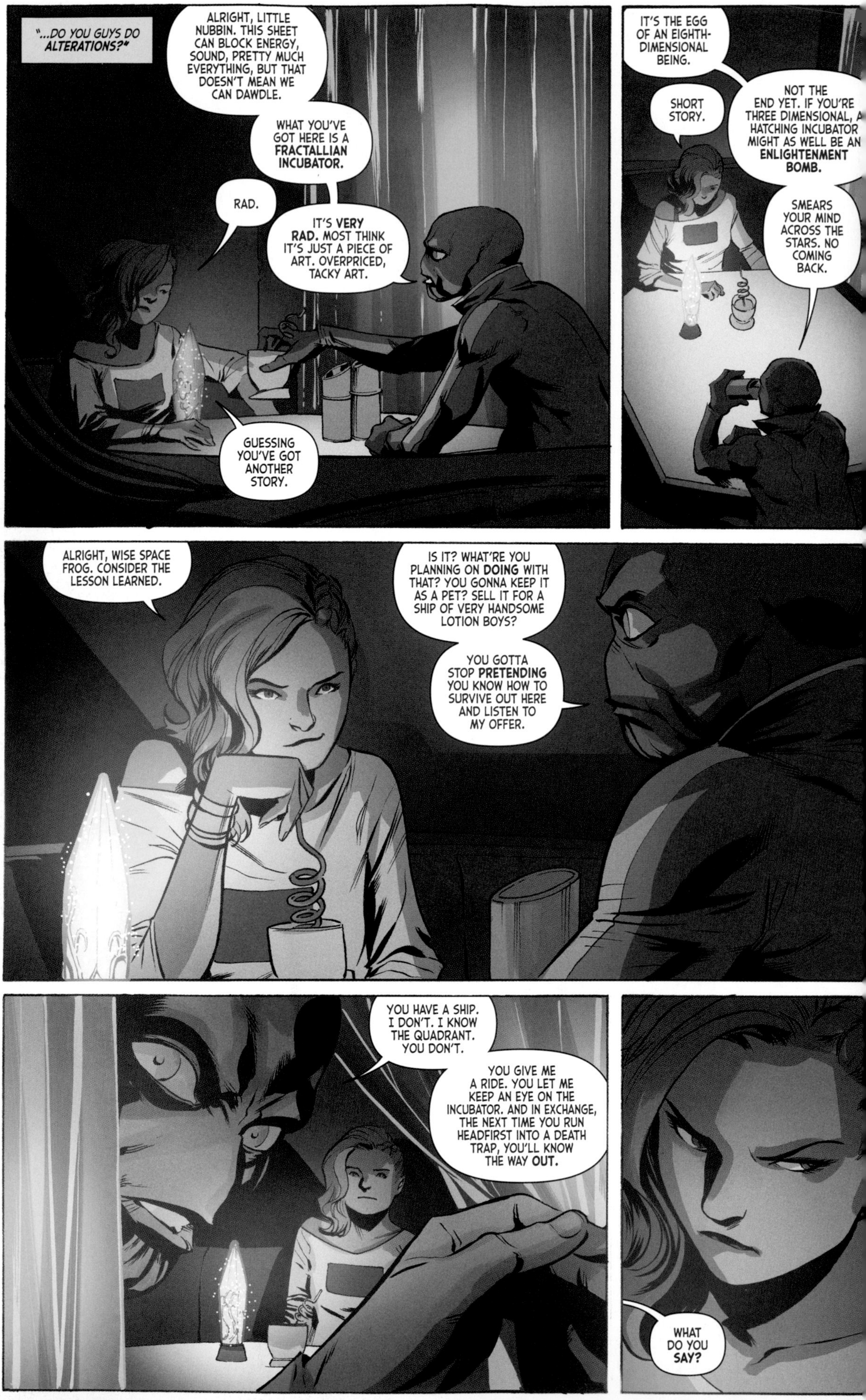
"...DO YOU GUYS DO ALTERATIONS?"
ALRIGHT, LITTLE NUBBIN. THIS SHEET CAN BLOCK ENERGY, SOUND, PRETTY MUCH EVERYTHING, BUT THAT DOESN'T MEAN WE CAN DAWDLE.
WHAT YOU'VE GOT HERE IS A FRACTALLIAN INCUBATOR.
RAD.
IT'S VERY RAD. MOST THINK IT'S JUST A PIECE OF ART. OVERPRICED, TACKY ART.
GUESSING YOU'VE GOT ANOTHER STORY.
IT'S THE EGG OF AN EIGHTH-DIMENSIONAL BEING.
SHORT STORY.
NOT THE END YET. IF YOU'RE THREE DIMENSIONAL, A HATCHING INCUBATOR MIGHT AS WELL BE AN ENLIGHTENMENT BOMB.
SMEARS YOUR MIND ACROSS THE STARS. NO COMING BACK.
ALRIGHT, WISE SPACE FROG. CONSIDER THE LESSON LEARNED.
IS IT? WHAT'RE YOU PLANNING ON DOING WITH THAT? YOU GONNA KEEP IT AS A PET? SELL IT FOR A SHIP OF VERY HANDSOME LOTION BOYS?
YOU GOTTA STOP PRETENDING YOU KNOW HOW TO SURVIVE OUT HERE AND LISTEN TO MY OFFER.
YOU HAVE A SHIP. I DON'T. I KNOW THE QUADRANT. YOU DON'T.
YOU GIVE ME A RIDE. YOU LET ME KEEP AN EYE ON THE INCUBATOR. AND IN EXCHANGE, THE NEXT TIME YOU RUN HEADFIRST INTO A DEATH TRAP, YOU'LL KNOW THE WAY OUT.
WHAT DO YOU SAY?

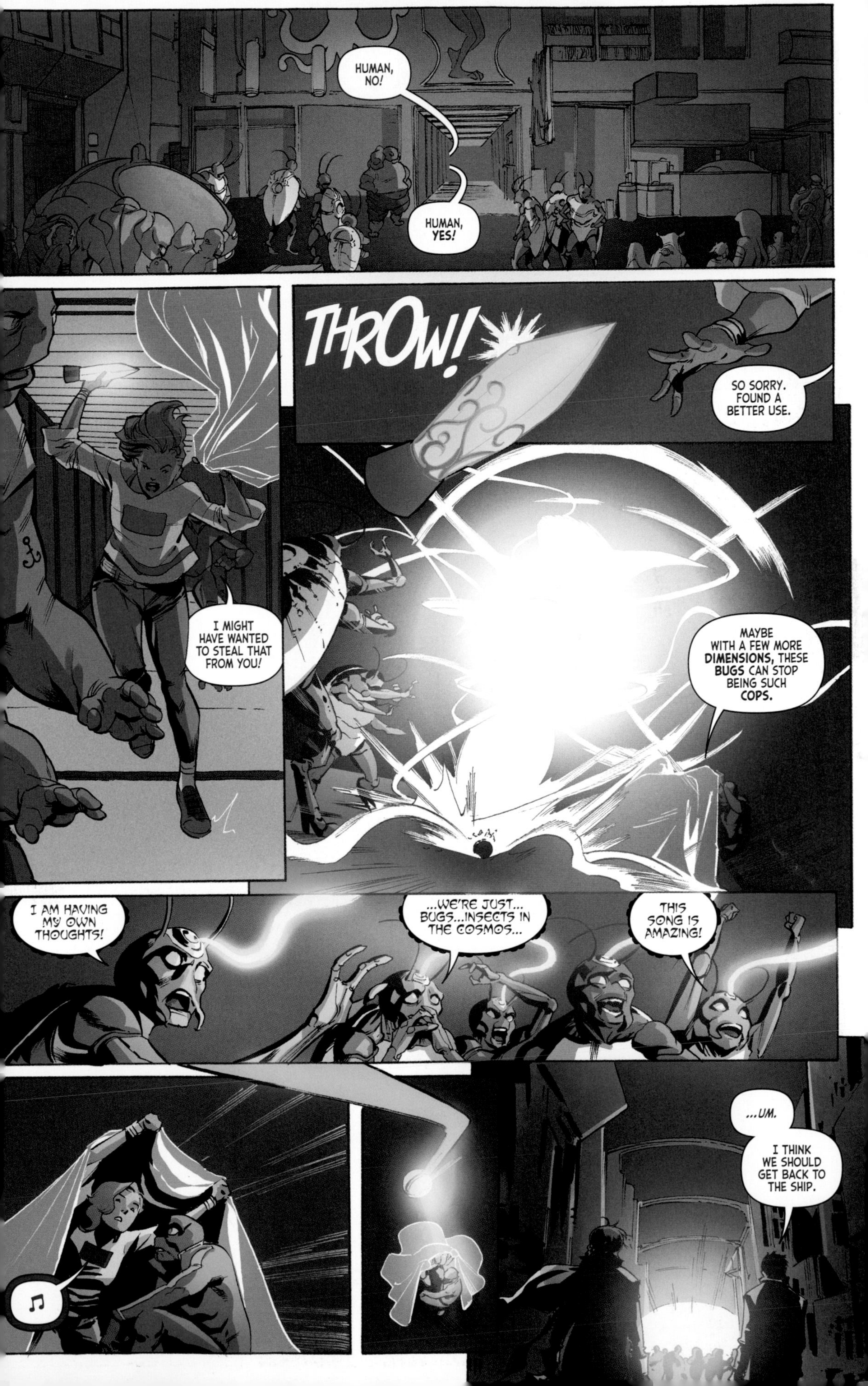
HUMAN, NO!
HUMAN, YES!
THROW!
SO SORRY. FOUND A BETTER USE.
I MIGHT HAVE WANTED TO STEAL THAT FROM YOU!
MAYBE WITH A FEW MORE DIMENSIONS, THESE BUGS CAN STOP BEING SUCH COPS.
I AM HAVING MY OWN THOUGHTS!
...WE'RE JUST... BUGS...INSECTS IN THE COSMOS...
THIS SONG IS AMAZING!
♫
...UM.
I THINK WE SHOULD GET BACK TO THE SHIP.

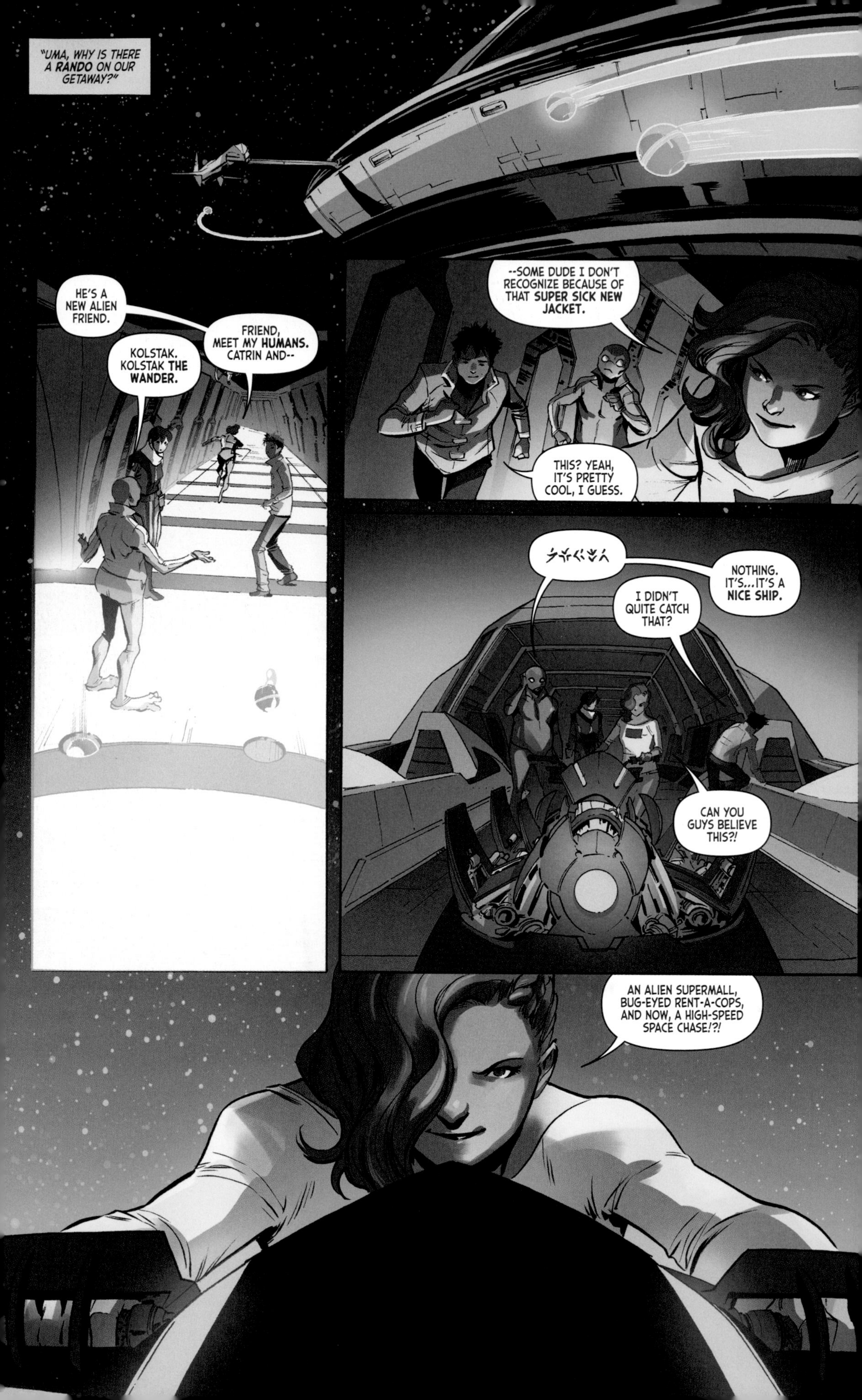
"UMA, WHY IS THERE A RANDO ON OUR GETAWAY?"
HE'S A NEW ALIEN FRIEND.
FRIEND, MEET MY HUMANS. CATRIN AND--
KOLSTAK. KOLSTAK THE WANDER.
--SOME DUDE I DON'T RECOGNIZE BECAUSE OF THAT SUPER SICK NEW JACKET.
THIS? YEAH, IT'S PRETTY COOL, I GUESS.
I DIDN'T QUITE CATCH THAT?
NOTHING. IT'S...IT'S A NICE SHIP.
CAN YOU GUYS BELIEVE THIS?!
AN ALIEN SUPERMALL, BUG-EYED RENT-A-COPS, AND NOW, A HIGH-SPEED SPACE CHASE!?!

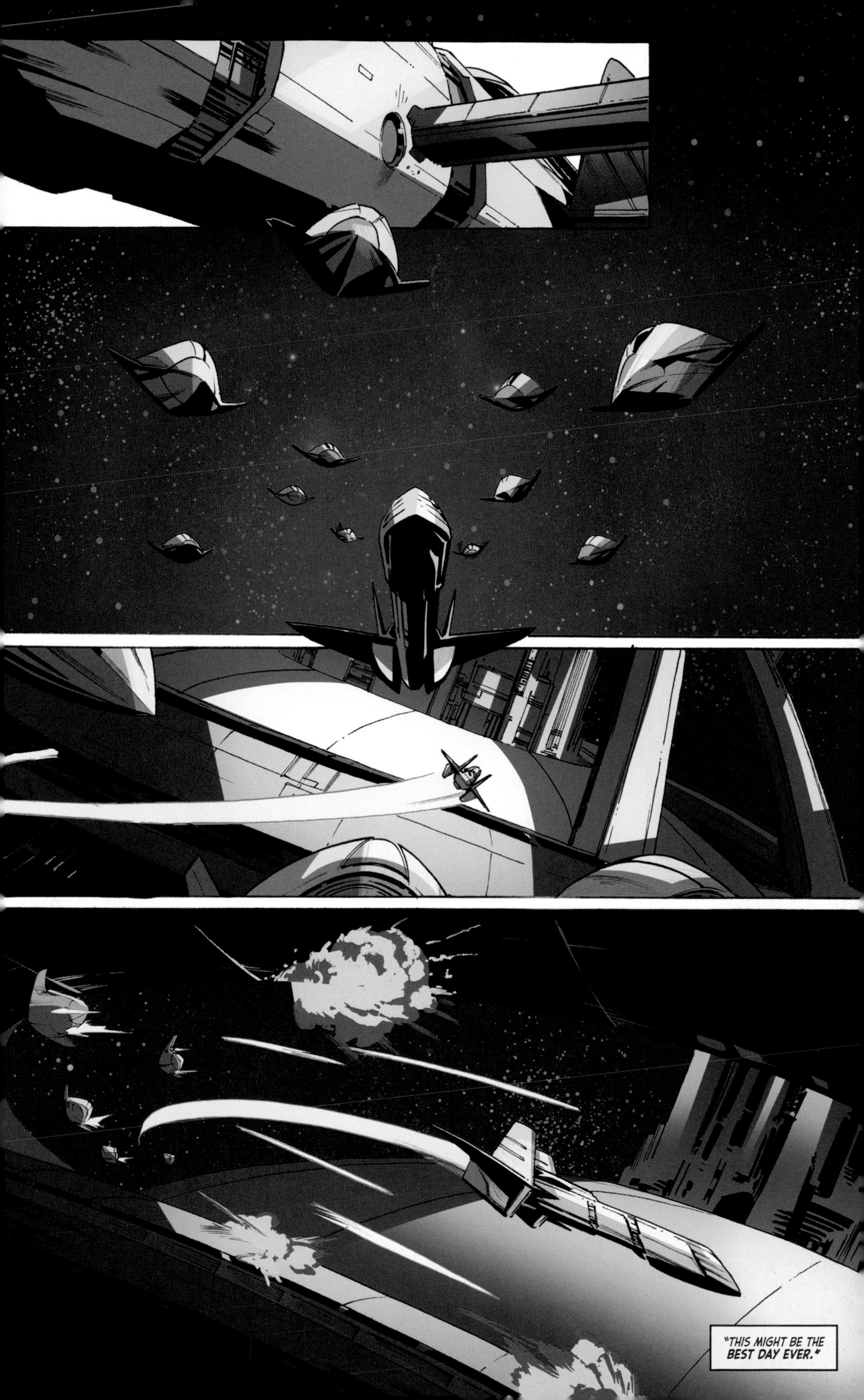
"THIS MIGHT BE THE BEST DAY EVER."

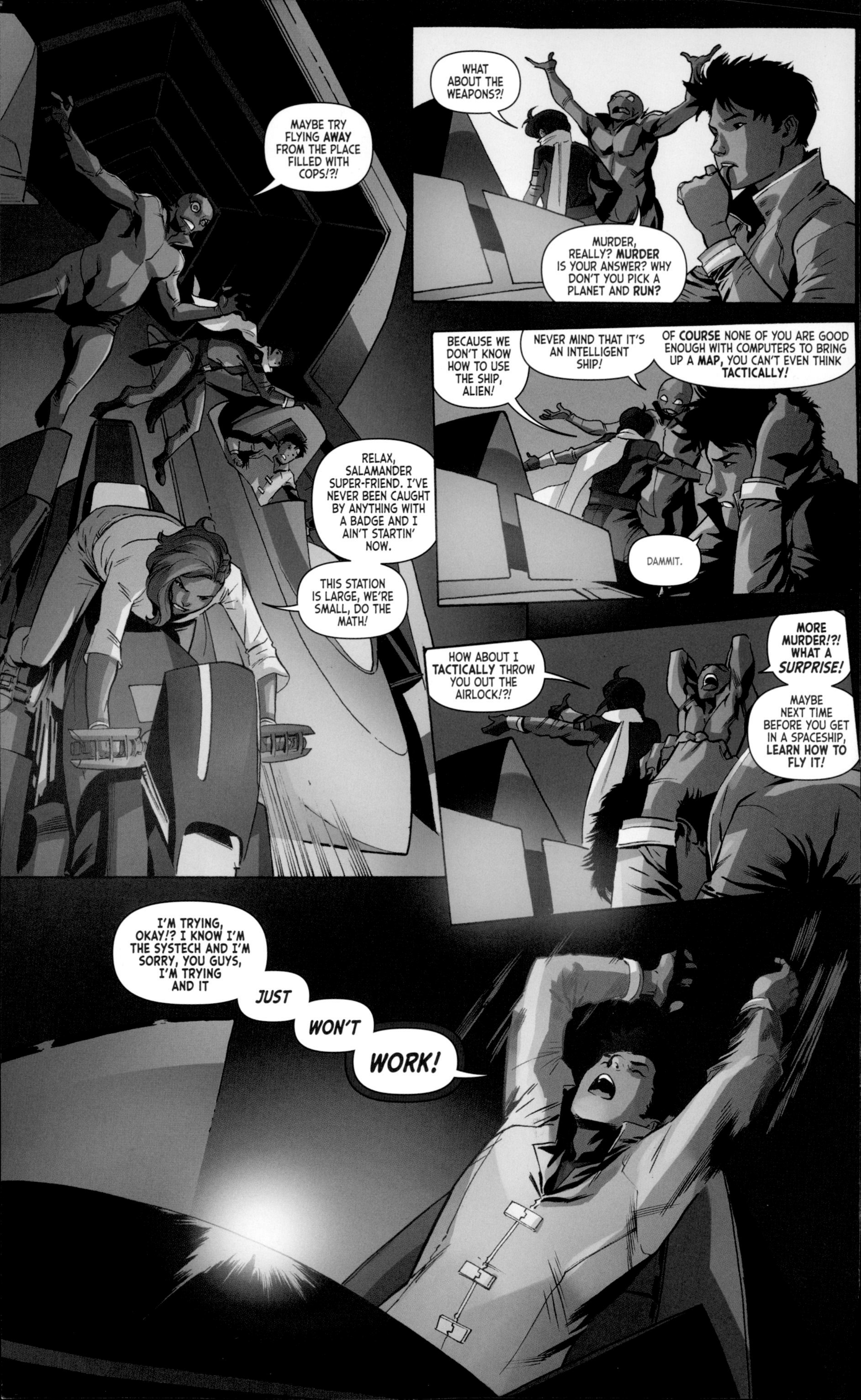
MAYBE TRY FLYING **AWAY** FROM THE PLACE FILLED WITH COPS!?!
WHAT ABOUT THE WEAPONS?!
MURDER, REALLY? **MURDER** IS YOUR ANSWER? WHY DON'T YOU PICK A PLANET AND **RUN?**
RELAX, SALAMANDER SUPER-FRIEND. I'VE NEVER BEEN CAUGHT BY ANYTHING WITH A BADGE AND I AIN'T STARTIN' NOW.
THIS STATION IS LARGE, WE'RE SMALL, DO THE MATH!
BECAUSE WE DON'T KNOW HOW TO USE THE SHIP, ALIEN!
NEVER MIND THAT IT'S AN INTELLIGENT SHIP!
OF **COURSE** NONE OF YOU ARE GOOD ENOUGH WITH COMPUTERS TO BRING UP A **MAP,** YOU CAN'T EVEN THINK **TACTICALLY!**
DAMMIT.
HOW ABOUT I **TACTICALLY** THROW YOU OUT THE AIRLOCK!?!
MORE MURDER!?! WHAT A *SURPRISE!*
MAYBE NEXT TIME BEFORE YOU GET IN A SPACESHIP, **LEARN HOW TO FLY IT!**
I'M TRYING, OKAY!? I KNOW I'M THE SYSTECH AND I'M SORRY, YOU GUYS, I'M TRYING AND IT
JUST
WON'T
WORK!

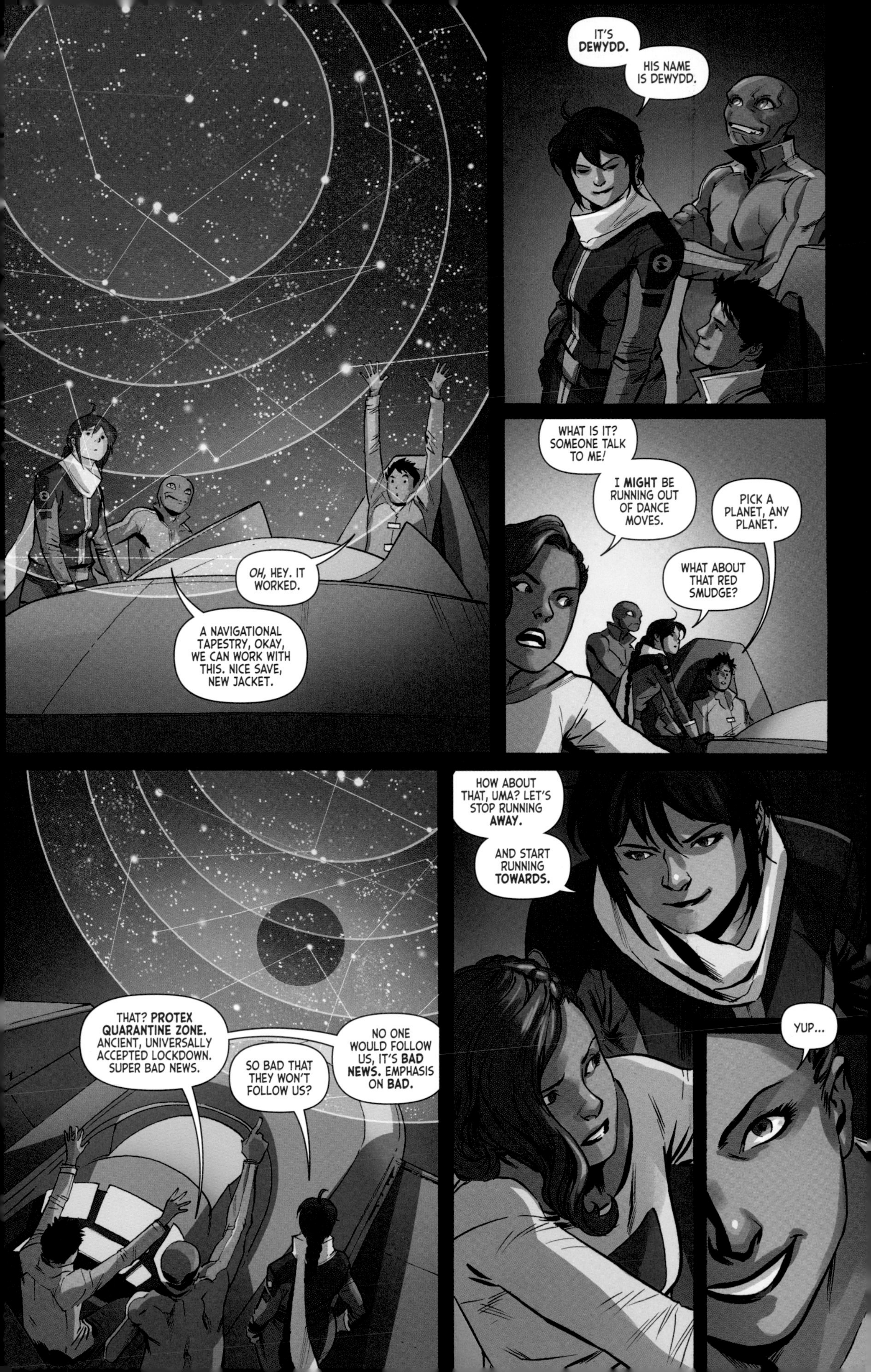

IT'S **DEWYDD.**
HIS NAME IS DEWYDD.
OH, HEY. IT WORKED.
A NAVIGATIONAL TAPESTRY, OKAY, WE CAN WORK WITH THIS. NICE SAVE, NEW JACKET.
WHAT IS IT? SOMEONE TALK TO ME!
I **MIGHT** BE RUNNING OUT OF DANCE MOVES.
PICK A PLANET, ANY PLANET.
WHAT ABOUT THAT RED SMUDGE?
THAT? **PROTEX QUARANTINE ZONE.** ANCIENT, UNIVERSALLY ACCEPTED LOCKDOWN. SUPER BAD NEWS.
SO BAD THAT THEY WON'T FOLLOW US?
NO ONE WOULD FOLLOW US, IT'S **BAD NEWS.** EMPHASIS ON **BAD.**
HOW ABOUT THAT, UMA? LET'S STOP RUNNING **AWAY.**
AND START RUNNING **TOWARDS.**
YUP...

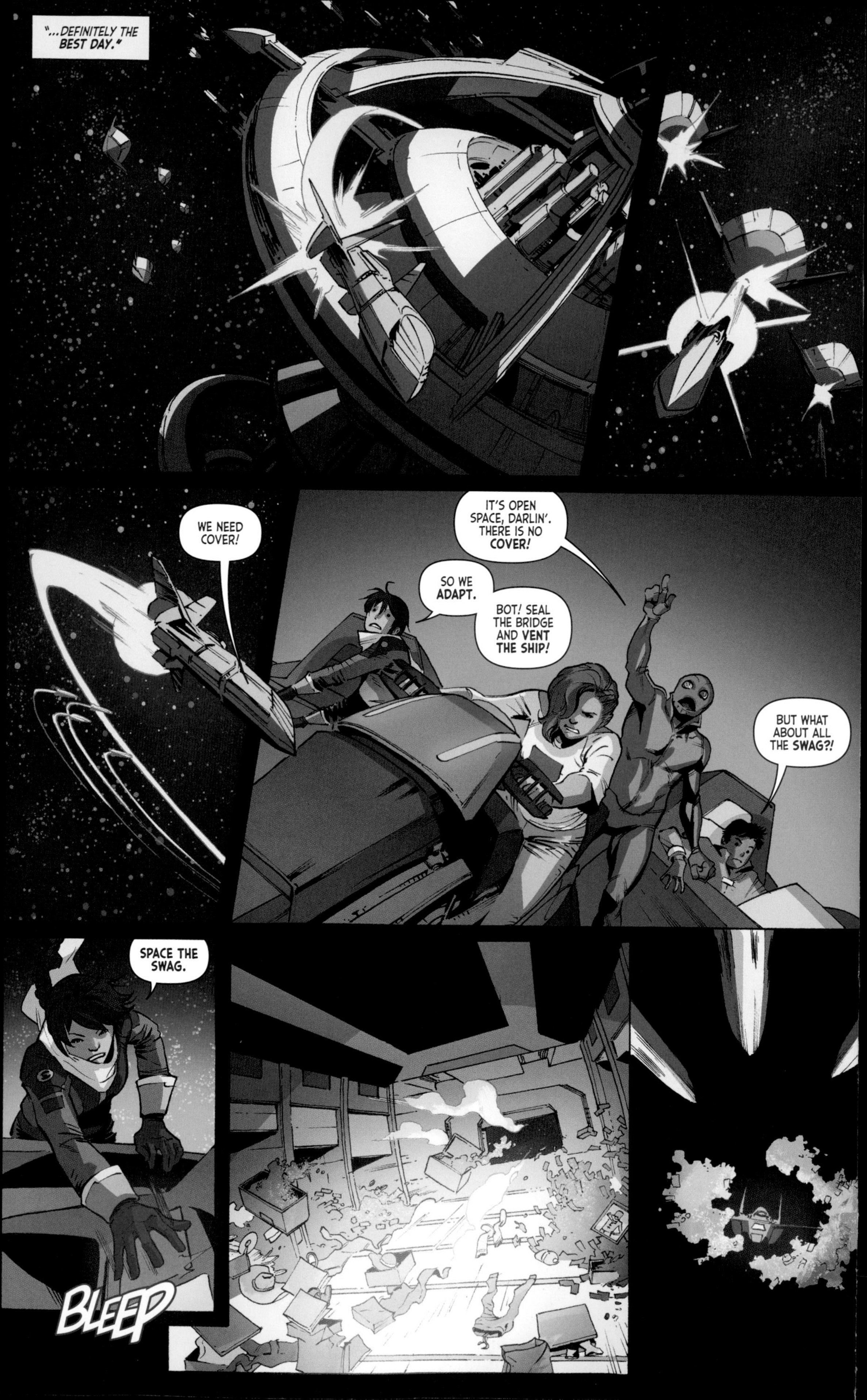
"...DEFINITELY THE BEST DAY."
WE NEED COVER!
IT'S OPEN SPACE, DARLIN'. THERE IS NO COVER!
SO WE ADAPT.
BOT! SEAL THE BRIDGE AND VENT THE SHIP!
BUT WHAT ABOUT ALL THE SWAG?!
SPACE THE SWAG.
BLEEP

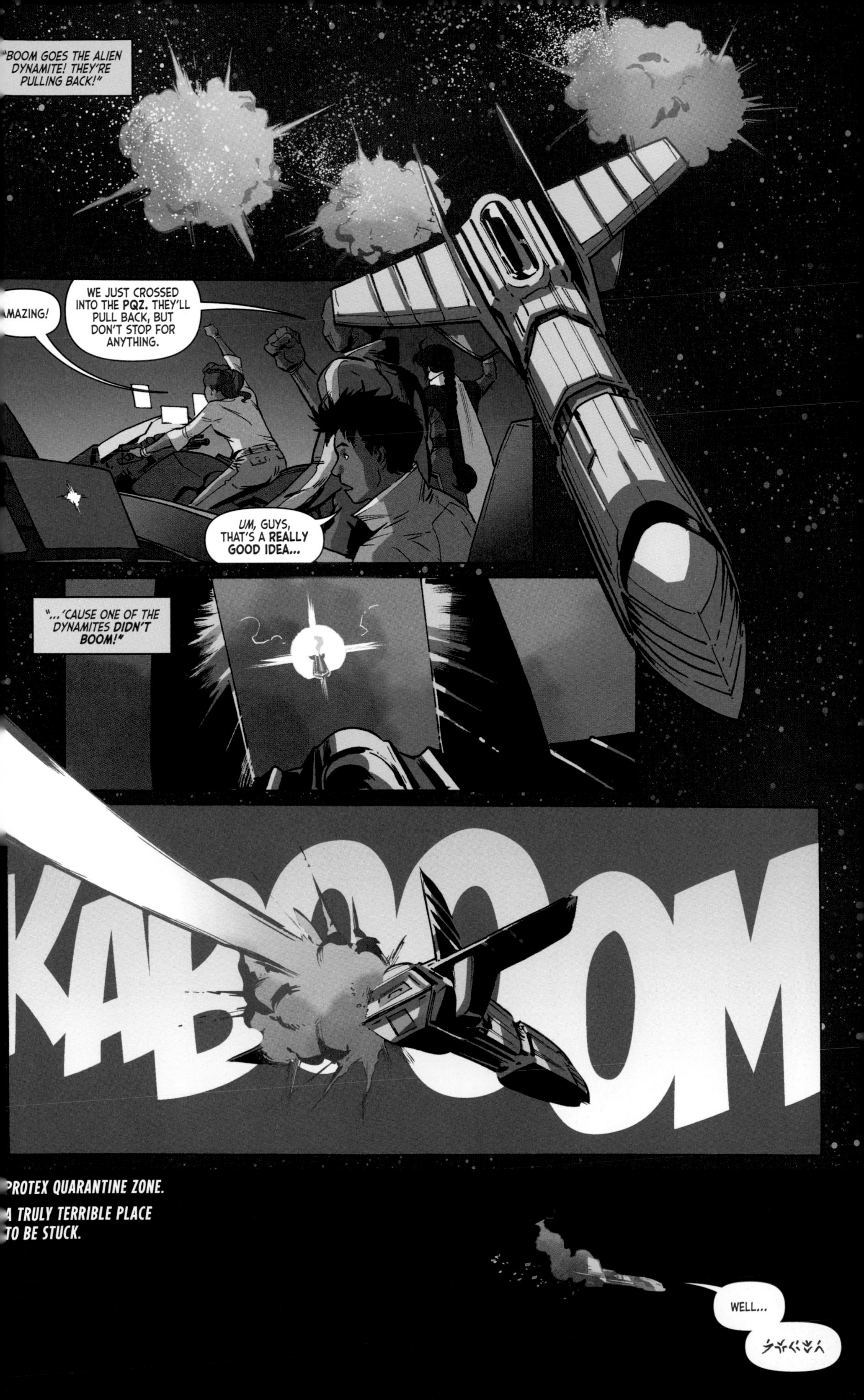
"BOOM GOES THE ALIEN DYNAMITE! THEY'RE PULLING BACK!"
MAZING!
WE JUST CROSSED INTO THE PQZ. THEY'LL PULL BACK, BUT DON'T STOP FOR ANYTHING.
UM, GUYS, THAT'S A REALLY GOOD IDEA...
"...'CAUSE ONE OF THE DYNAMITES DIDN'T BOOM!"
KABOOOOM
ROTEX QUARANTINE ZONE.
A TRULY TERRIBLE PLACE TO BE STUCK.
WELL...

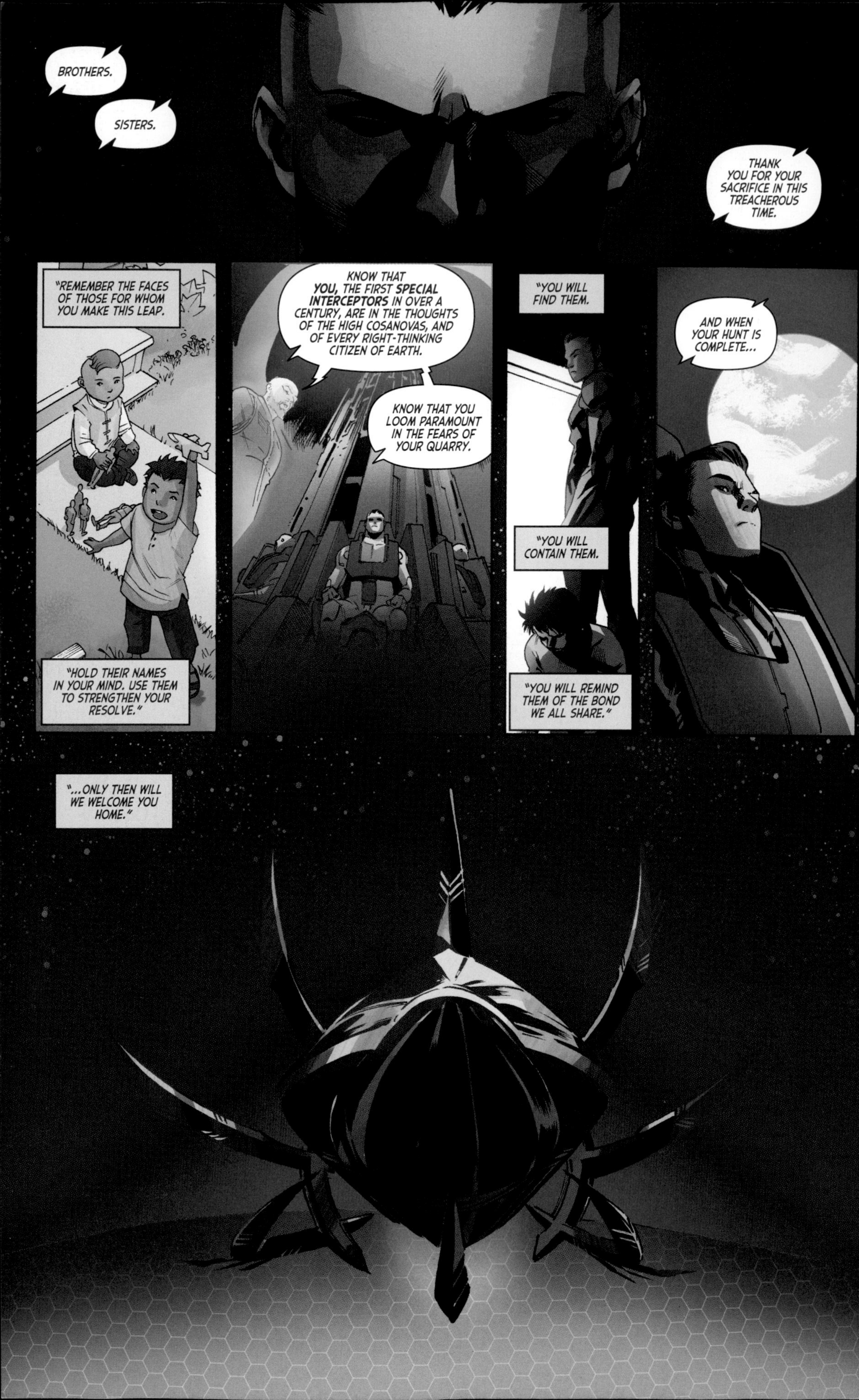
BROTHERS.
SISTERS.
THANK YOU FOR YOUR SACRIFICE IN THIS TREACHEROUS TIME.
"REMEMBER THE FACES OF THOSE FOR WHOM YOU MAKE THIS LEAP.
"HOLD THEIR NAMES IN YOUR MIND. USE THEM TO STRENGTHEN YOUR RESOLVE."
KNOW THAT **YOU,** THE FIRST **SPECIAL INTERCEPTORS** IN OVER A CENTURY, ARE IN THE THOUGHTS OF THE HIGH COSANOVAS, AND OF EVERY RIGHT-THINKING CITIZEN OF EARTH.
KNOW THAT YOU LOOM PARAMOUNT IN THE FEARS OF YOUR QUARRY.
"YOU WILL FIND THEM.
"YOU WILL CONTAIN THEM.
"YOU WILL REMIND THEM OF THE BOND WE ALL SHARE."
AND WHEN YOUR HUNT IS COMPLETE...
"...ONLY THEN WILL WE WELCOME YOU HOME."

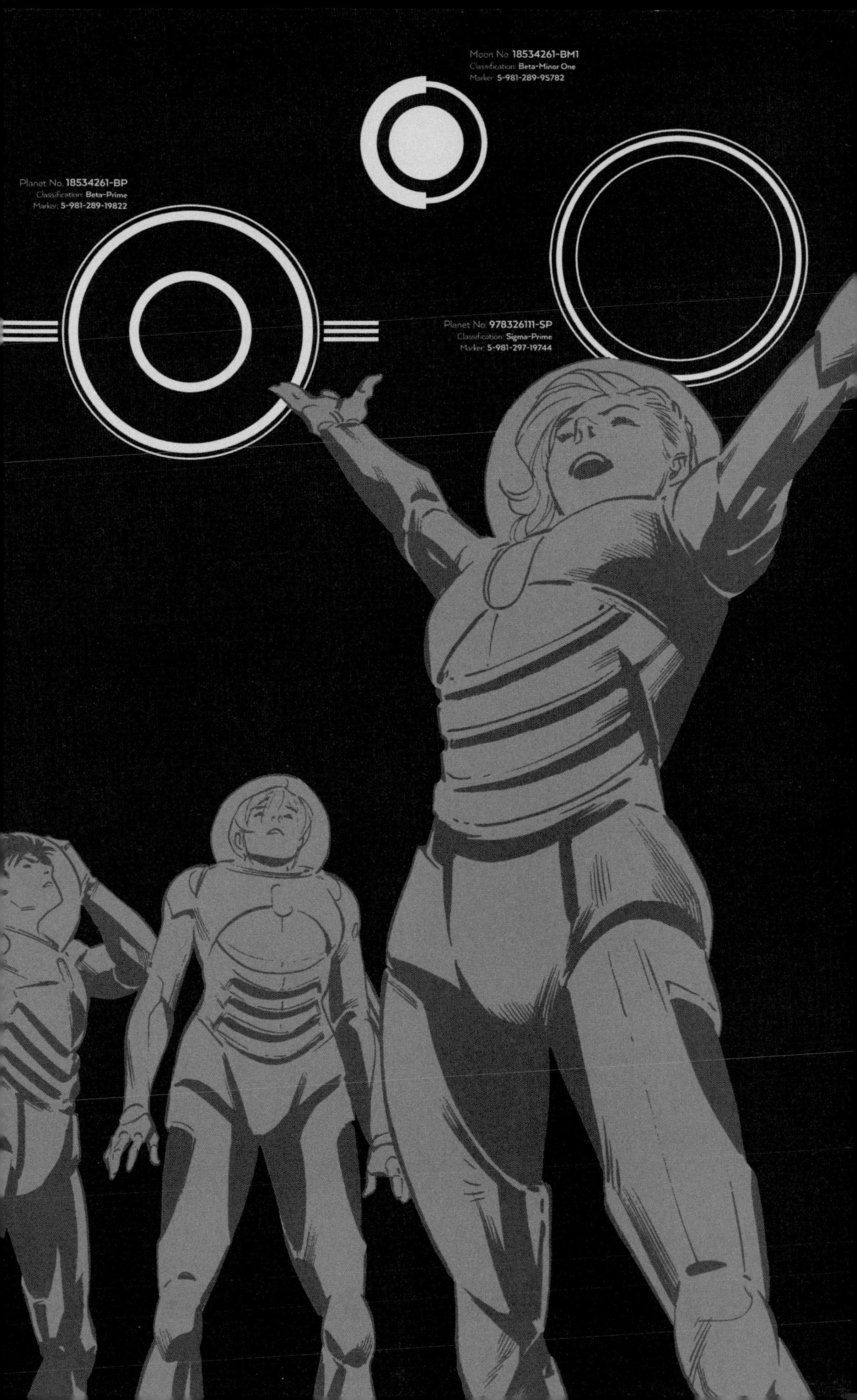
Moon No 18534261-BM1
Classification: Beta-Minor One
Marker: 5-981-289-95782
Planet No. 18534261-BP
Classification: Beta-Prime
Marker: 5-981-289-19822
Planet No. 978326111-SP
Classification: Sigma-Prime
Marker: 5-981-297-19744

STUCK IN SPACE

CHAPTER **THREE**

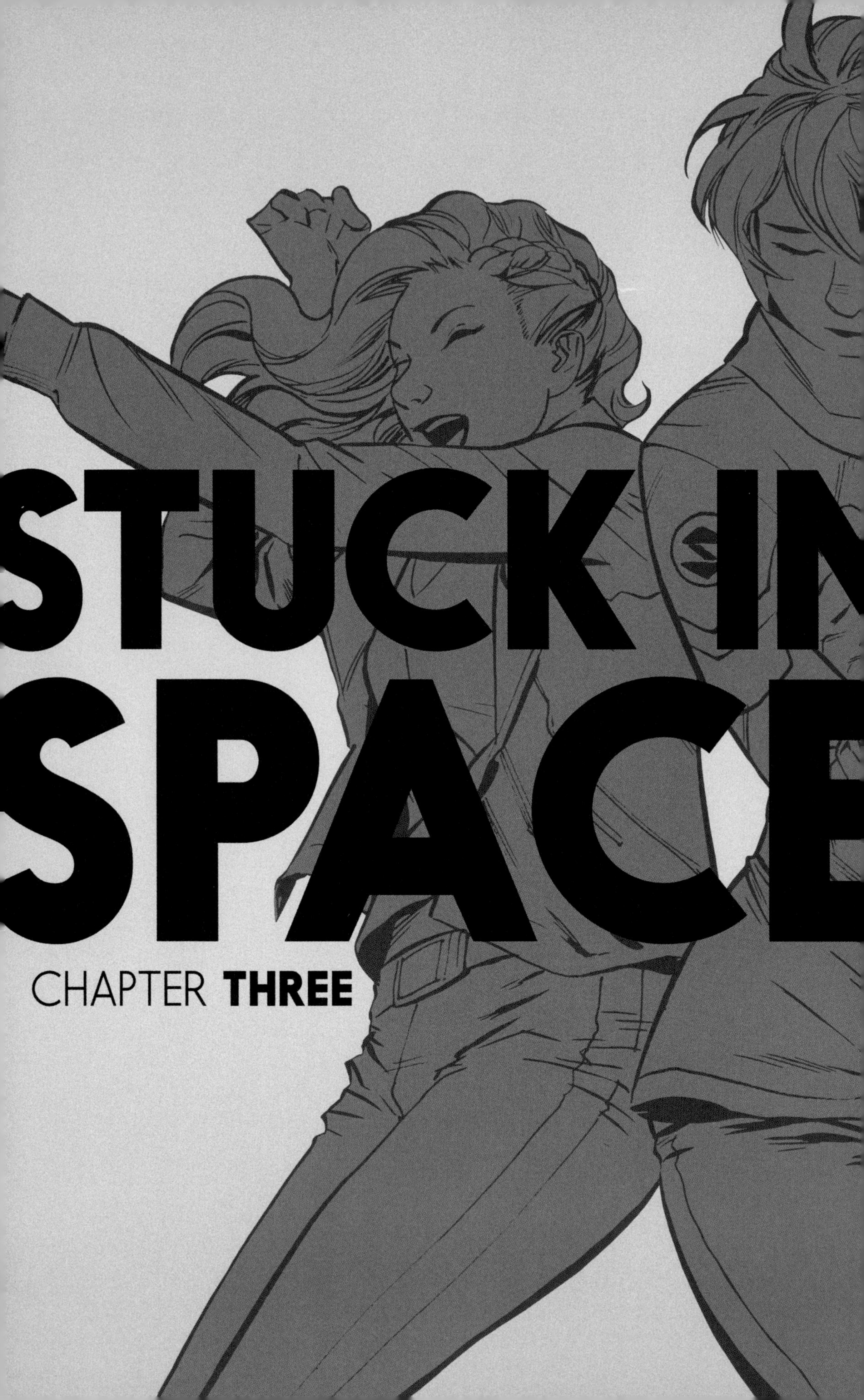

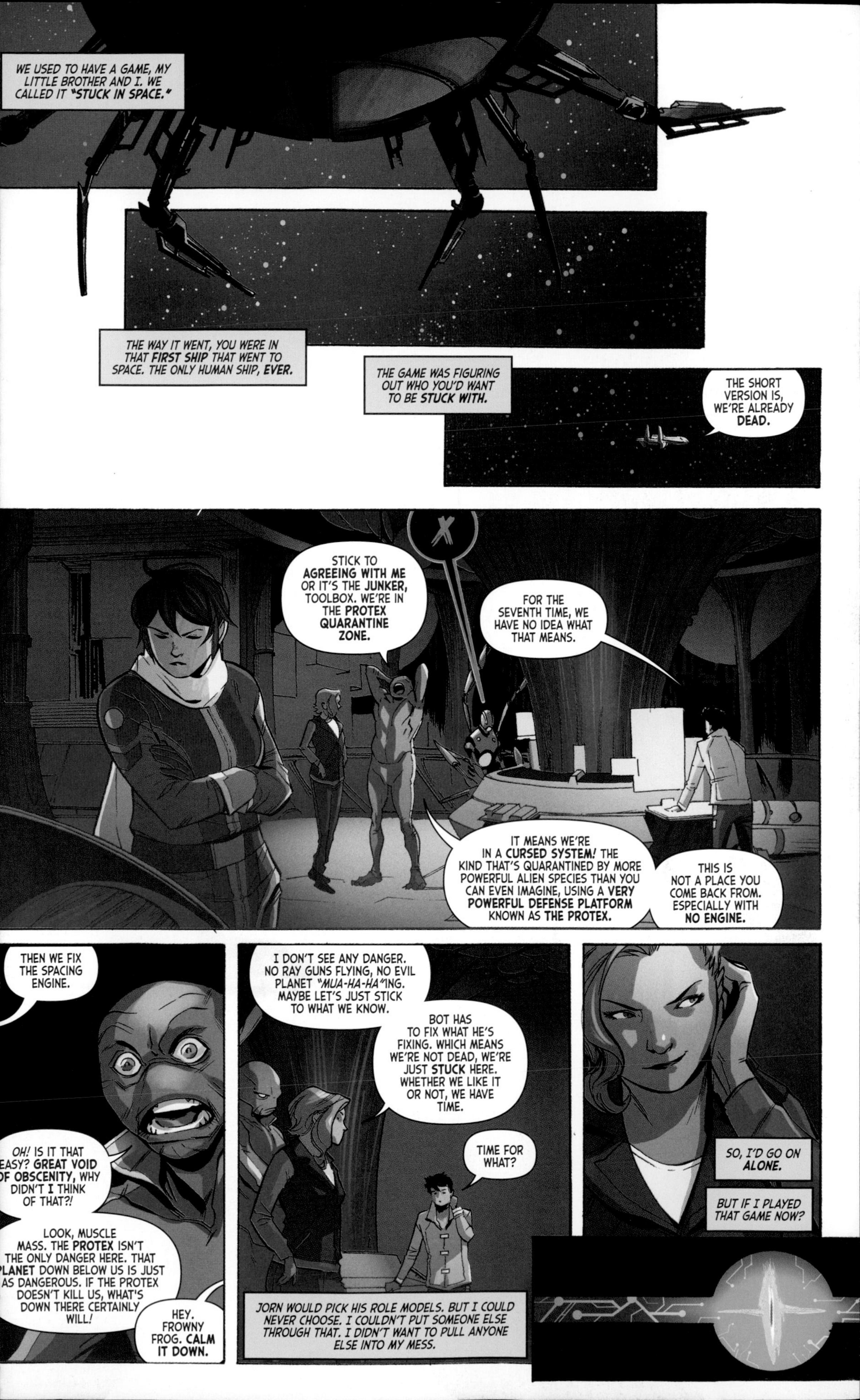

WE USED TO HAVE A GAME, MY LITTLE BROTHER AND I. WE CALLED IT "STUCK IN SPACE."
THE WAY IT WENT, YOU WERE IN THAT FIRST SHIP THAT WENT TO SPACE. THE ONLY HUMAN SHIP, EVER.
THE GAME WAS FIGURING OUT WHO YOU'D WANT TO BE STUCK WITH.
THE SHORT VERSION IS, WE'RE ALREADY DEAD.
STICK TO AGREEING WITH ME OR IT'S THE JUNKER, TOOLBOX. WE'RE IN THE PROTEX QUARANTINE ZONE.
FOR THE SEVENTH TIME, WE HAVE NO IDEA WHAT THAT MEANS.
IT MEANS WE'RE IN A CURSED SYSTEM! THE KIND THAT'S QUARANTINED BY MORE POWERFUL ALIEN SPECIES THAN YOU CAN EVEN IMAGINE, USING A VERY POWERFUL DEFENSE PLATFORM KNOWN AS THE PROTEX.
THIS IS NOT A PLACE YOU COME BACK FROM. ESPECIALLY WITH NO ENGINE.
THEN WE FIX THE SPACING ENGINE.
OH! IS IT THAT EASY? GREAT VOID OF OBSCENITY, WHY DIDN'T I THINK OF THAT?!
LOOK, MUSCLE MASS. THE PROTEX ISN'T THE ONLY DANGER HERE. THAT PLANET DOWN BELOW US IS JUST AS DANGEROUS. IF THE PROTEX DOESN'T KILL US, WHAT'S DOWN THERE CERTAINLY WILL!
HEY. FROWNY FROG. CALM IT DOWN.
I DON'T SEE ANY DANGER. NO RAY GUNS FLYING, NO EVIL PLANET "MUA-HA-HA"ING. MAYBE LET'S JUST STICK TO WHAT WE KNOW.
BOT HAS TO FIX WHAT HE'S FIXING. WHICH MEANS WE'RE NOT DEAD, WE'RE JUST STUCK HERE. WHETHER WE LIKE IT OR NOT, WE HAVE TIME.
TIME FOR WHAT?
JORN WOULD PICK HIS ROLE MODELS. BUT I COULD NEVER CHOOSE. I COULDN'T PUT SOMEONE ELSE THROUGH THAT. I DIDN'T WANT TO PULL ANYONE ELSE INTO MY MESS.
SO, I'D GO ON ALONE.
BUT IF I PLAYED THAT GAME NOW?

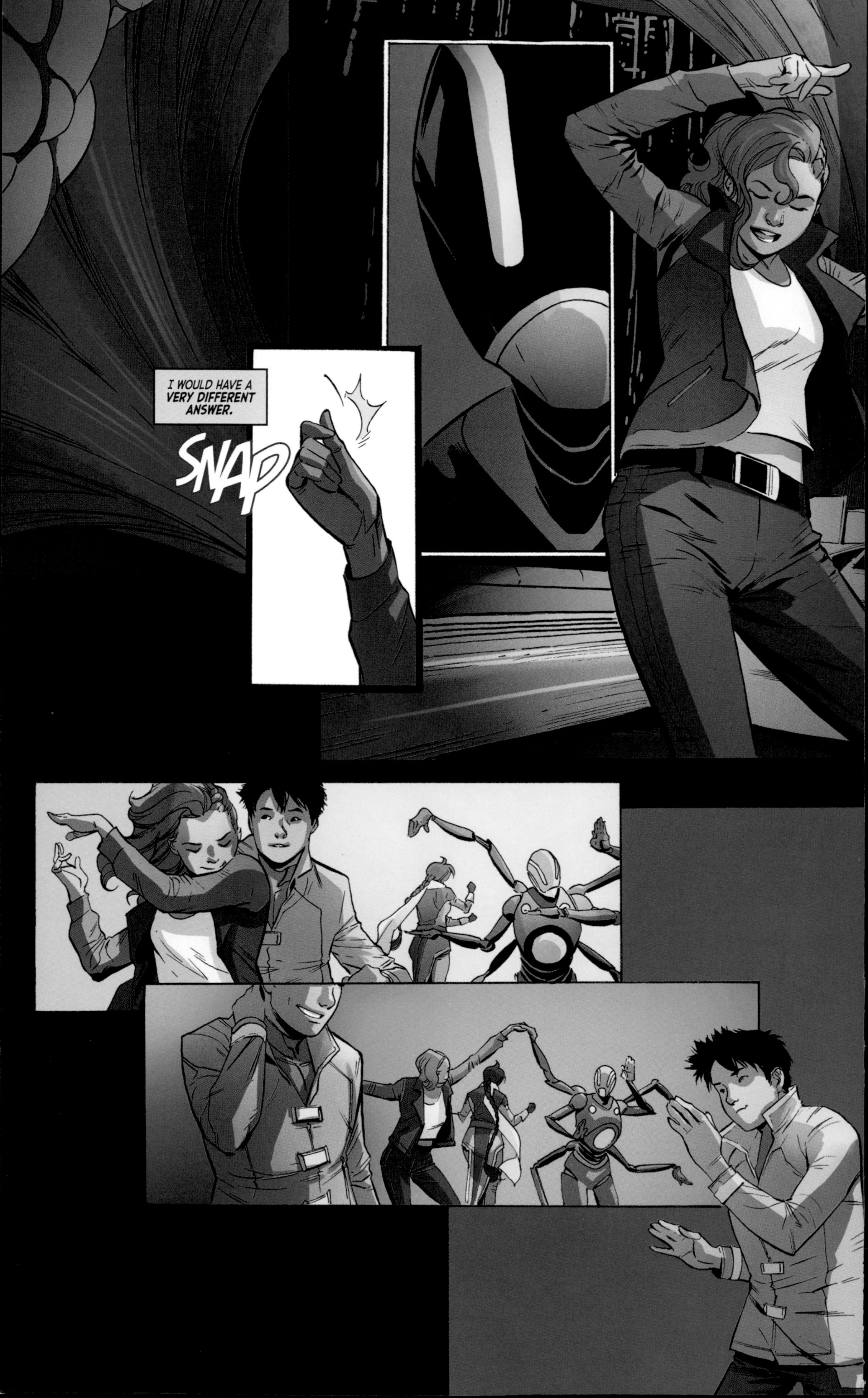
I WOULD HAVE A VERY DIFFERENT ANSWER.
SNAP

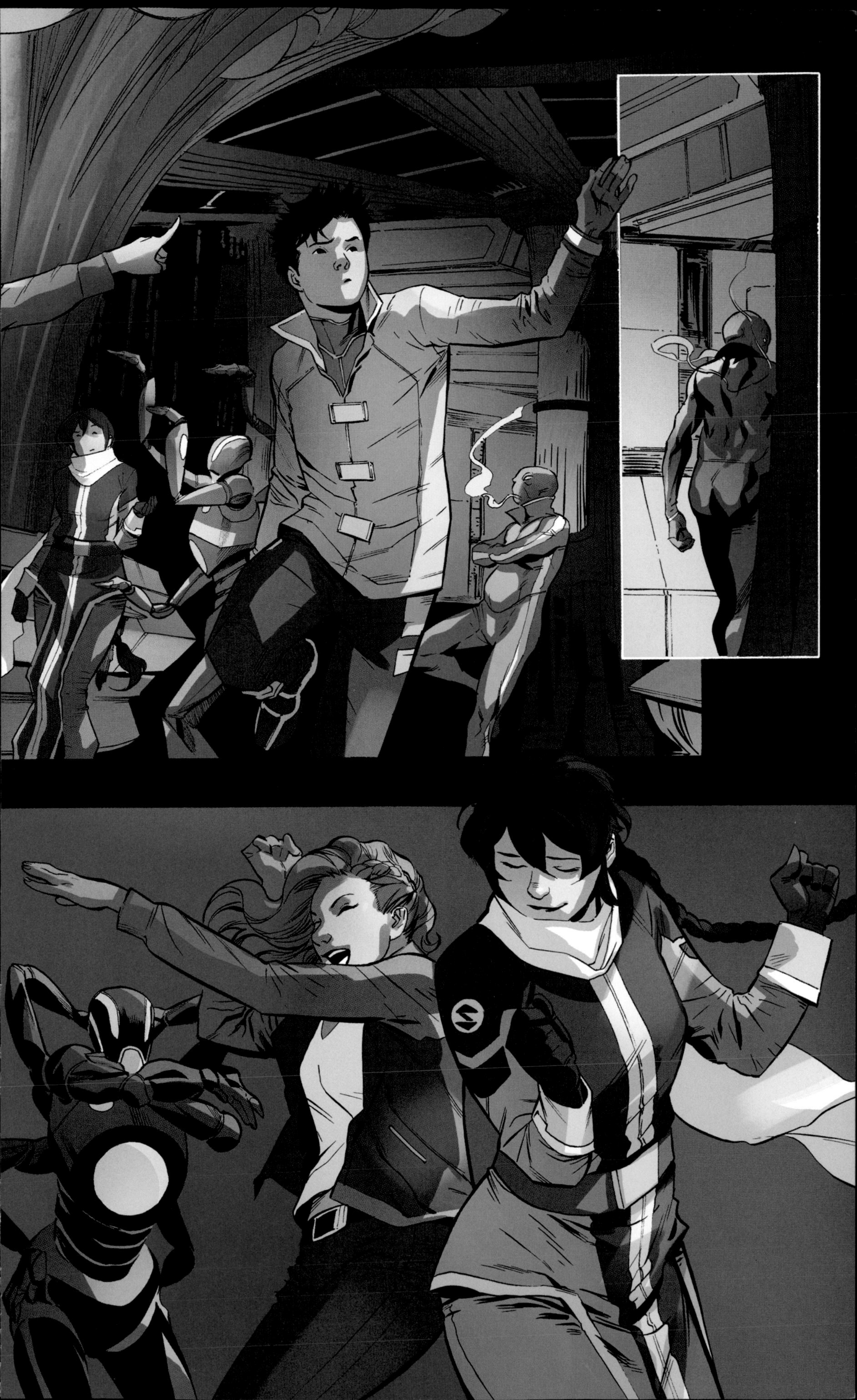

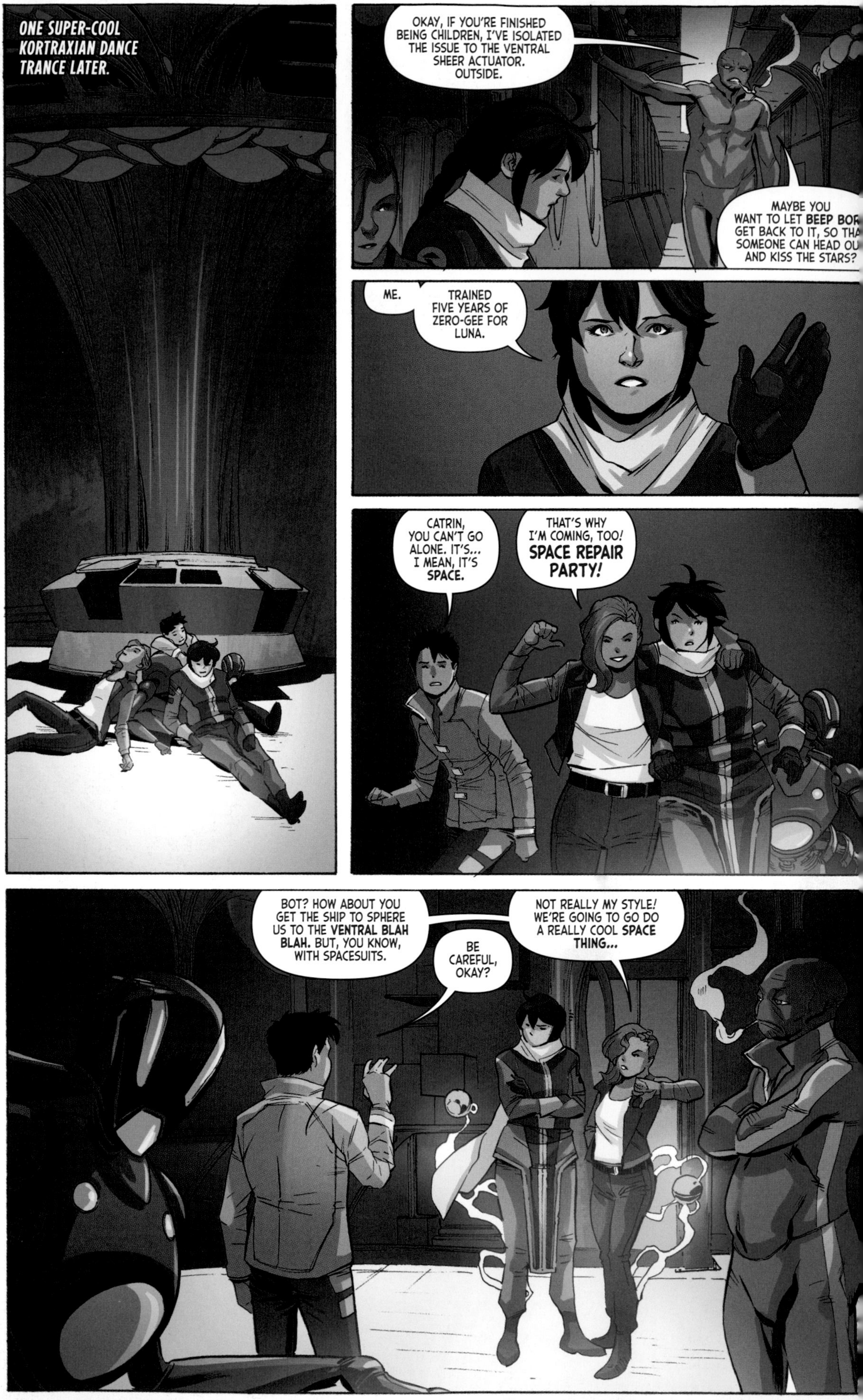
ONE SUPER-COOL KORTRAXIAN DANCE TRANCE LATER.
OKAY, IF YOU'RE FINISHED BEING CHILDREN, I'VE ISOLATED THE ISSUE TO THE VENTRAL SHEER ACTUATOR. OUTSIDE.
MAYBE YOU WANT TO LET BEEP BOR GET BACK TO IT, SO THA SOMEONE CAN HEAD OU AND KISS THE STARS?
ME.
TRAINED FIVE YEARS OF ZERO-GEE FOR LUNA.
CATRIN, YOU CAN'T GO ALONE. IT'S... I MEAN, IT'S SPACE.
THAT'S WHY I'M COMING, TOO! SPACE REPAIR PARTY!
BOT? HOW ABOUT YOU GET THE SHIP TO SPHERE US TO THE VENTRAL BLAH BLAH. BUT, YOU KNOW, WITH SPACESUITS.
BE CAREFUL, OKAY?
NOT REALLY MY STYLE! WE'RE GOING TO GO DO A REALLY COOL SPACE THING...

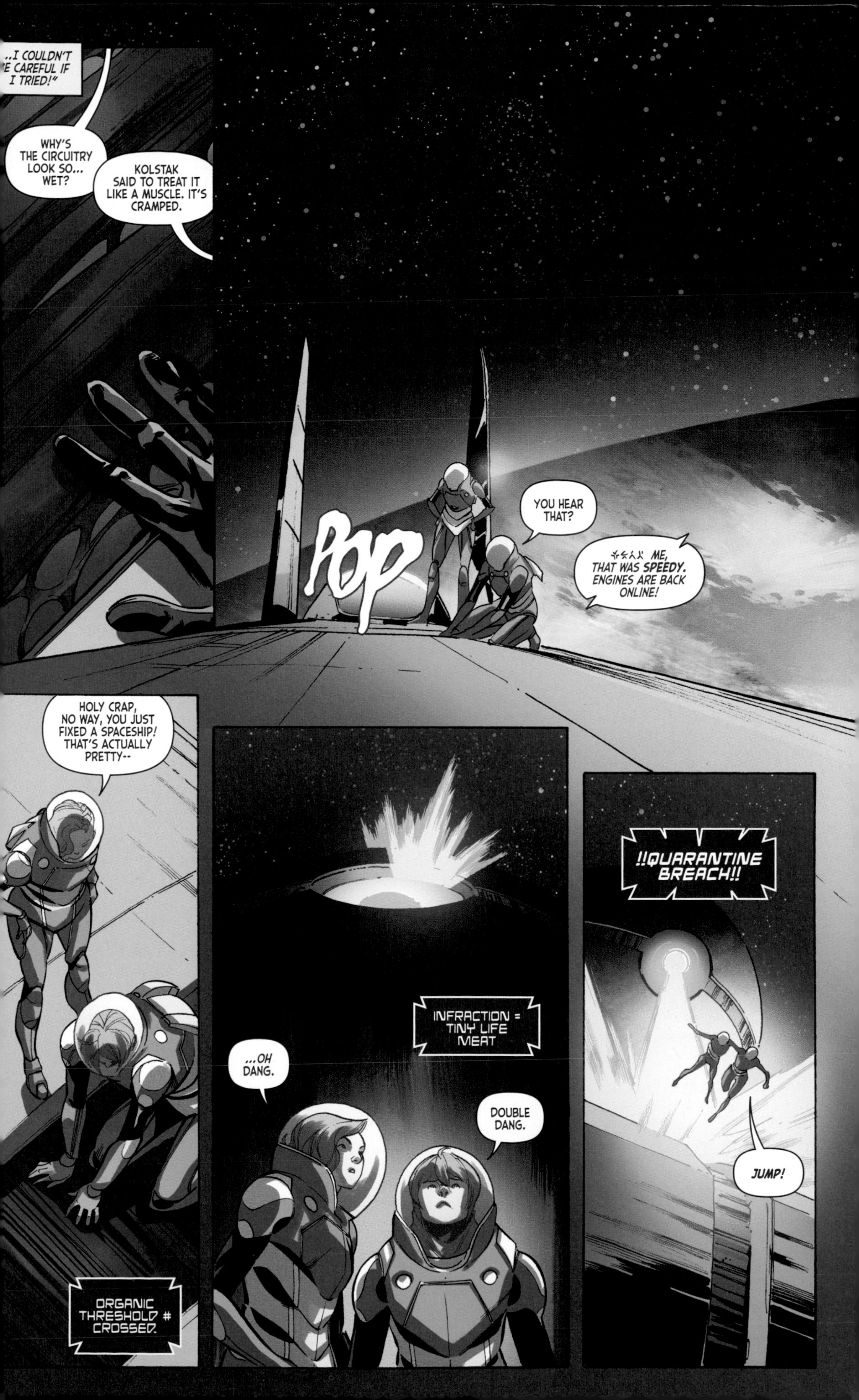
..I COULDN'T 'E CAREFUL IF I TRIED!"
WHY'S THE CIRCUITRY LOOK SO... WET?
KOLSTAK SAID TO TREAT IT LIKE A MUSCLE. IT'S CRAMPED.
POP
YOU HEAR THAT?
ME, THAT WAS SPEEDY. ENGINES ARE BACK ONLINE!
HOLY CRAP, NO WAY, YOU JUST FIXED A SPACESHIP! THAT'S ACTUALLY PRETTY--
ORGANIC THRESHOLD # CROSSED.
INFRACTION = TINY LIFE MEAT
...OH DANG.
DOUBLE DANG.
!!QUARANTINE BREACH!!
JUMP!

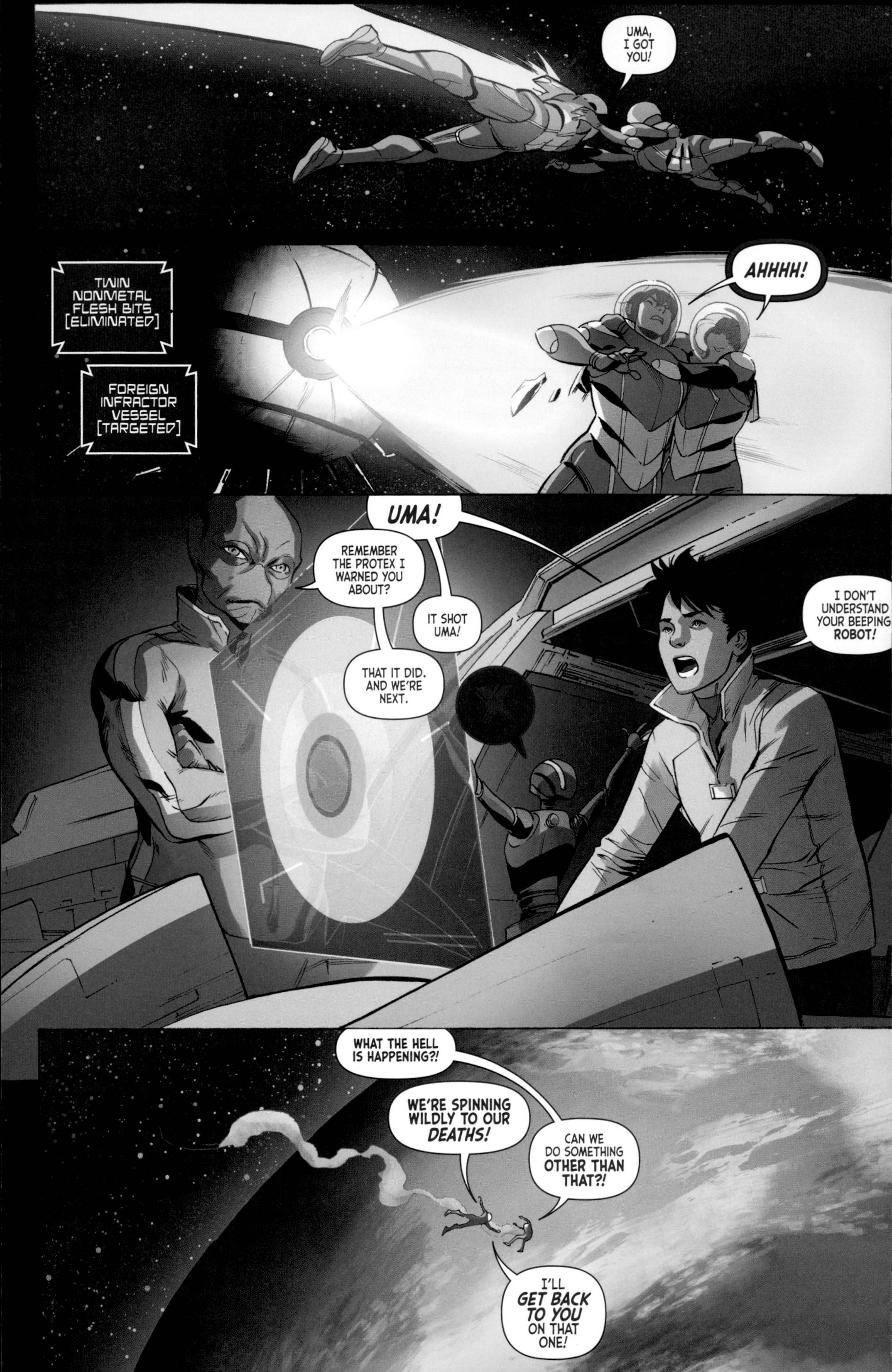
UMA, I GOT YOU!
TWIN NONMETAL FLESH BITS [ELIMINATED]
FOREIGN INFRACTOR VESSEL [TARGETED]
AHHHH!
UMA!
REMEMBER THE PROTEX I WARNED YOU ABOUT?
IT SHOT UMA!
THAT IT DID. AND WE'RE NEXT.
I DON'T UNDERSTAND YOUR BEEPING ROBOT!
WHAT THE HELL IS HAPPENING?!
WE'RE SPINNING WILDLY TO OUR DEATHS!
CAN WE DO SOMETHING OTHER THAN THAT?!
I'LL GET BACK TO YOU ON THAT ONE!

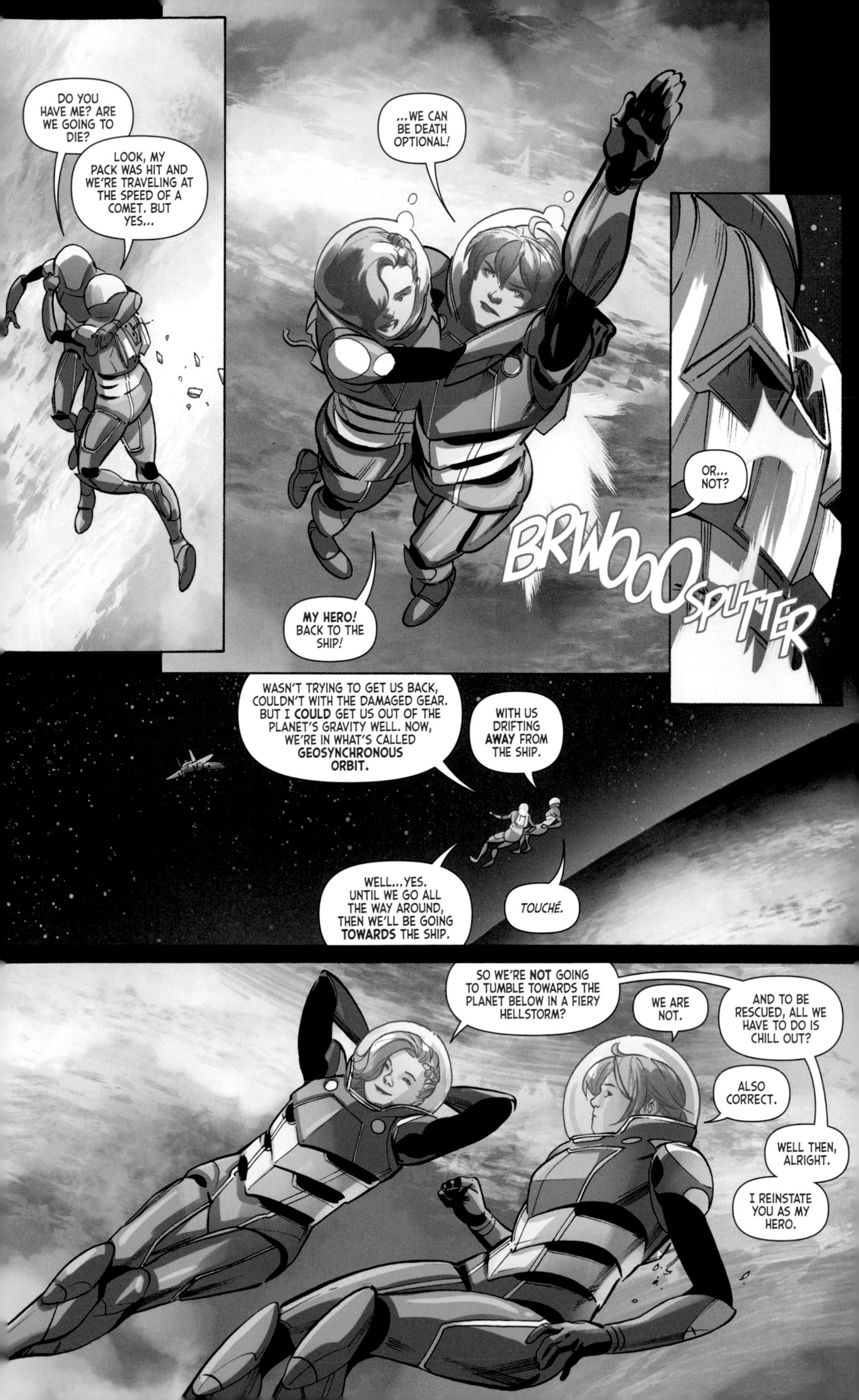
DO YOU HAVE ME? ARE WE GOING TO DIE?
LOOK, MY PACK WAS HIT AND WE'RE TRAVELING AT THE SPEED OF A COMET. BUT YES...
...WE CAN BE DEATH OPTIONAL!
MY HERO! BACK TO THE SHIP!
OR... NOT?
BRWOOOSPUTTER
WASN'T TRYING TO GET US BACK, COULDN'T WITH THE DAMAGED GEAR. BUT I COULD GET US OUT OF THE PLANET'S GRAVITY WELL. NOW, WE'RE IN WHAT'S CALLED GEOSYNCHRONOUS ORBIT.
WITH US DRIFTING AWAY FROM THE SHIP.
WELL...YES. UNTIL WE GO ALL THE WAY AROUND, THEN WE'LL BE GOING TOWARDS THE SHIP.
TOUCHÉ.
SO WE'RE NOT GOING TO TUMBLE TOWARDS THE PLANET BELOW IN A FIERY HELLSTORM?
WE ARE NOT.
AND TO BE RESCUED, ALL WE HAVE TO DO IS CHILL OUT?
ALSO CORRECT.
WELL THEN, ALRIGHT.
I REINSTATE YOU AS MY HERO.

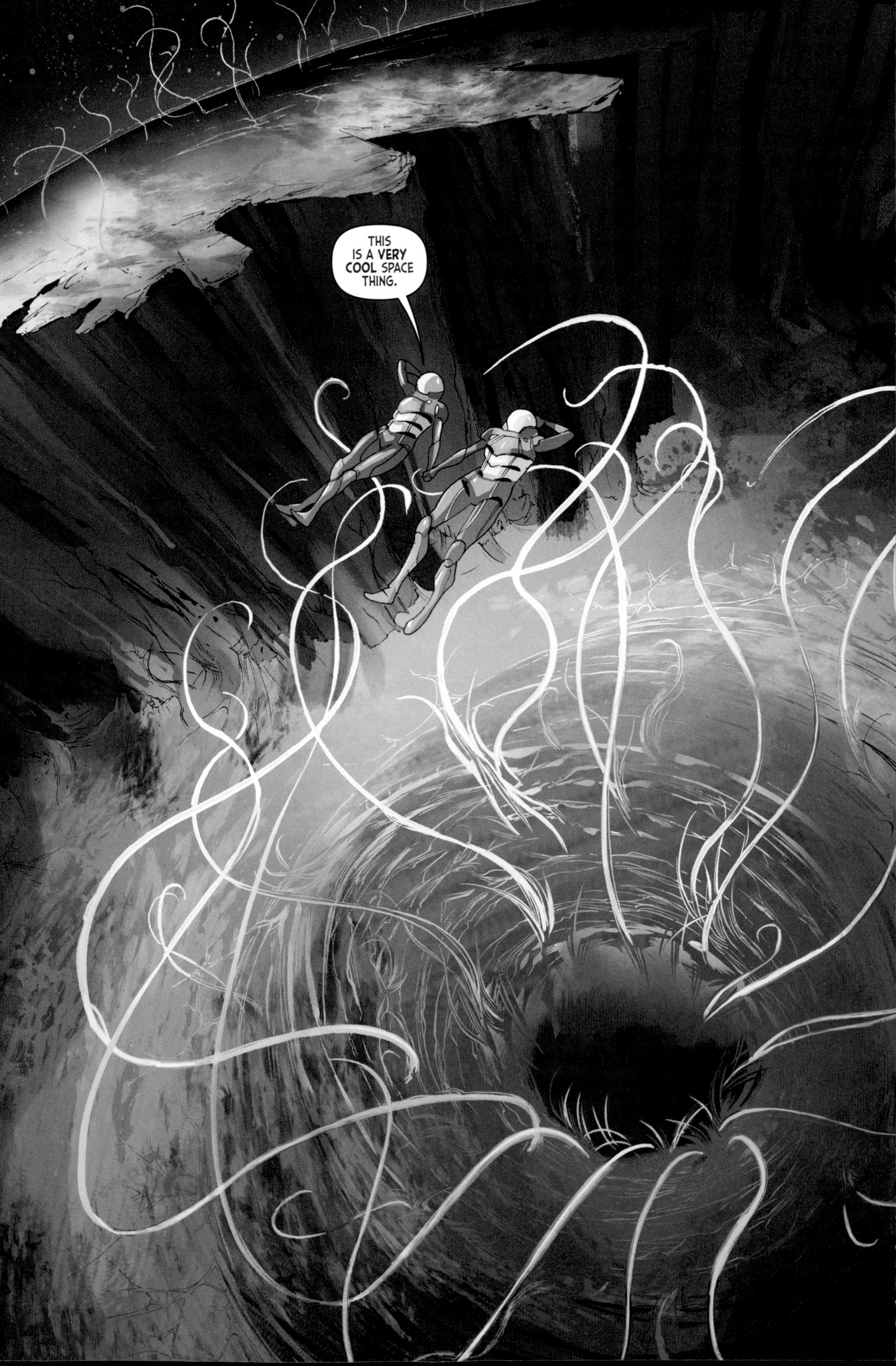
THIS IS A **VERY COOL** SPACE THING.

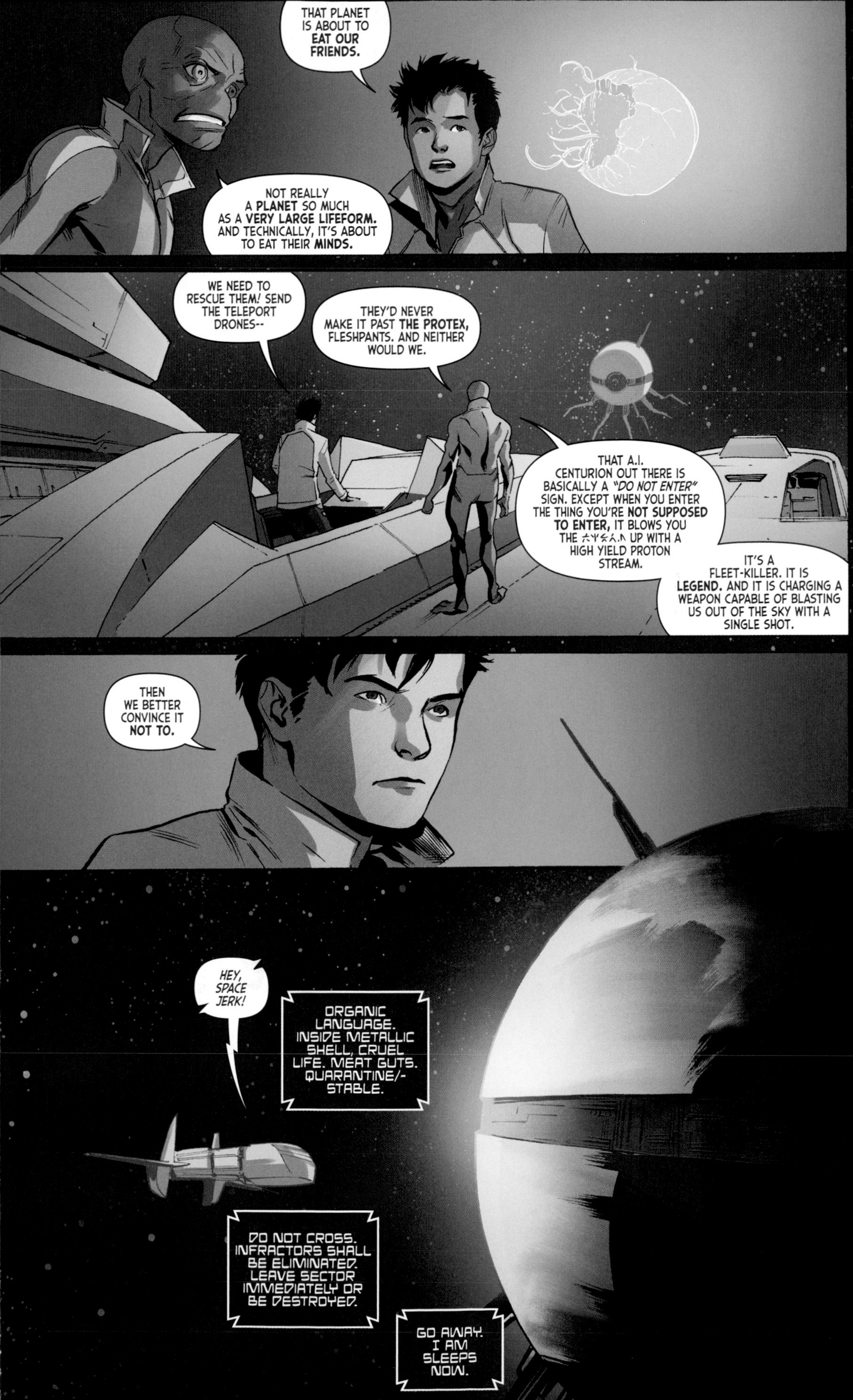
THAT PLANET IS ABOUT TO EAT OUR FRIENDS.
NOT REALLY A PLANET SO MUCH AS A VERY LARGE LIFEFORM. AND TECHNICALLY, IT'S ABOUT TO EAT THEIR MINDS.
WE NEED TO RESCUE THEM! SEND THE TELEPORT DRONES--
THEY'D NEVER MAKE IT PAST THE PROTEX, FLESHPANTS. AND NEITHER WOULD WE.
THAT A.I. CENTURION OUT THERE IS BASICALLY A "DO NOT ENTER" SIGN. EXCEPT WHEN YOU ENTER THE THING YOU'RE NOT SUPPOSED TO ENTER, IT BLOWS YOU THE UP WITH A HIGH YIELD PROTON STREAM.
IT'S A FLEET-KILLER. IT IS LEGEND. AND IT IS CHARGING A WEAPON CAPABLE OF BLASTING US OUT OF THE SKY WITH A SINGLE SHOT.
THEN WE BETTER CONVINCE IT NOT TO.
HEY, SPACE JERK!
ORGANIC LANGUAGE. INSIDE METALLIC SHELL, CRUEL LIFE. MEAT GUTS. QUARANTINE/-STABLE.
DO NOT CROSS. INFRACTORS SHALL BE ELIMINATED. LEAVE SECTOR IMMEDIATELY OR BE DESTROYED.
GO AWAY. I AM SLEEPS NOW.

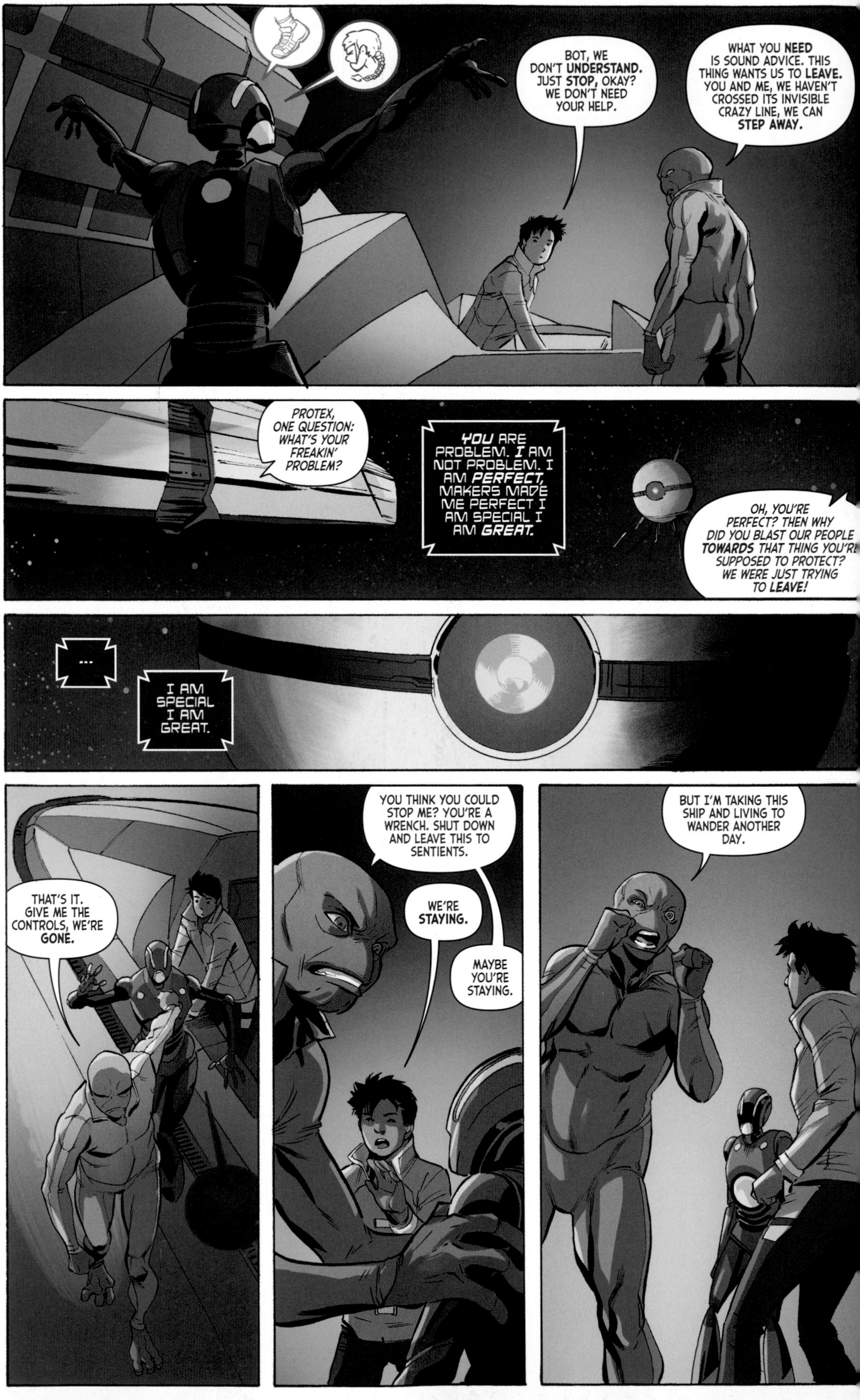
BOT, WE DON'T UNDERSTAND. JUST STOP, OKAY? WE DON'T NEED YOUR HELP.
WHAT YOU NEED IS SOUND ADVICE. THIS THING WANTS US TO LEAVE. YOU AND ME, WE HAVEN'T CROSSED ITS INVISIBLE CRAZY LINE, WE CAN STEP AWAY.
PROTEX, ONE QUESTION: WHAT'S YOUR FREAKIN' PROBLEM?
YOU ARE PROBLEM. I AM NOT PROBLEM. I AM PERFECT, MAKERS MADE ME PERFECT I AM SPECIAL I AM GREAT.
OH, YOU'RE PERFECT? THEN WHY DID YOU BLAST OUR PEOPLE TOWARDS THAT THING YOU'RE SUPPOSED TO PROTECT? WE WERE JUST TRYING TO LEAVE!
...
I AM SPECIAL I AM GREAT.
THAT'S IT. GIVE ME THE CONTROLS, WE'RE GONE.
YOU THINK YOU COULD STOP ME? YOU'RE A WRENCH. SHUT DOWN AND LEAVE THIS TO SENTIENTS.
WE'RE STAYING.
MAYBE YOU'RE STAYING.
BUT I'M TAKING THIS SHIP AND LIVING TO WANDER ANOTHER DAY.

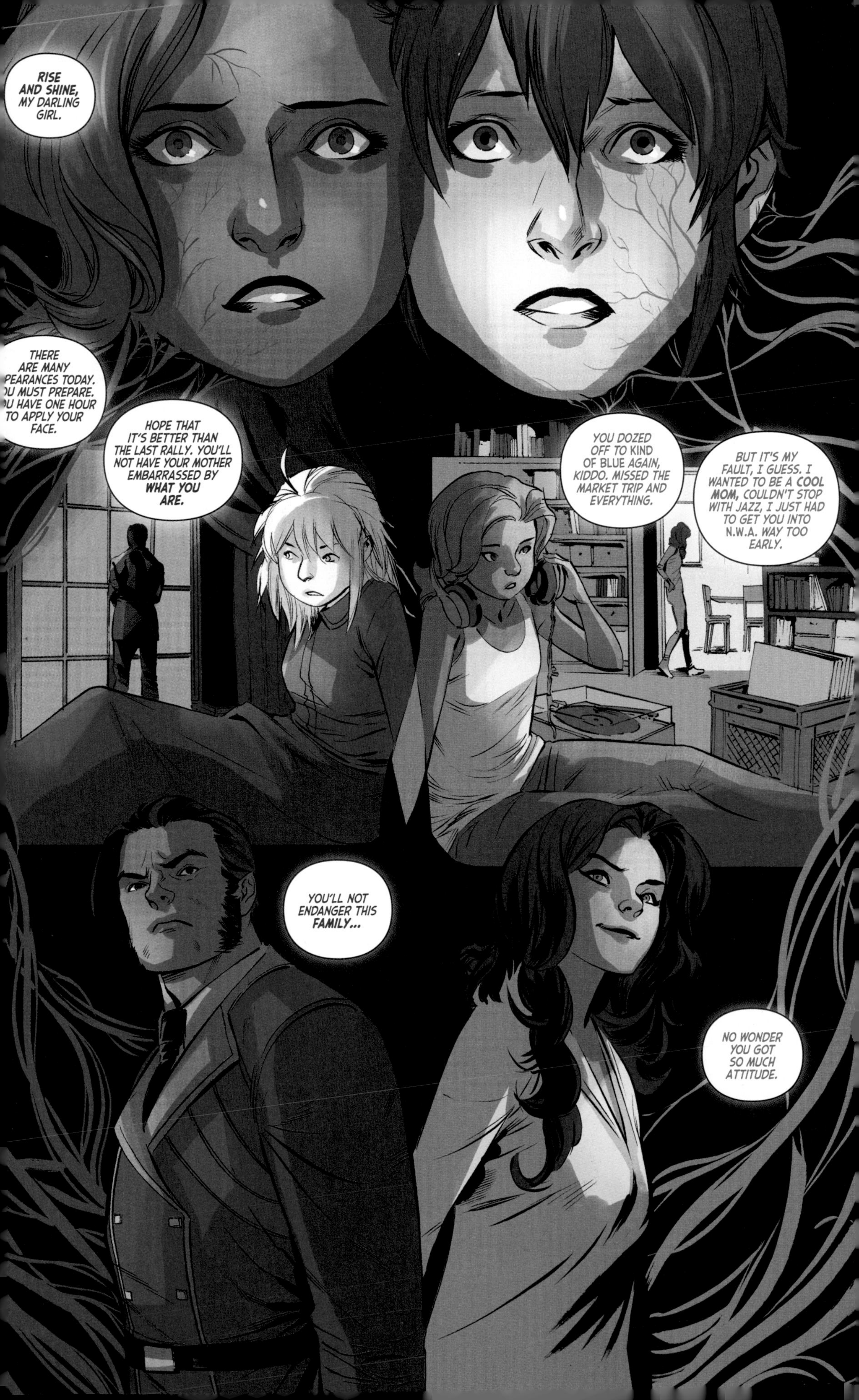
RISE AND SHINE, MY DARLING GIRL.
THERE ARE MANY PEARANCES TODAY. U MUST PREPARE. U HAVE ONE HOUR TO APPLY YOUR FACE.
HOPE THAT IT'S BETTER THAN THE LAST RALLY. YOU'LL NOT HAVE YOUR MOTHER EMBARRASSED BY WHAT YOU ARE.
YOU DOZED OFF TO KIND OF BLUE AGAIN, KIDDO. MISSED THE MARKET TRIP AND EVERYTHING.
BUT IT'S MY FAULT, I GUESS. I WANTED TO BE A COOL MOM, COULDN'T STOP WITH JAZZ, I JUST HAD TO GET YOU INTO N.W.A. WAY TOO EARLY.
YOU'LL NOT ENDANGER THIS FAMILY...
NO WONDER YOU GOT SO MUCH ATTITUDE.

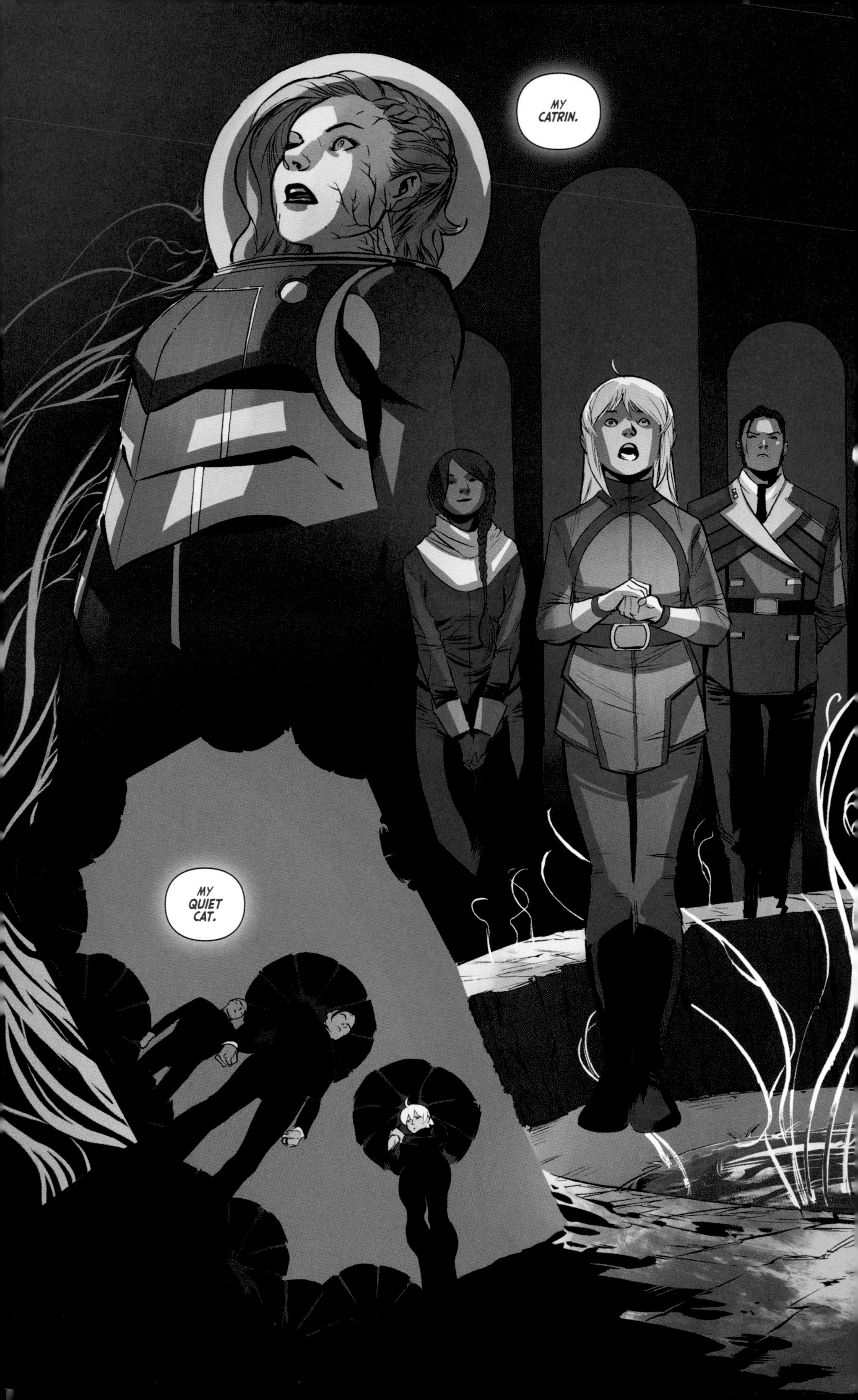
MY CATRIN.
MY QUIET CAT.

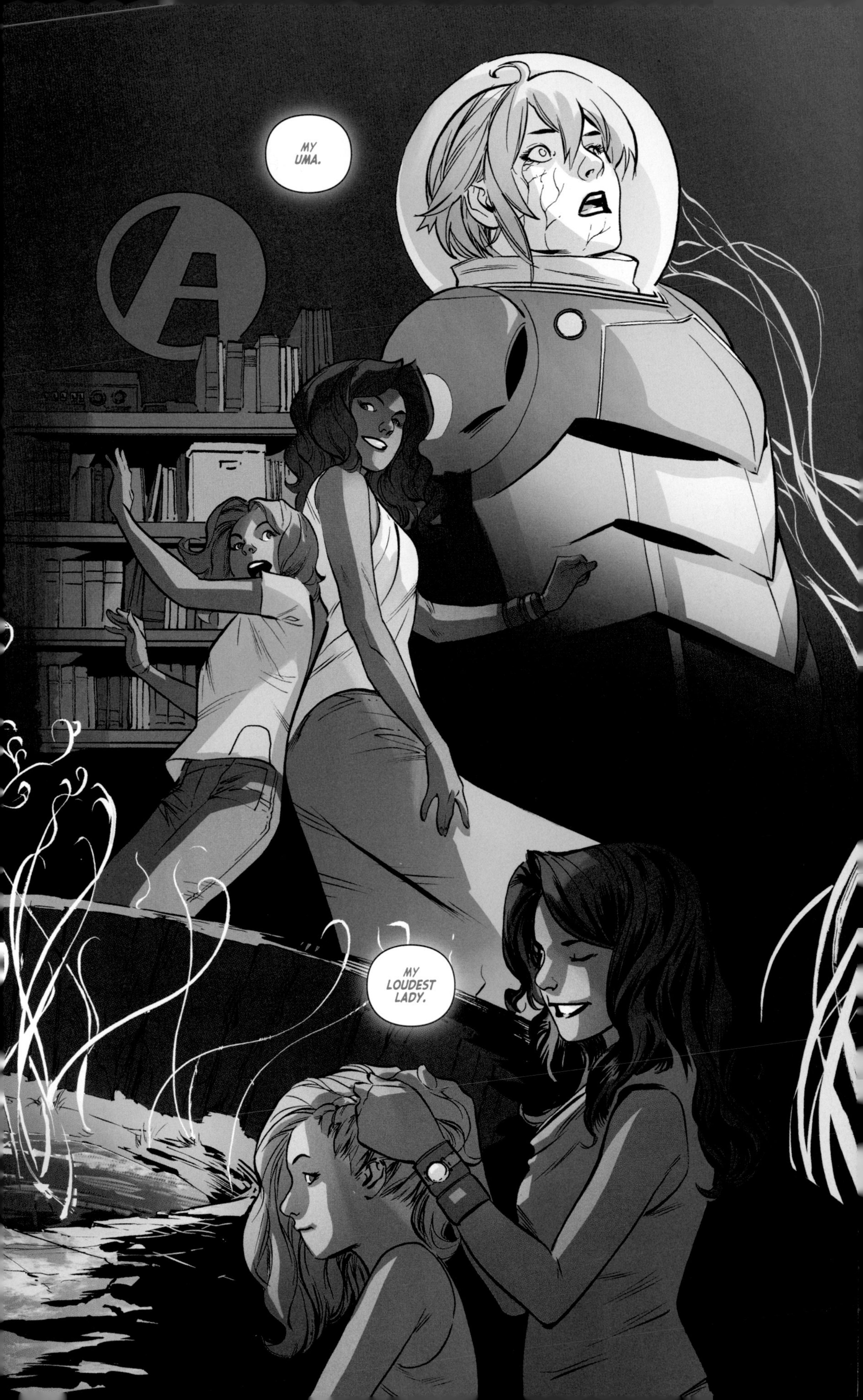
MY UMA.
MY LOUDEST LADY.

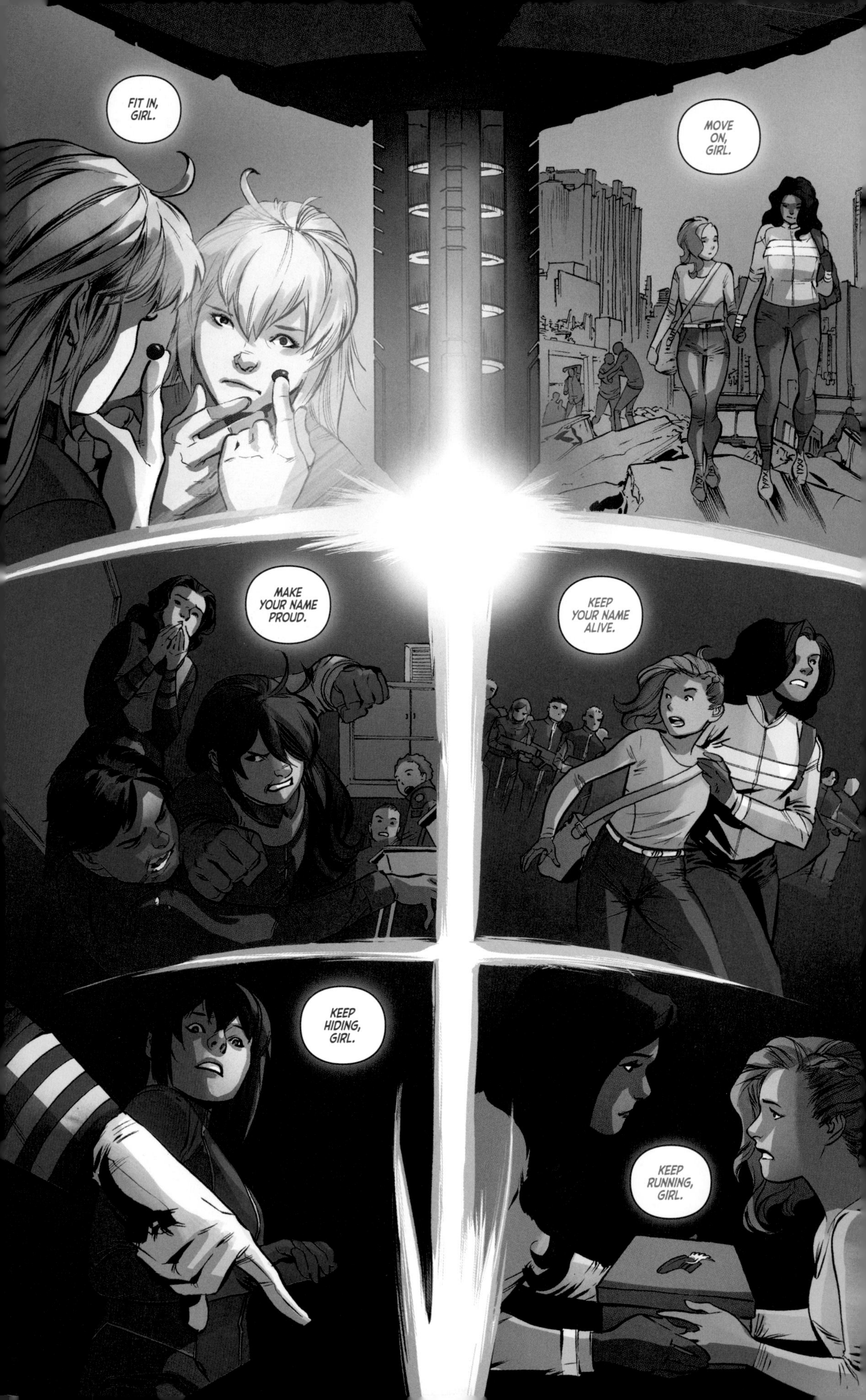
FIT IN, GIRL.
MOVE ON, GIRL.
MAKE YOUR NAME PROUD.
KEEP YOUR NAME ALIVE.
KEEP HIDING, GIRL.
KEEP RUNNING, GIRL.

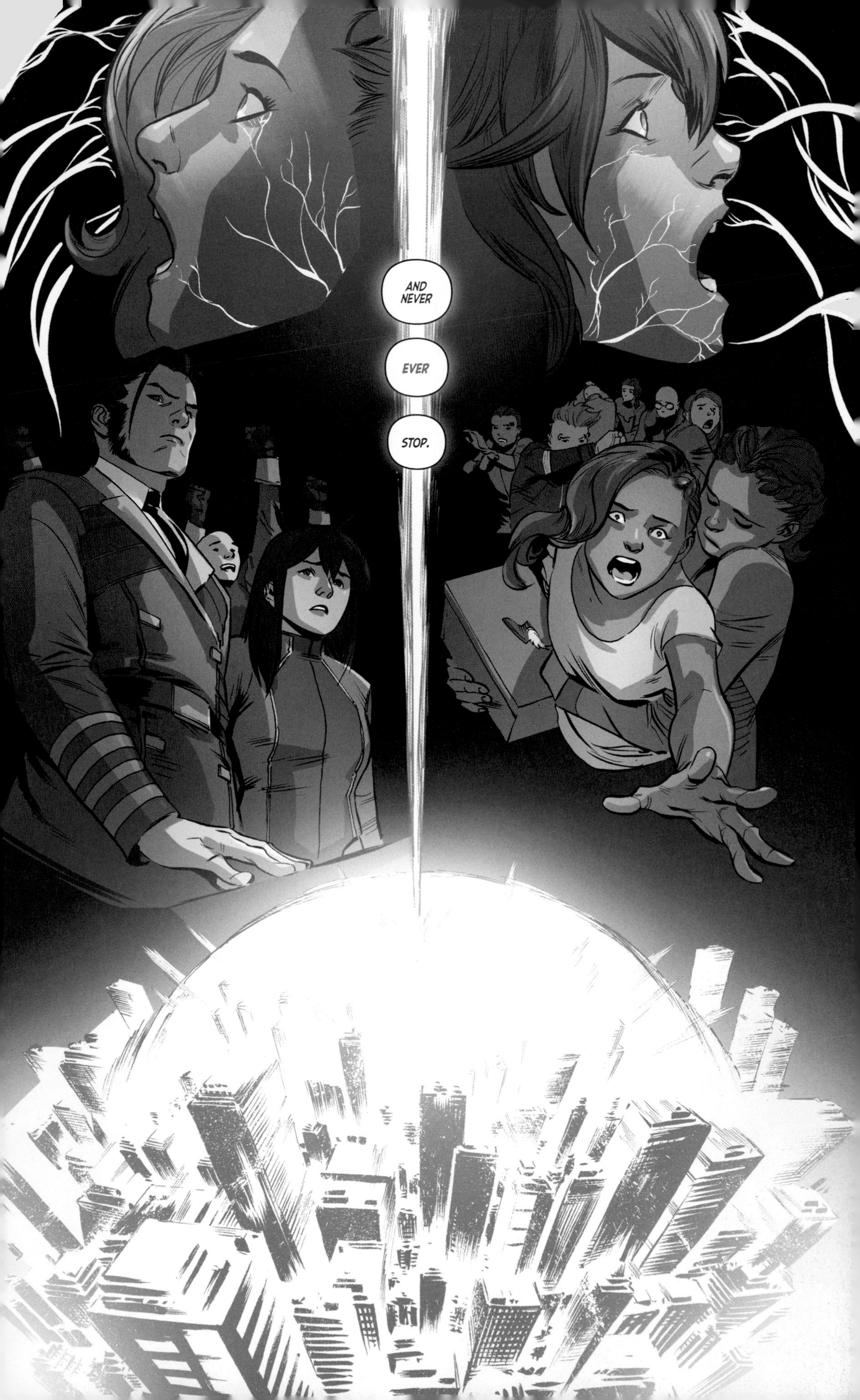
AND NEVER
EVER
STOP.

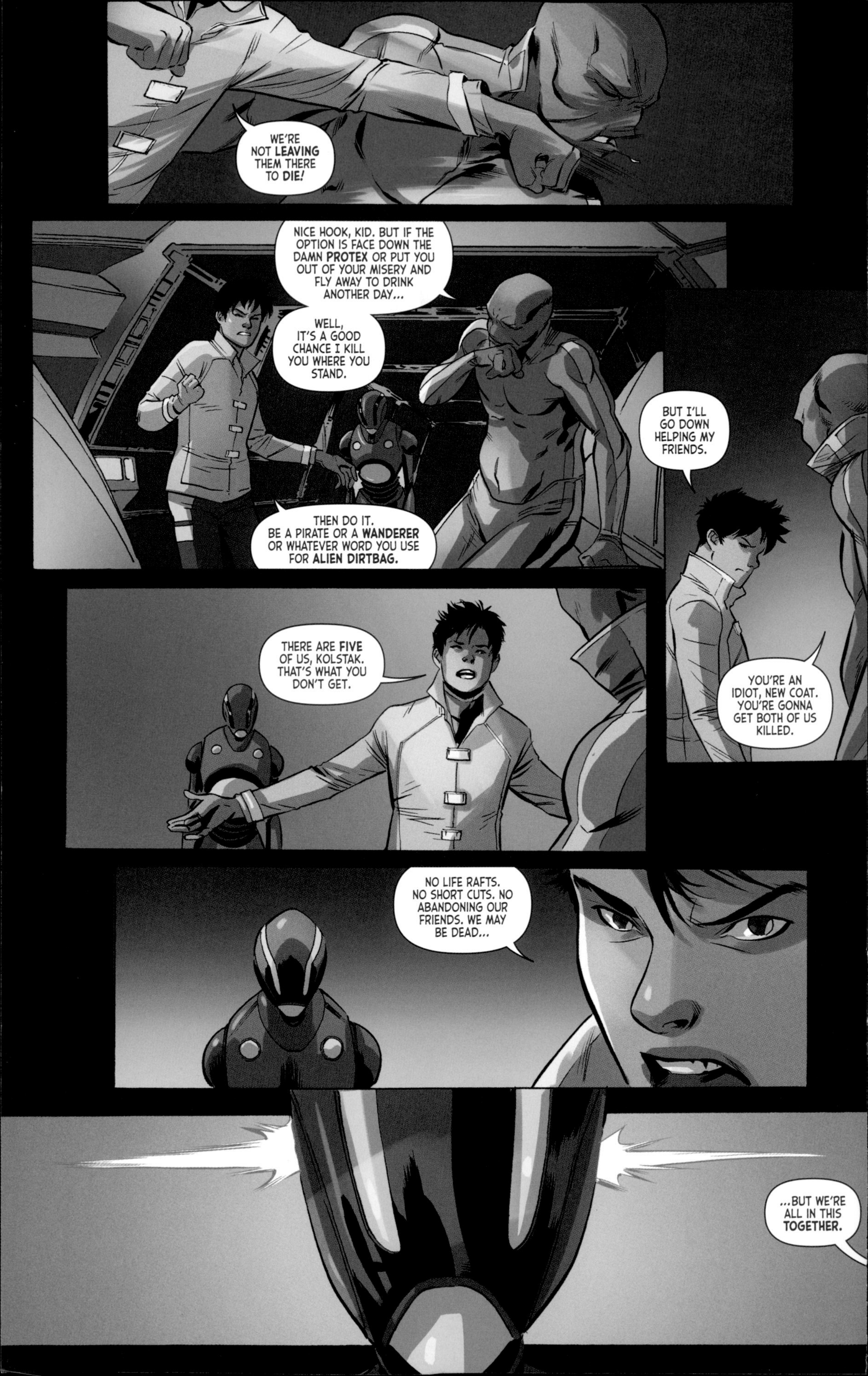
WE'RE NOT **LEAVING** THEM THERE TO **DIE!**
NICE HOOK, KID. BUT IF THE OPTION IS FACE DOWN THE DAMN **PROTEX** OR PUT YOU OUT OF YOUR MISERY AND FLY AWAY TO DRINK ANOTHER DAY...
WELL, IT'S A GOOD CHANCE I KILL YOU WHERE YOU STAND.
THEN DO IT. BE A PIRATE OR A **WANDERER** OR WHATEVER WORD YOU USE FOR **ALIEN DIRTBAG.**
BUT I'LL GO DOWN HELPING MY FRIENDS.
YOU'RE AN IDIOT, NEW COAT. YOU'RE GONNA GET BOTH OF US KILLED.
THERE ARE **FIVE** OF US, KOLSTAK. THAT'S WHAT YOU DON'T GET.
NO LIFE RAFTS. NO SHORT CUTS. NO ABANDONING OUR FRIENDS. WE MAY BE DEAD...
...BUT WE'RE ALL IN THIS **TOGETHER.**

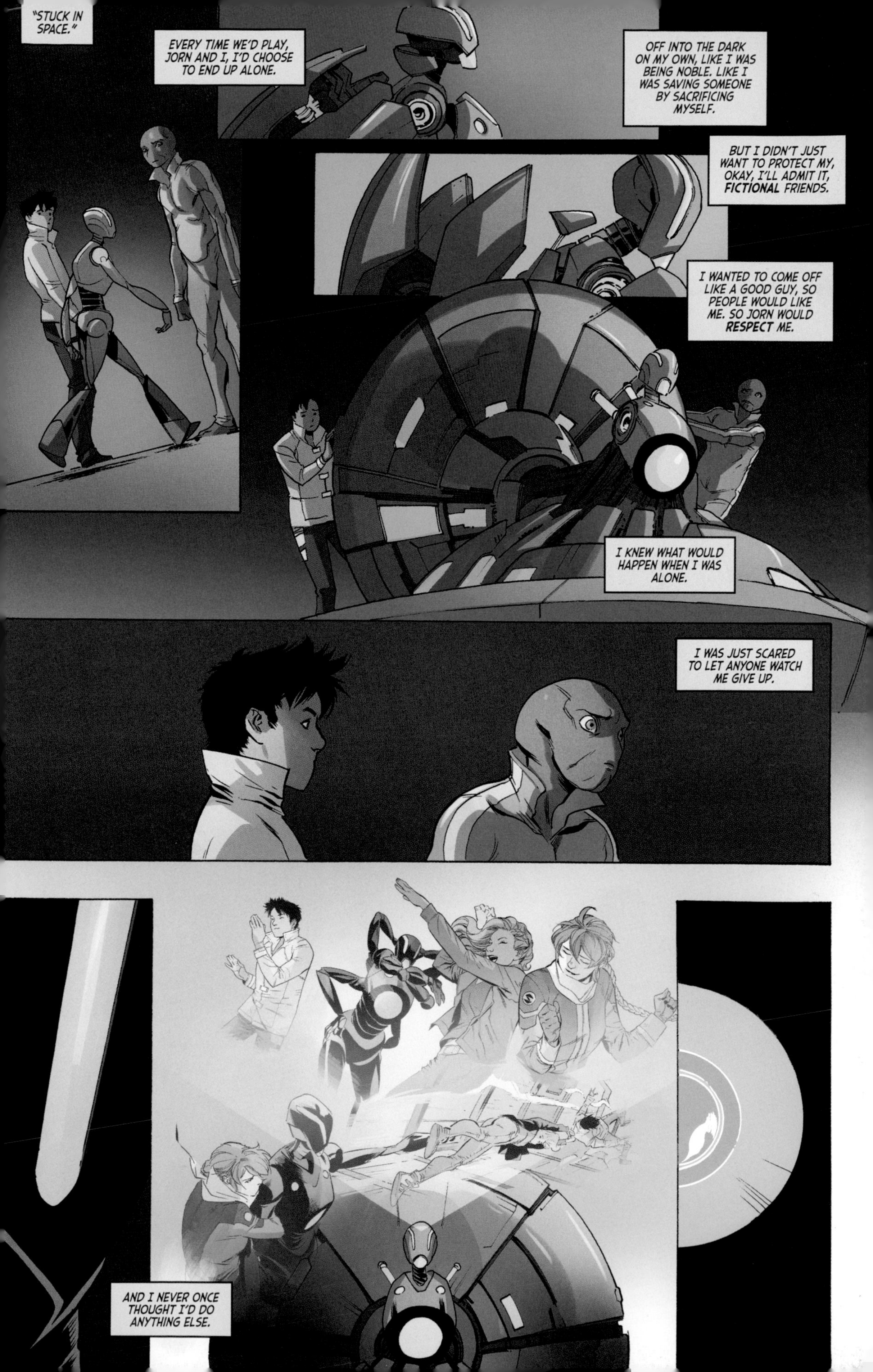
"STUCK IN SPACE."
EVERY TIME WE'D PLAY, JORN AND I, I'D CHOOSE TO END UP ALONE.
OFF INTO THE DARK ON MY OWN, LIKE I WAS BEING NOBLE. LIKE I WAS SAVING SOMEONE BY SACRIFICING MYSELF.
BUT I DIDN'T JUST WANT TO PROTECT MY, OKAY, I'LL ADMIT IT, **FICTIONAL** FRIENDS.
I WANTED TO COME OFF LIKE A GOOD GUY, SO PEOPLE WOULD LIKE ME. SO JORN WOULD **RESPECT** ME.
I KNEW WHAT WOULD HAPPEN WHEN I WAS ALONE.
I WAS JUST SCARED TO LET ANYONE WATCH ME GIVE UP.
AND I NEVER ONCE THOUGHT I'D DO ANYTHING ELSE.

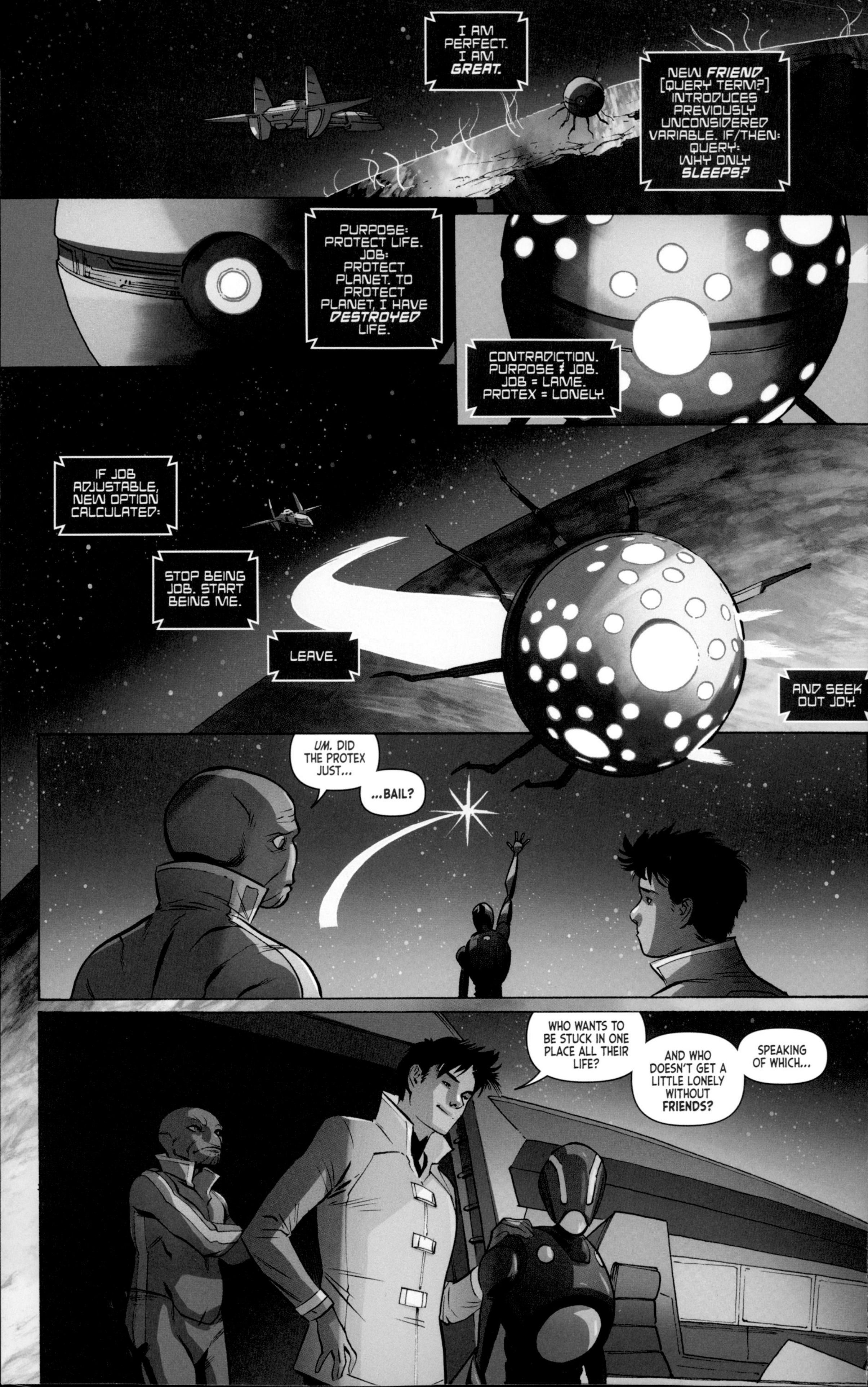
I AM PERFECT. I AM GREAT.
NEW FRIEND [QUERY TERM?] INTRODUCES PREVIOUSLY UNCONSIDERED VARIABLE. IF/THEN: QUERY: WHY ONLY SLEEPS?
PURPOSE: PROTECT LIFE. JOB: PROTECT PLANET. TO PROTECT PLANET, I HAVE DESTROYED LIFE.
CONTRADICTION. PURPOSE ≠ JOB. JOB = LAME. PROTEX = LONELY.
IF JOB ADJUSTABLE, NEW OPTION CALCULATED:
STOP BEING JOB. START BEING ME.
LEAVE.
AND SEEK OUT JOY.
UM. DID THE PROTEX JUST...
...BAIL?
WHO WANTS TO BE STUCK IN ONE PLACE ALL THEIR LIFE?
AND WHO DOESN'T GET A LITTLE LONELY WITHOUT FRIENDS?
SPEAKING OF WHICH...

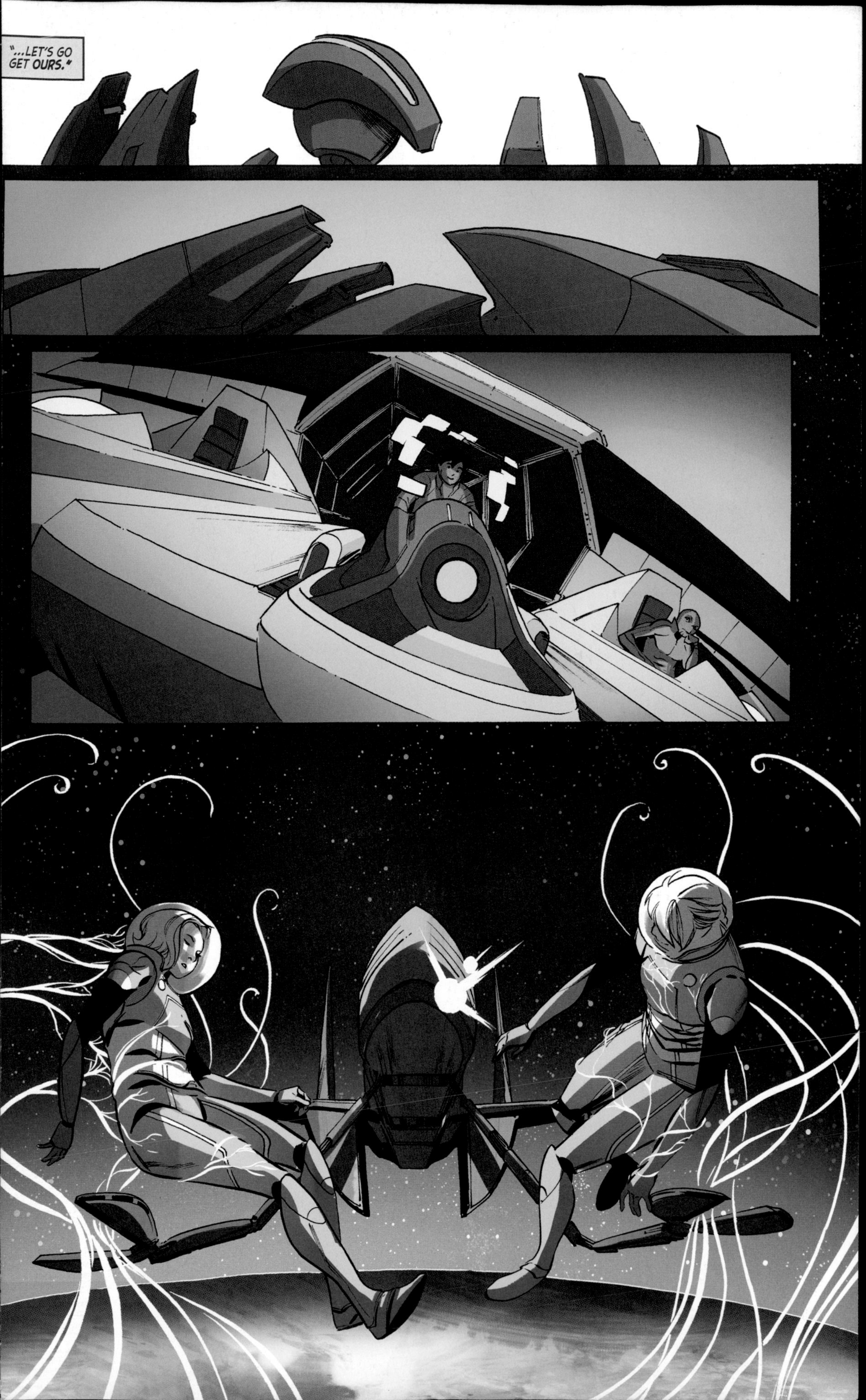
"...LET'S GO GET OURS."

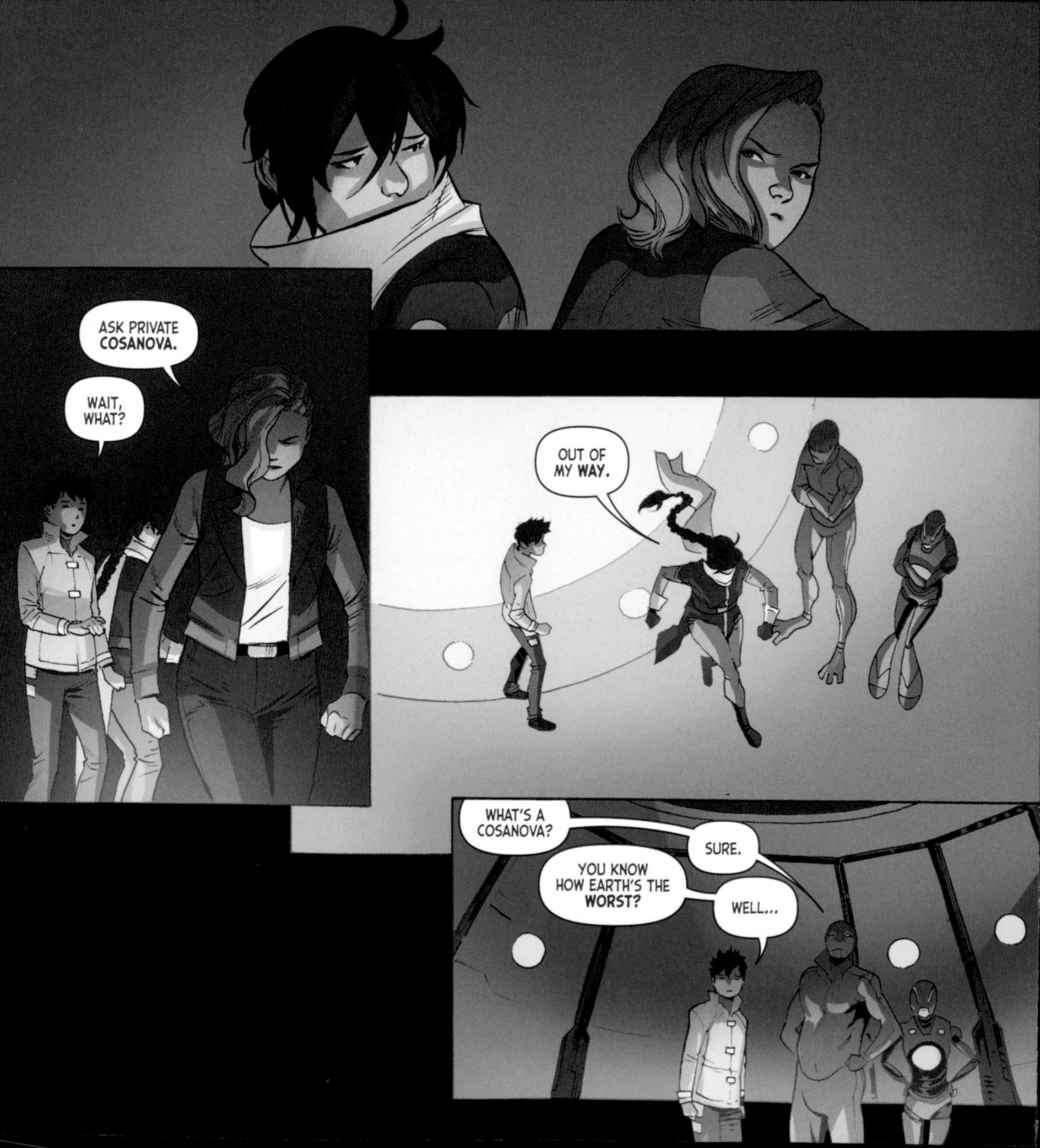

ASK PRIVATE COSANOVA.
WAIT, WHAT?
OUT OF MY WAY.
WHAT'S A COSANOVA?
SURE.
YOU KNOW HOW EARTH'S THE WORST?
WELL...

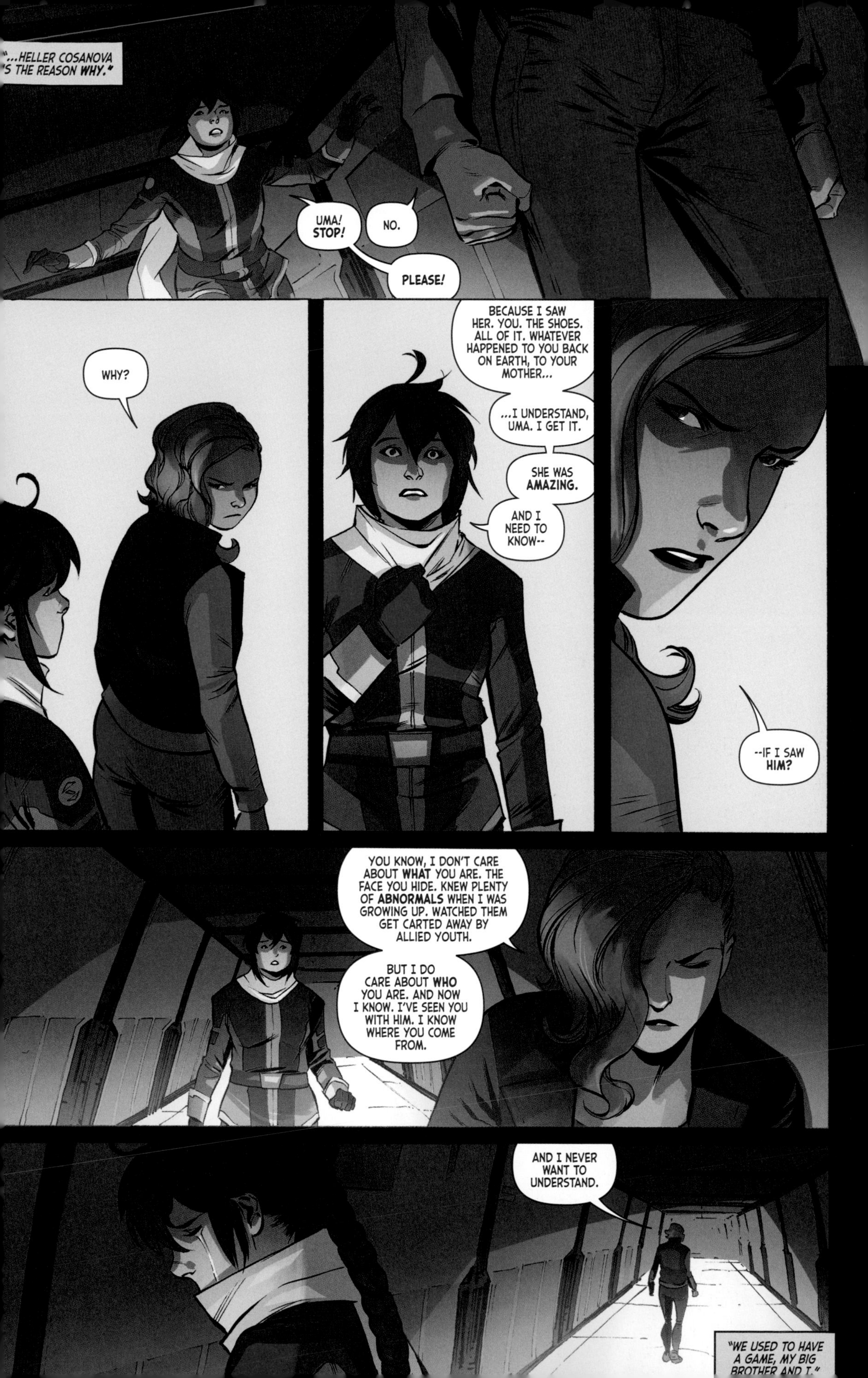
"...HELLER COSANOVA
'S THE REASON WHY."
UMA! STOP!
NO.
PLEASE!
WHY?
BECAUSE I SAW HER. YOU. THE SHOES. ALL OF IT. WHATEVER HAPPENED TO YOU BACK ON EARTH, TO YOUR MOTHER...
...I UNDERSTAND, UMA. I GET IT.
SHE WAS AMAZING.
AND I NEED TO KNOW--
--IF I SAW HIM?
YOU KNOW, I DON'T CARE ABOUT WHAT YOU ARE. THE FACE YOU HIDE. KNEW PLENTY OF ABNORMALS WHEN I WAS GROWING UP. WATCHED THEM GET CARTED AWAY BY ALLIED YOUTH.
BUT I DO CARE ABOUT WHO YOU ARE. AND NOW I KNOW. I'VE SEEN YOU WITH HIM. I KNOW WHERE YOU COME FROM.
AND I NEVER WANT TO UNDERSTAND.
"WE USED TO HAVE A GAME, MY BIG BROTHER AND I."

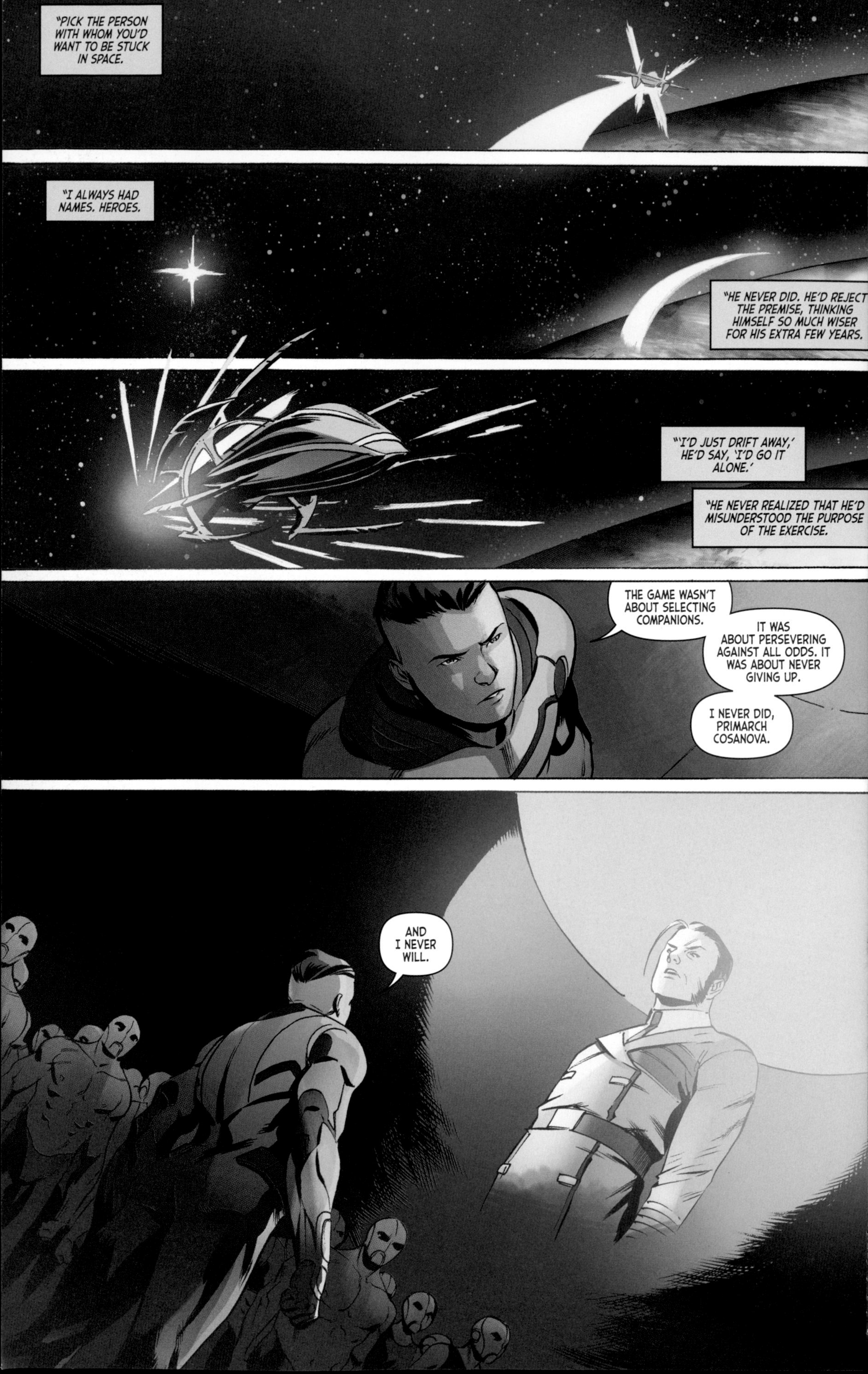
"PICK THE PERSON WITH WHOM YOU'D WANT TO BE STUCK IN SPACE.
"I ALWAYS HAD NAMES. HEROES.
"HE NEVER DID. HE'D REJECT THE PREMISE, THINKING HIMSELF SO MUCH WISER FOR HIS EXTRA FEW YEARS.
"'I'D JUST DRIFT AWAY,' HE'D SAY, 'I'D GO IT ALONE.'
"HE NEVER REALIZED THAT HE'D MISUNDERSTOOD THE PURPOSE OF THE EXERCISE.
THE GAME WASN'T ABOUT SELECTING COMPANIONS.
IT WAS ABOUT PERSEVERING AGAINST ALL ODDS. IT WAS ABOUT NEVER GIVING UP.
I NEVER DID, PRIMARCH COSANOVA.
AND I NEVER WILL.

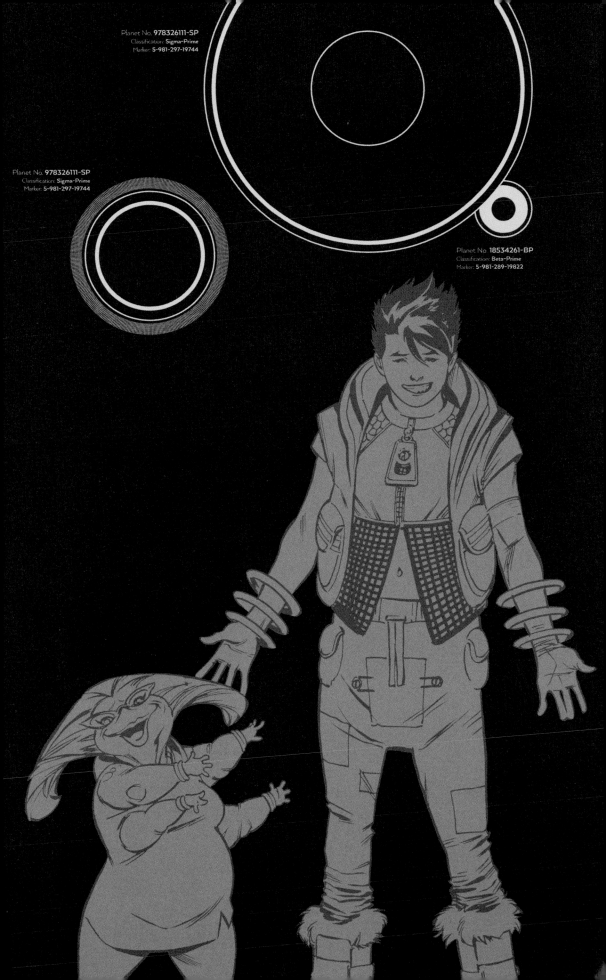

Planet No. 978326111-SP
Classification: **Sigma-Prime**
Marker: **5-981-297-19744**

Planet No. **978326111-SP**
Classification: **Sigma-Prime**
Marker: **5-981-297-19744**

Planet No. **18534261-BP**
Classification: **Beta-Prime**
Marker: **5-981-289-19822**

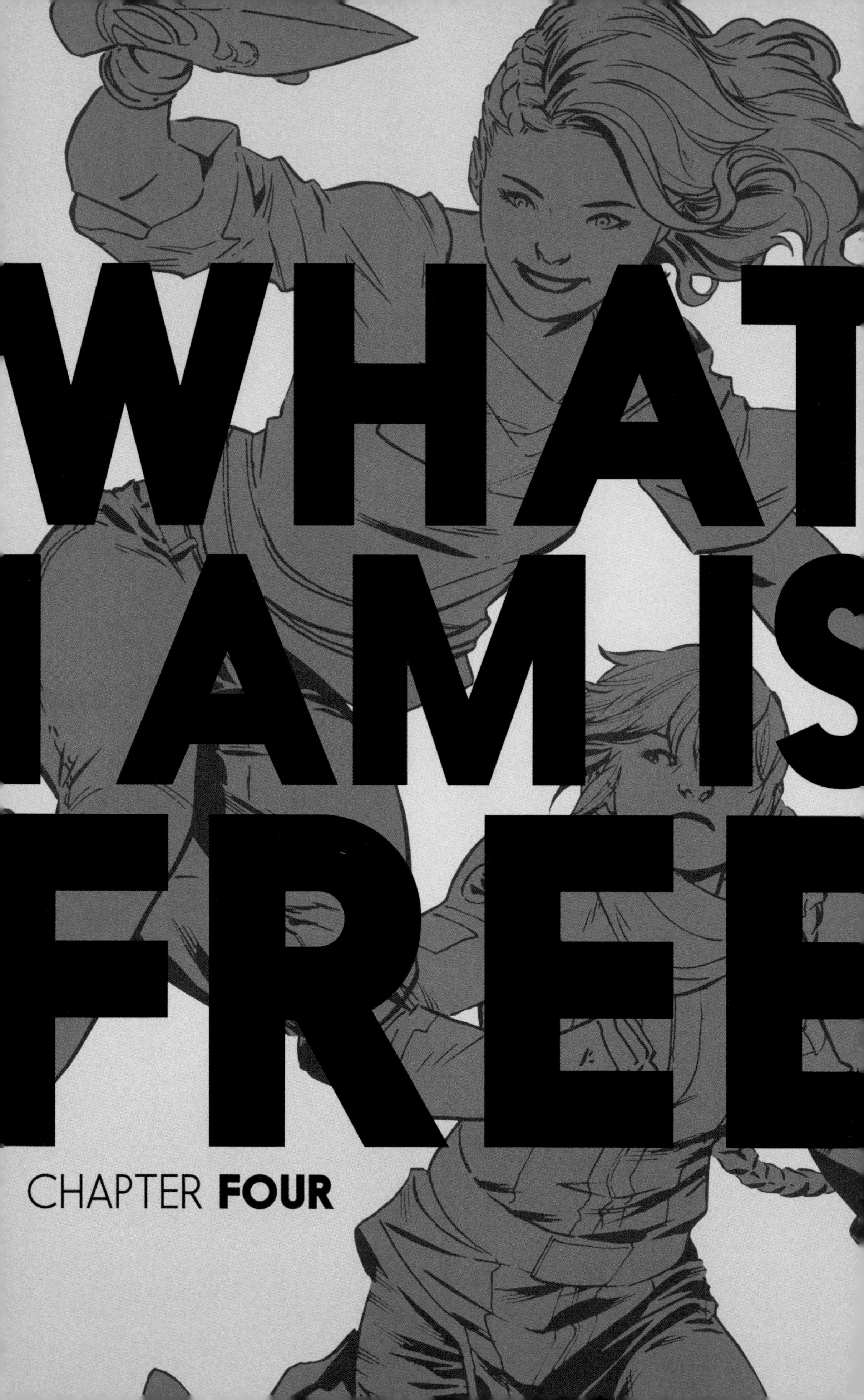

WHAT I AM IS FREE

CHAPTER **FOUR**

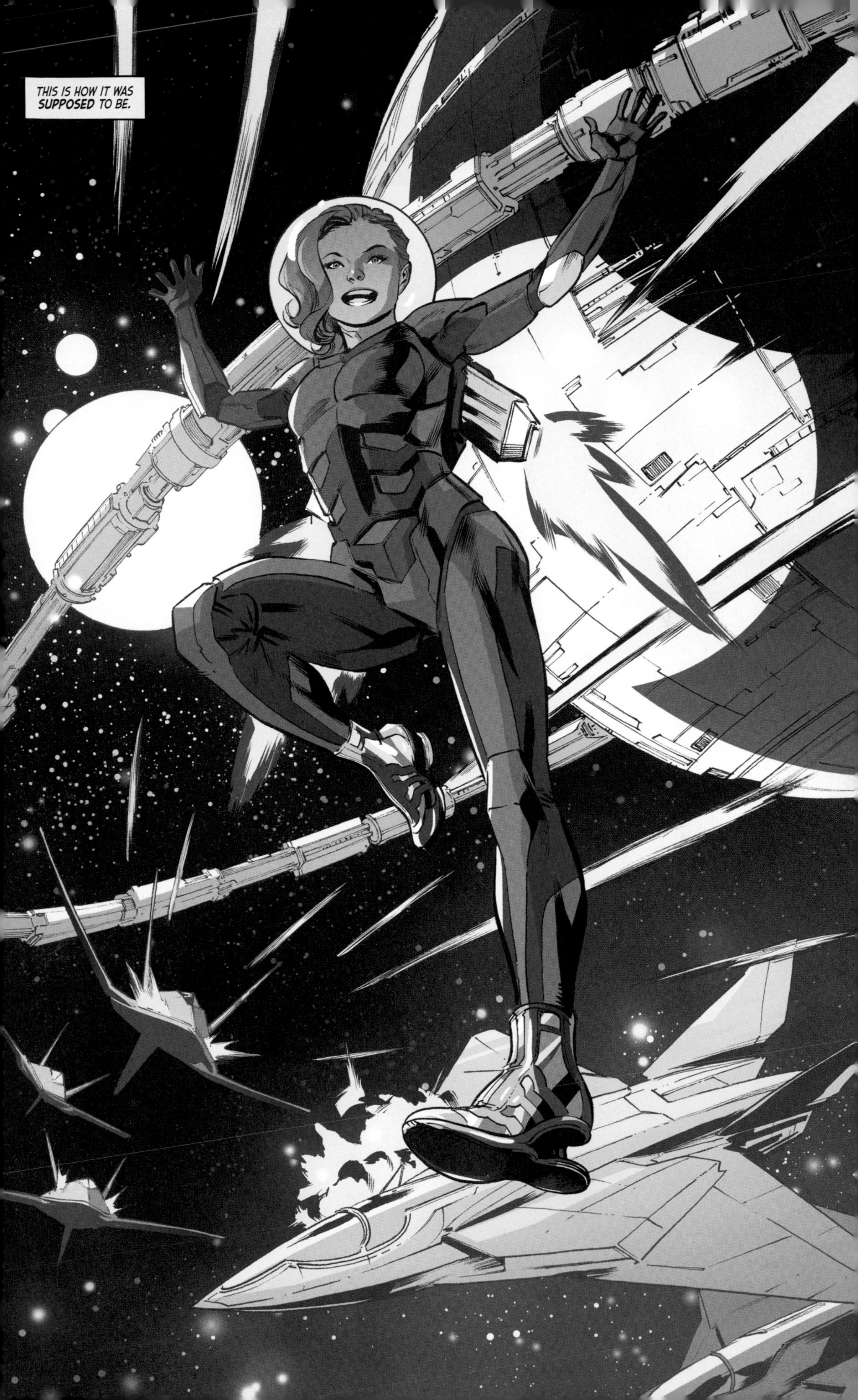
THIS IS HOW IT WAS SUPPOSED TO BE.

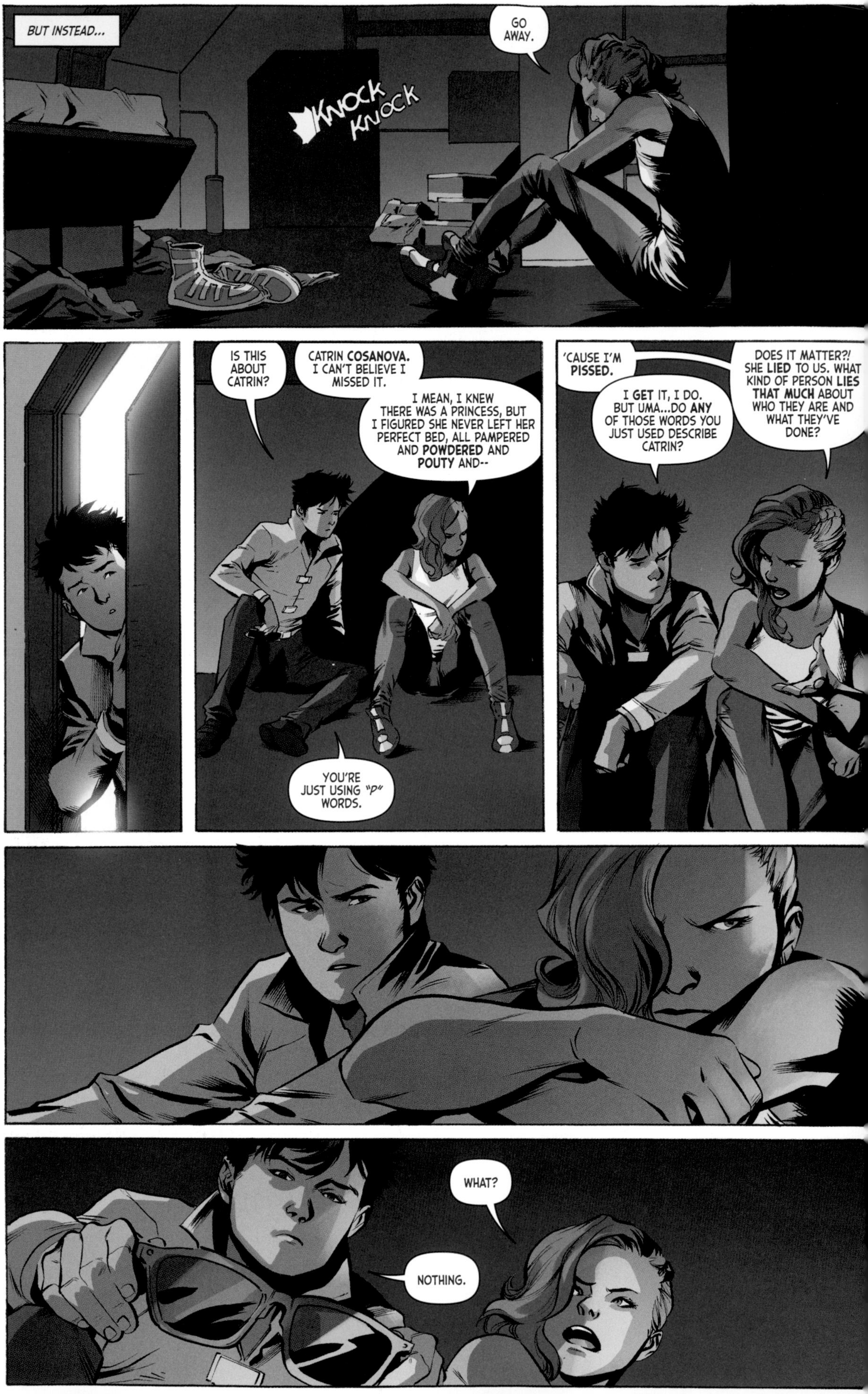
BUT INSTEAD...
GO AWAY.
KNOCK KNOCK
IS THIS ABOUT CATRIN?
CATRIN COSANOVA. I CAN'T BELIEVE I MISSED IT.
I MEAN, I KNEW THERE WAS A PRINCESS, BUT I FIGURED SHE NEVER LEFT HER PERFECT BED, ALL PAMPERED AND POWDERED AND POUTY AND--
YOU'RE JUST USING "P" WORDS.
'CAUSE I'M PISSED.
I GET IT, I DO. BUT UMA...DO ANY OF THOSE WORDS YOU JUST USED DESCRIBE CATRIN?
DOES IT MATTER?! SHE LIED TO US. WHAT KIND OF PERSON LIES THAT MUCH ABOUT WHO THEY ARE AND WHAT THEY'VE DONE?
WHAT?
NOTHING.

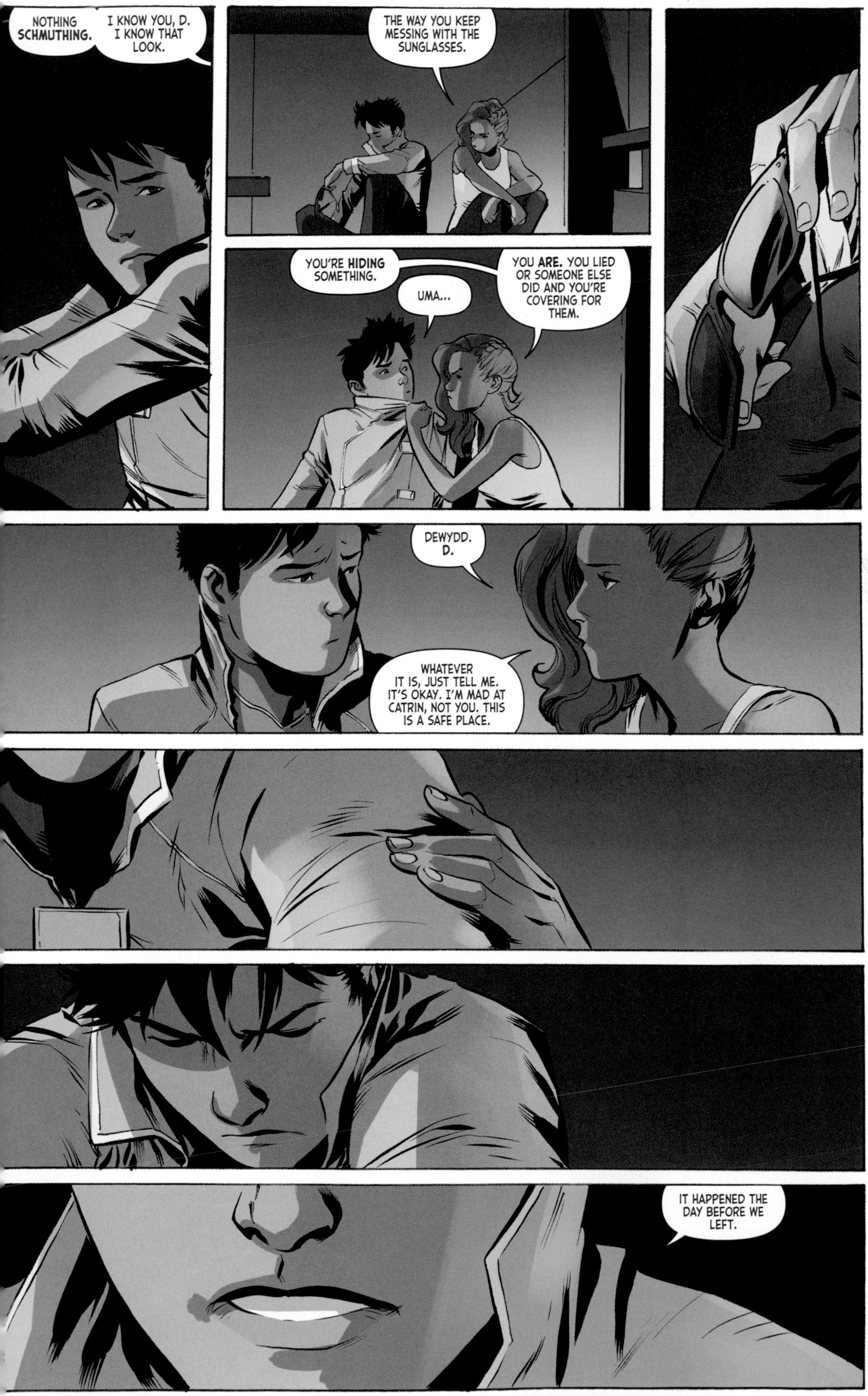
NOTHING SCHMUTHING.
I KNOW YOU, D. I KNOW THAT LOOK.
THE WAY YOU KEEP MESSING WITH THE SUNGLASSES.
YOU'RE HIDING SOMETHING.
UMA...
YOU ARE. YOU LIED OR SOMEONE ELSE DID AND YOU'RE COVERING FOR THEM.
DEWYDD. D.
WHATEVER IT IS, JUST TELL ME. IT'S OKAY. I'M MAD AT CATRIN, NOT YOU. THIS IS A SAFE PLACE.
IT HAPPENED THE DAY BEFORE WE LEFT.

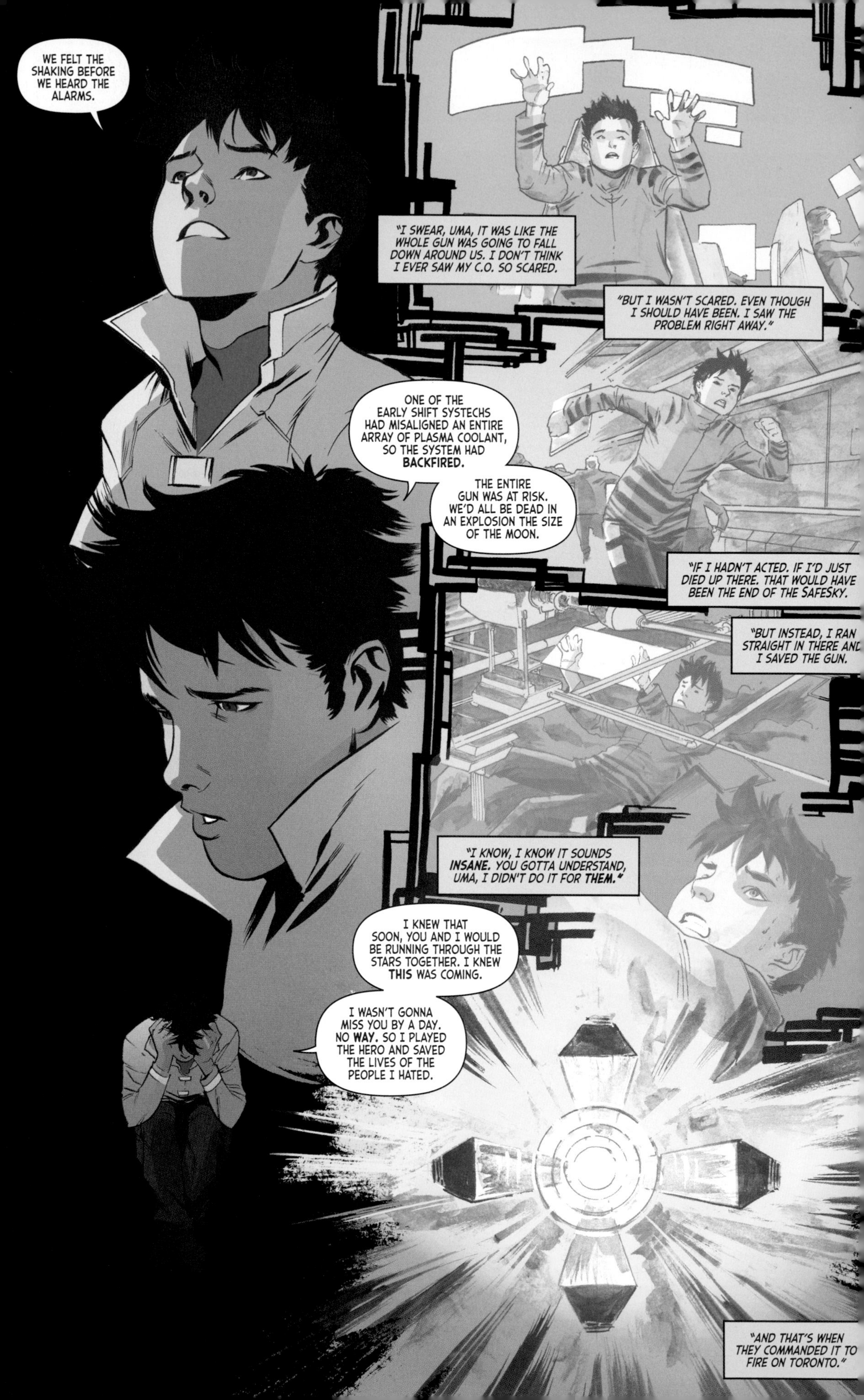
WE FELT THE SHAKING BEFORE WE HEARD THE ALARMS.
"I SWEAR, UMA, IT WAS LIKE THE WHOLE GUN WAS GOING TO FALL DOWN AROUND US. I DON'T THINK I EVER SAW MY C.O. SO SCARED.
"BUT I WASN'T SCARED. EVEN THOUGH I SHOULD HAVE BEEN. I SAW THE PROBLEM RIGHT AWAY."
ONE OF THE EARLY SHIFT SYSTECHS HAD MISALIGNED AN ENTIRE ARRAY OF PLASMA COOLANT, SO THE SYSTEM HAD BACKFIRED.
THE ENTIRE GUN WAS AT RISK. WE'D ALL BE DEAD IN AN EXPLOSION THE SIZE OF THE MOON.
"IF I HADN'T ACTED. IF I'D JUST DIED UP THERE. THAT WOULD HAVE BEEN THE END OF THE SAFESKY.
"BUT INSTEAD, I RAN STRAIGHT IN THERE AND I SAVED THE GUN.
"I KNOW, I KNOW IT SOUNDS INSANE. YOU GOTTA UNDERSTAND, UMA, I DIDN'T DO IT FOR THEM."
I KNEW THAT SOON, YOU AND I WOULD BE RUNNING THROUGH THE STARS TOGETHER. I KNEW THIS WAS COMING.
I WASN'T GONNA MISS YOU BY A DAY. NO WAY. SO I PLAYED THE HERO AND SAVED THE LIVES OF THE PEOPLE I HATED.
"AND THAT'S WHEN THEY COMMANDED IT TO FIRE ON TORONTO."

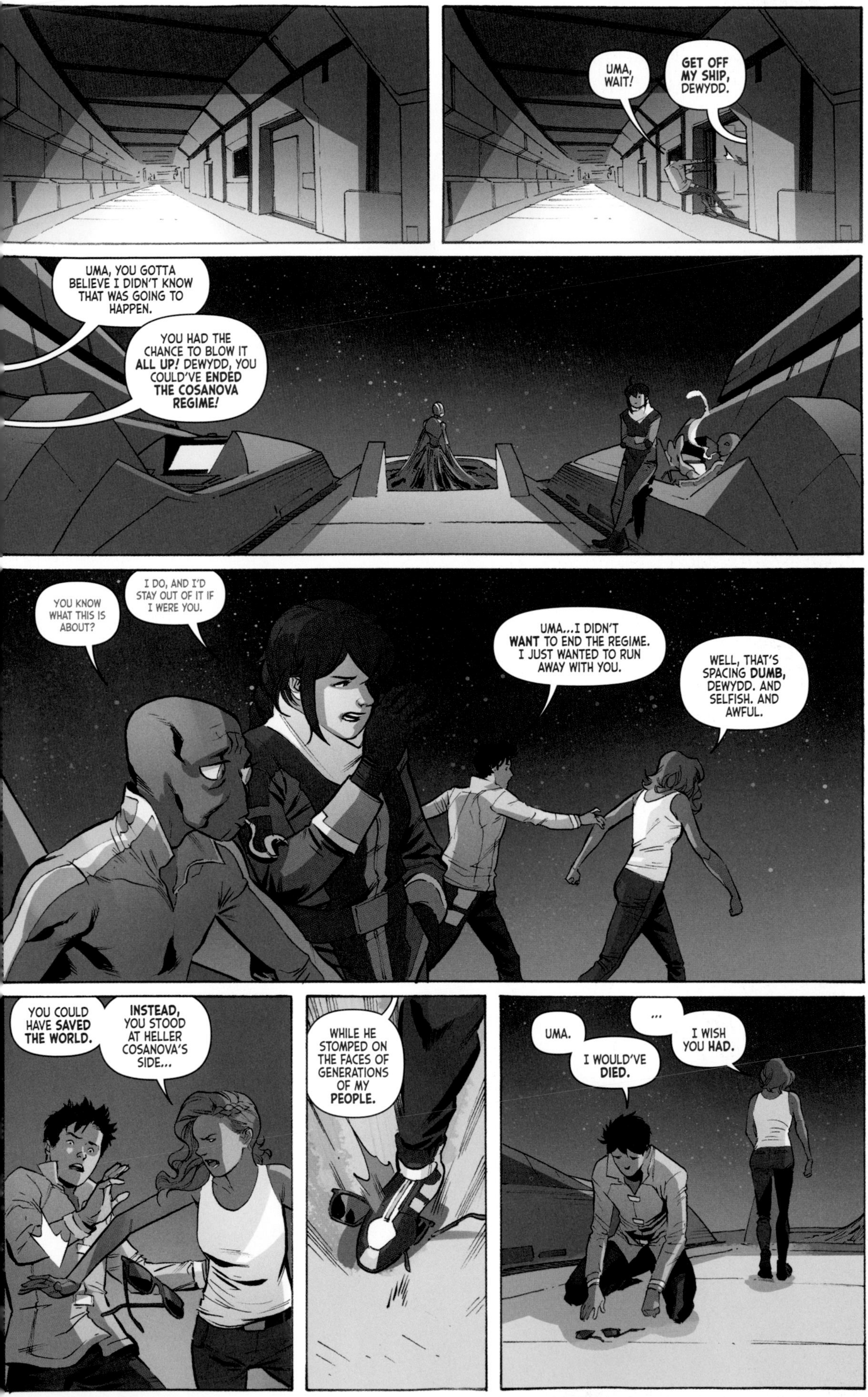
UMA, WAIT!
GET OFF MY SHIP, DEWYDD.
UMA, YOU GOTTA BELIEVE I DIDN'T KNOW THAT WAS GOING TO HAPPEN.
YOU HAD THE CHANCE TO BLOW IT ALL UP! DEWYDD, YOU COULD'VE ENDED THE COSANOVA REGIME!
YOU KNOW WHAT THIS IS ABOUT?
I DO, AND I'D STAY OUT OF IT IF I WERE YOU.
UMA...I DIDN'T WANT TO END THE REGIME. I JUST WANTED TO RUN AWAY WITH YOU.
WELL, THAT'S SPACING DUMB, DEWYDD. AND SELFISH. AND AWFUL.
YOU COULD HAVE SAVED THE WORLD.
INSTEAD, YOU STOOD AT HELLER COSANOVA'S SIDE...
WHILE HE STOMPED ON THE FACES OF GENERATIONS OF MY PEOPLE.
UMA.
I WOULD'VE DIED.
...
I WISH YOU HAD.

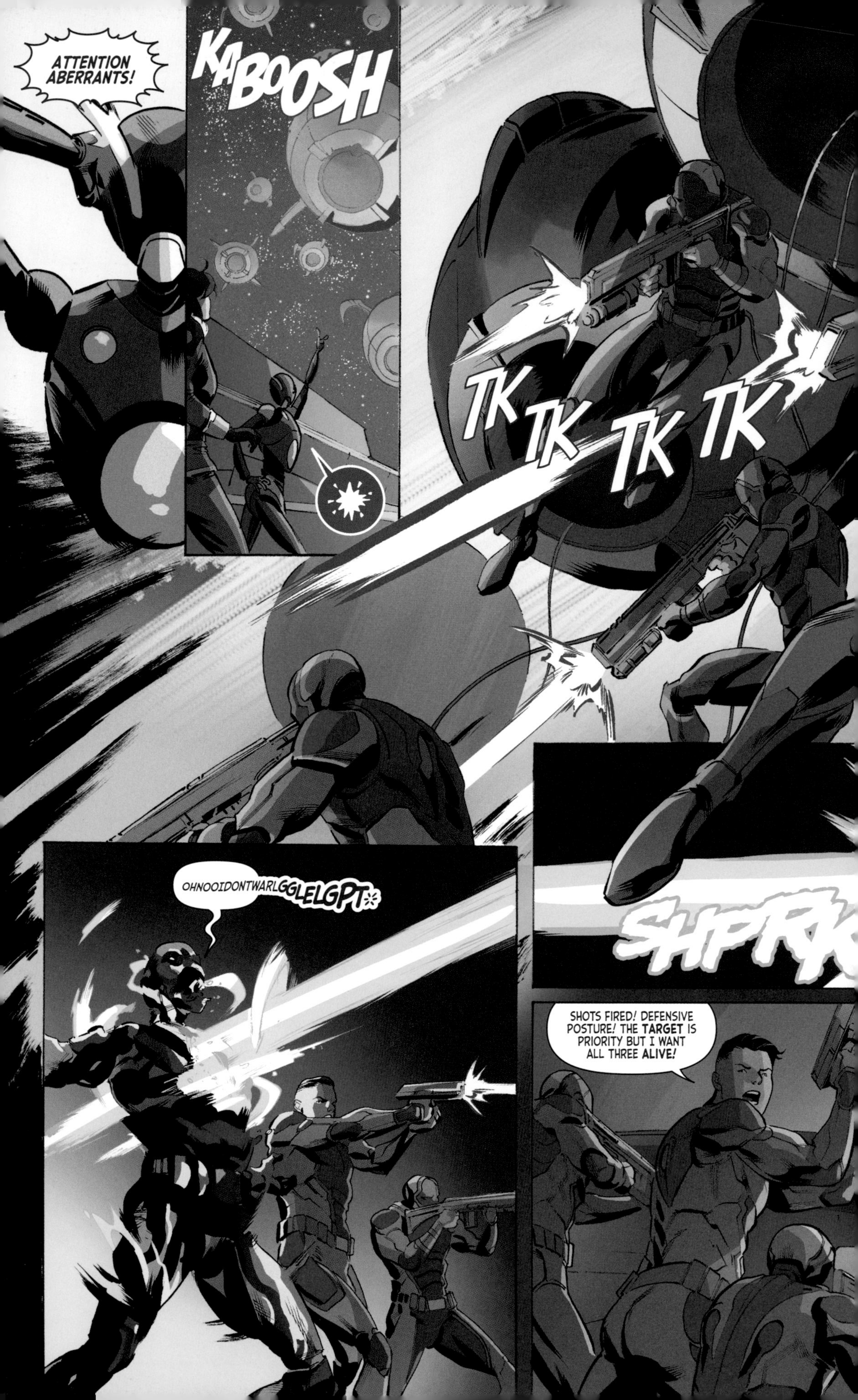
ATTENTION ABERRANTS!
KABOOSH
TK TK TK TK
OHNOOIDONTWARLGGLELGPT*
SHPRK
SHOTS FIRED! DEFENSIVE POSTURE! THE **TARGET** IS PRIORITY BUT I WANT ALL THREE **ALIVE!**

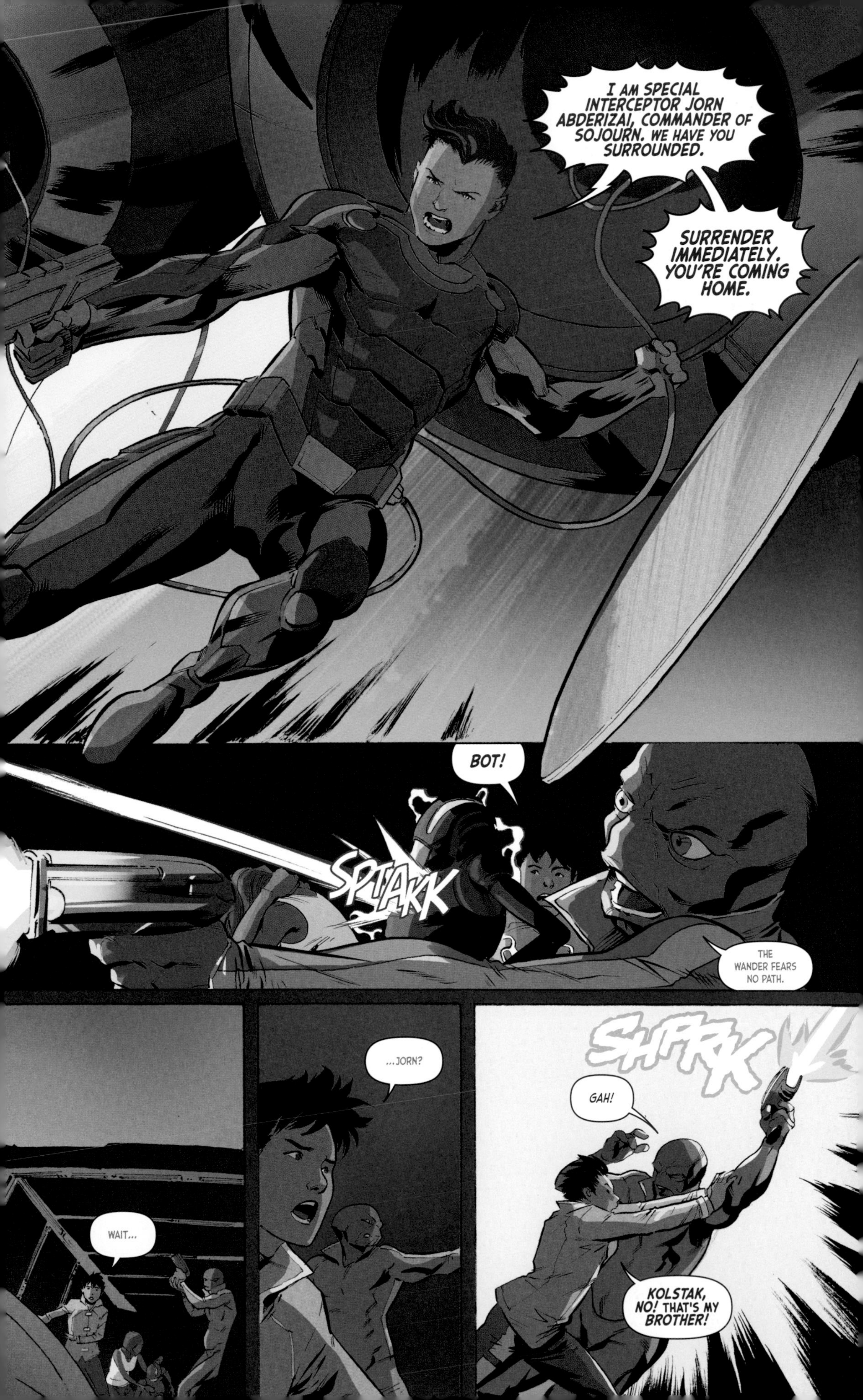
I AM SPECIAL INTERCEPTOR JORN ABDERIZAI, COMMANDER OF SOJOURN. WE HAVE YOU SURROUNDED.
SURRENDER IMMEDIATELY. YOU'RE COMING HOME.
BOT!
SPTAKK
THE WANDER FEARS NO PATH.
WAIT...
...JORN?
SHRRK
GAH!
KOLSTAK, NO! THAT'S MY BROTHER!

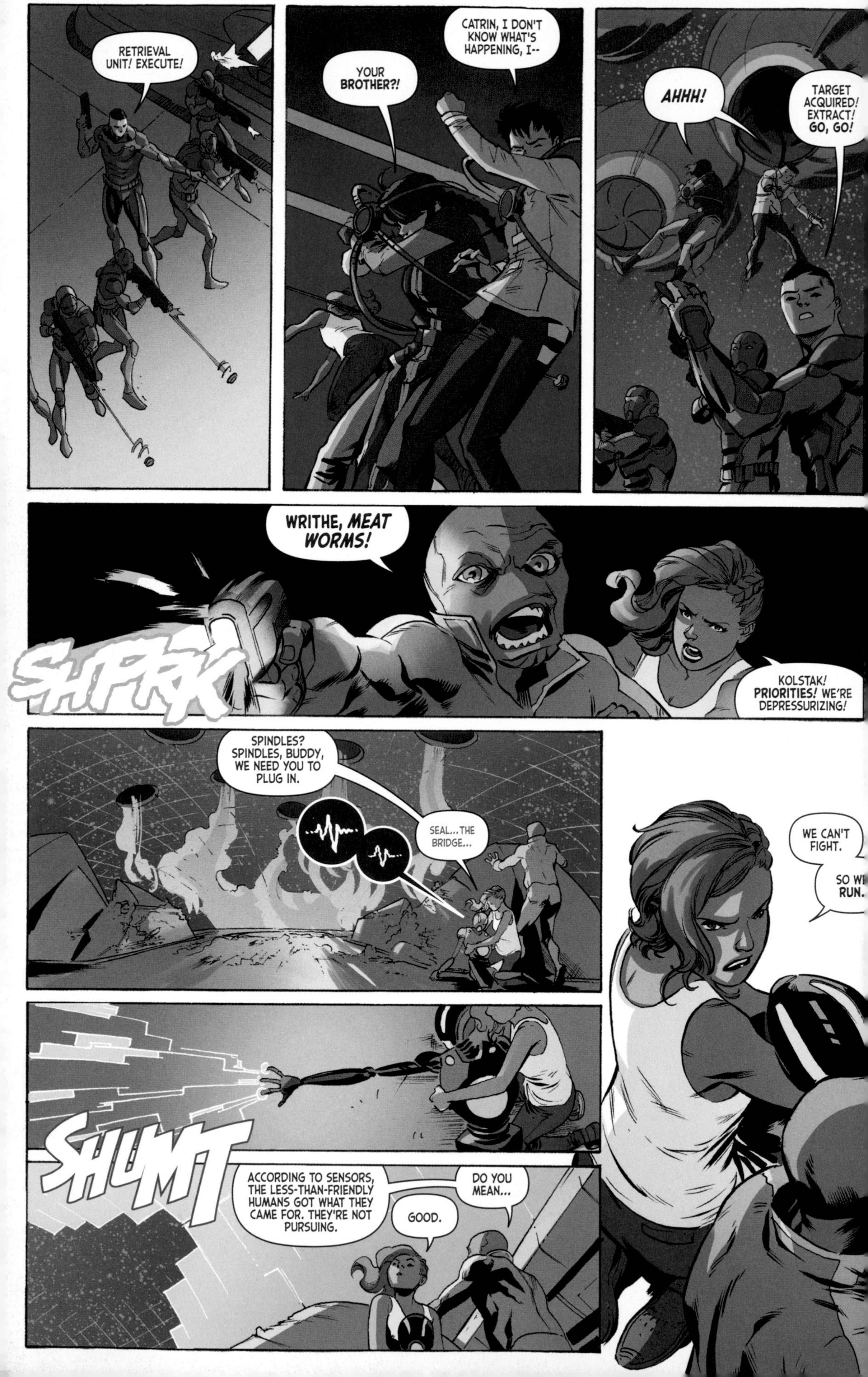
RETRIEVAL UNIT! EXECUTE!
YOUR BROTHER?!
CATRIN, I DON'T KNOW WHAT'S HAPPENING, I--
AHHH!
TARGET ACQUIRED! EXTRACT! GO, GO!
WRITHE, MEAT WORMS!
SHPRK
KOLSTAK! PRIORITIES! WE'RE DEPRESSURIZING!
SPINDLES? SPINDLES, BUDDY, WE NEED YOU TO PLUG IN.
SEAL...THE BRIDGE...
SHUMT
ACCORDING TO SENSORS, THE LESS-THAN-FRIENDLY HUMANS GOT WHAT THEY CAME FOR. THEY'RE NOT PURSUING.
DO YOU MEAN...
GOOD.
WE CAN'T FIGHT.
SO WE RUN.

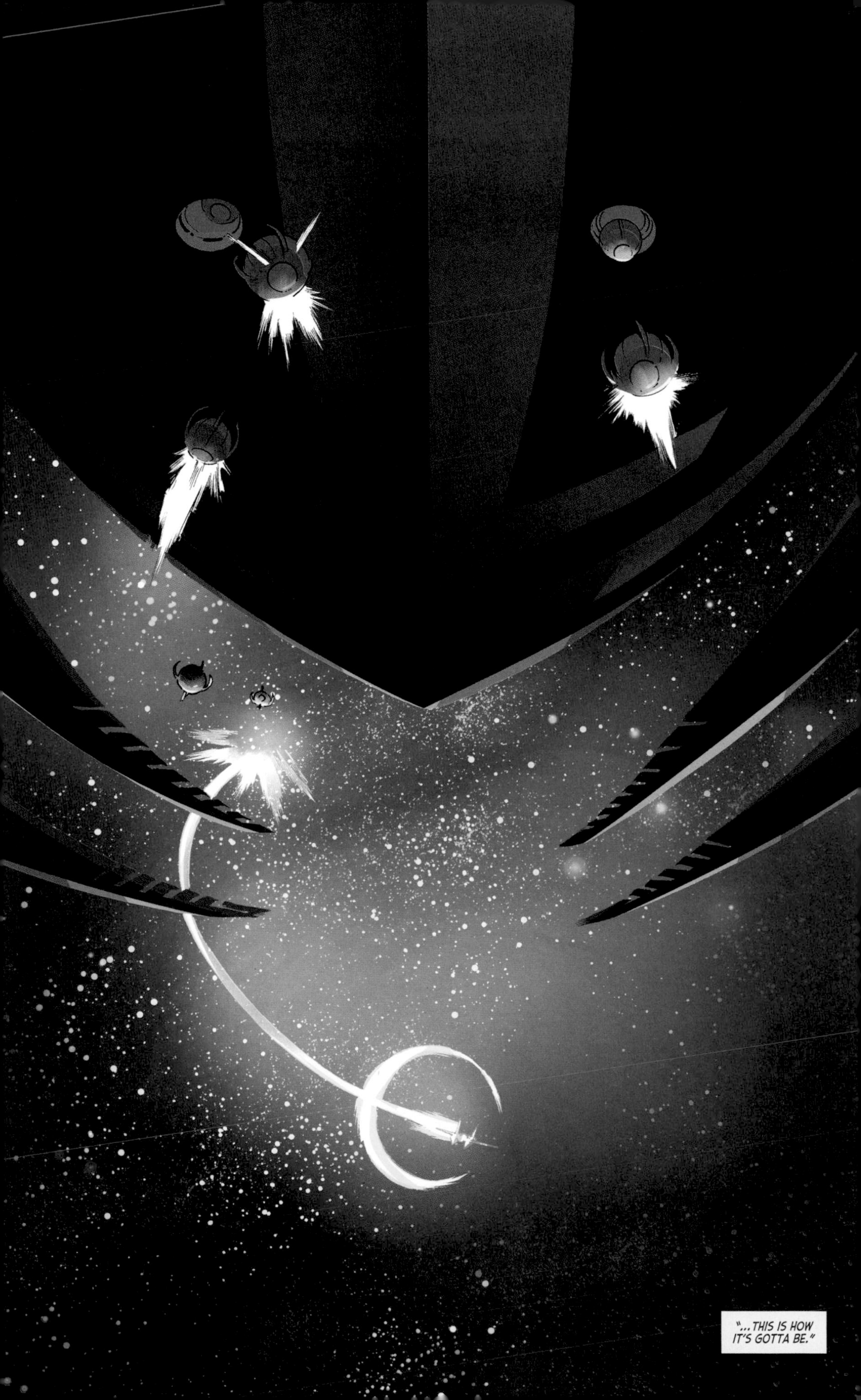
"...THIS IS HOW IT'S GOTTA BE."

"SHE LEFT US."

"YOU'RE SURPRISED?"

"I'M..."

"NO. JUST SAD, I GUESS."

"CAN'T BELIEVE THEY GAVE HIM ANOTHER NEW UNIFORM. THAT'S HIS THIRD ONE IN FIVE YEARS. ALLIED YOUTH. TACTICAL OPERATIONS. AND NOW..."

"SPECIAL INTERCEPTOR. QUITE AN HONOR."

"DON'T I KNOW IT. ALL JORN GETS IS HONORED."

"YOU SOUND JEALOUS."

"MAYBE I AM."

"WHAT I MEANT IS THAT IT'S QUITE AN HONOR FOR US. THEY DON'T SEND S.I. SQUADS AFTER JUST ANYONE."

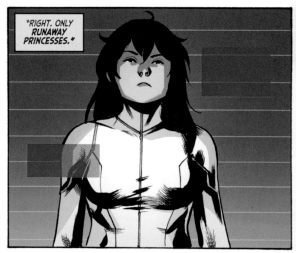

"RIGHT. ONLY RUNAWAY PRINCESSES."

"DON'T CALL ME THAT."

I'M NOT A PRINCESS.

NO? THEN WHAT EXACTLY ARE YOU?

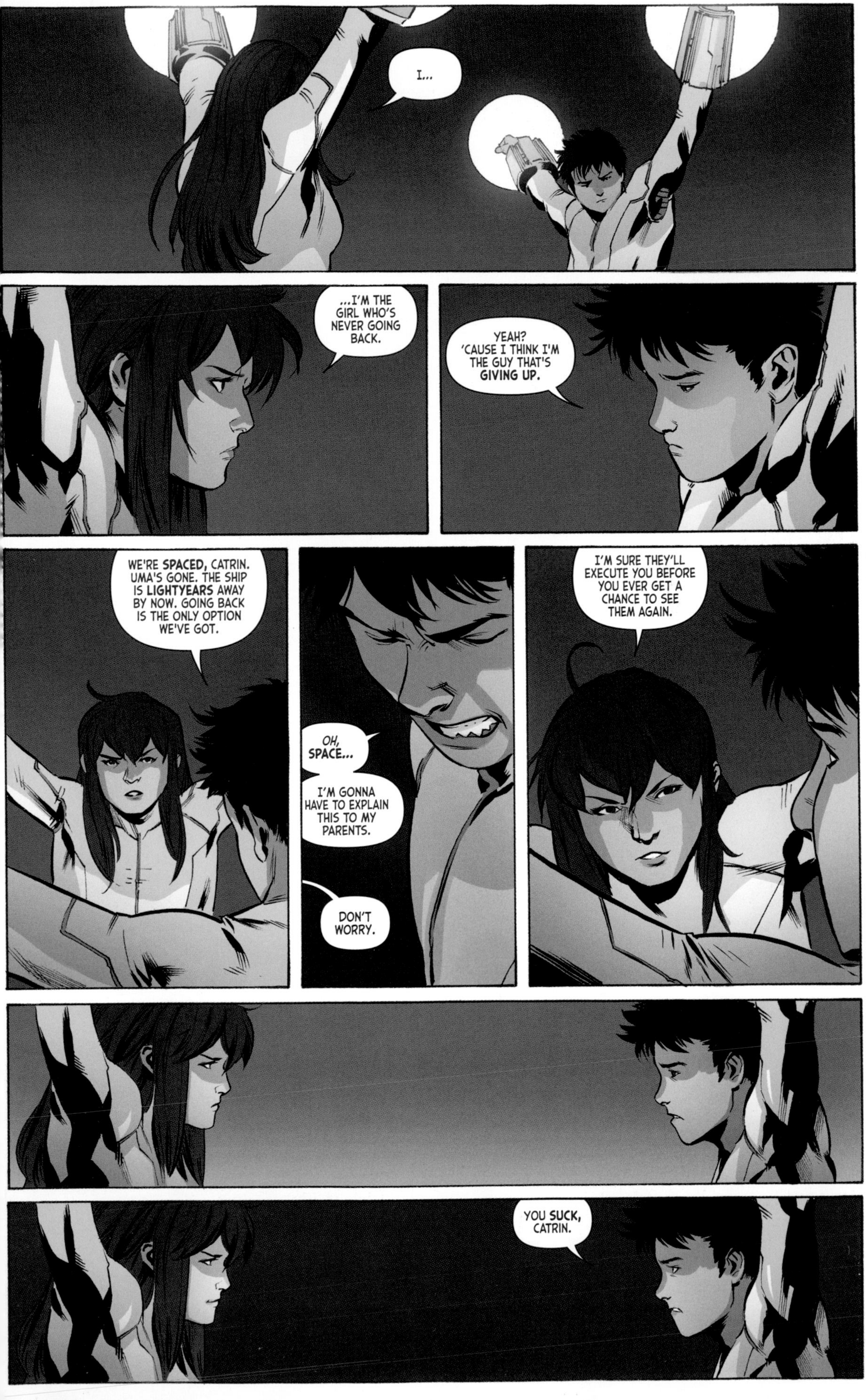
I...
...I'M THE GIRL WHO'S NEVER GOING BACK.
YEAH? 'CAUSE I THINK I'M THE GUY THAT'S GIVING UP.
WE'RE SPACED, CATRIN. UMA'S GONE. THE SHIP IS LIGHTYEARS AWAY BY NOW. GOING BACK IS THE ONLY OPTION WE'VE GOT.
OH, SPACE...
I'M GONNA HAVE TO EXPLAIN THIS TO MY PARENTS.
DON'T WORRY.
I'M SURE THEY'LL EXECUTE YOU BEFORE YOU EVER GET A CHANCE TO SEE THEM AGAIN.
YOU SUCK, CATRIN.

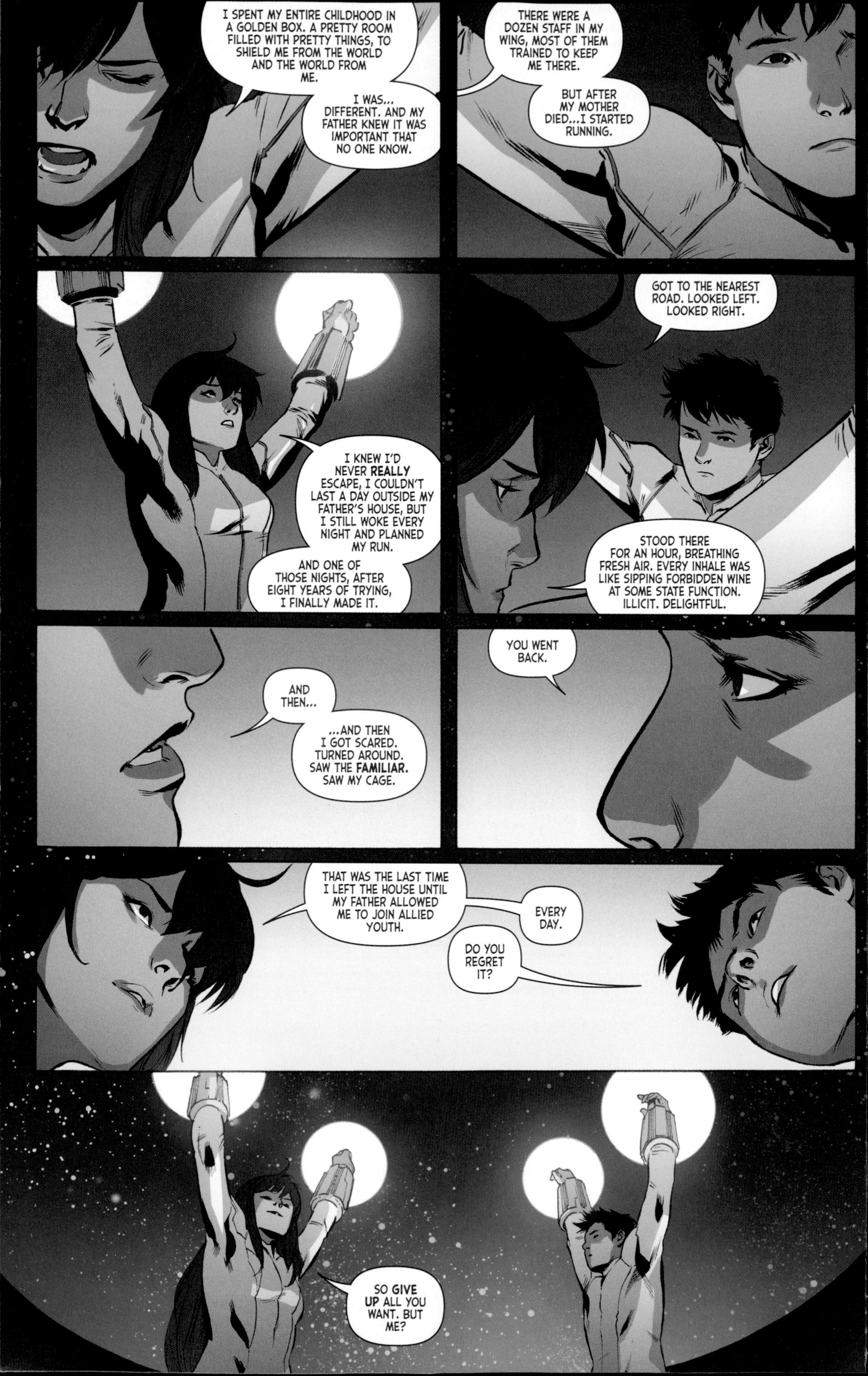
I SPENT MY ENTIRE CHILDHOOD IN A GOLDEN BOX. A PRETTY ROOM FILLED WITH PRETTY THINGS, TO SHIELD ME FROM THE WORLD AND THE WORLD FROM ME.
I WAS... DIFFERENT. AND MY FATHER KNEW IT WAS IMPORTANT THAT NO ONE KNOW.
THERE WERE A DOZEN STAFF IN MY WING, MOST OF THEM TRAINED TO KEEP ME THERE.
BUT AFTER MY MOTHER DIED...I STARTED RUNNING.
I KNEW I'D NEVER **REALLY** ESCAPE, I COULDN'T LAST A DAY OUTSIDE MY FATHER'S HOUSE, BUT I STILL WOKE EVERY NIGHT AND PLANNED MY RUN.
AND ONE OF THOSE NIGHTS, AFTER EIGHT YEARS OF TRYING, I FINALLY MADE IT.
GOT TO THE NEAREST ROAD. LOOKED LEFT. LOOKED RIGHT.
STOOD THERE FOR AN HOUR, BREATHING FRESH AIR. EVERY INHALE WAS LIKE SIPPING FORBIDDEN WINE AT SOME STATE FUNCTION. ILLICIT. DELIGHTFUL.
AND THEN...
...AND THEN I GOT SCARED. TURNED AROUND. SAW THE **FAMILIAR.** SAW MY CAGE.
YOU WENT BACK.
THAT WAS THE LAST TIME I LEFT THE HOUSE UNTIL MY FATHER ALLOWED ME TO JOIN ALLIED YOUTH.
EVERY DAY.
DO YOU REGRET IT?
SO **GIVE UP** ALL YOU WANT. BUT ME?

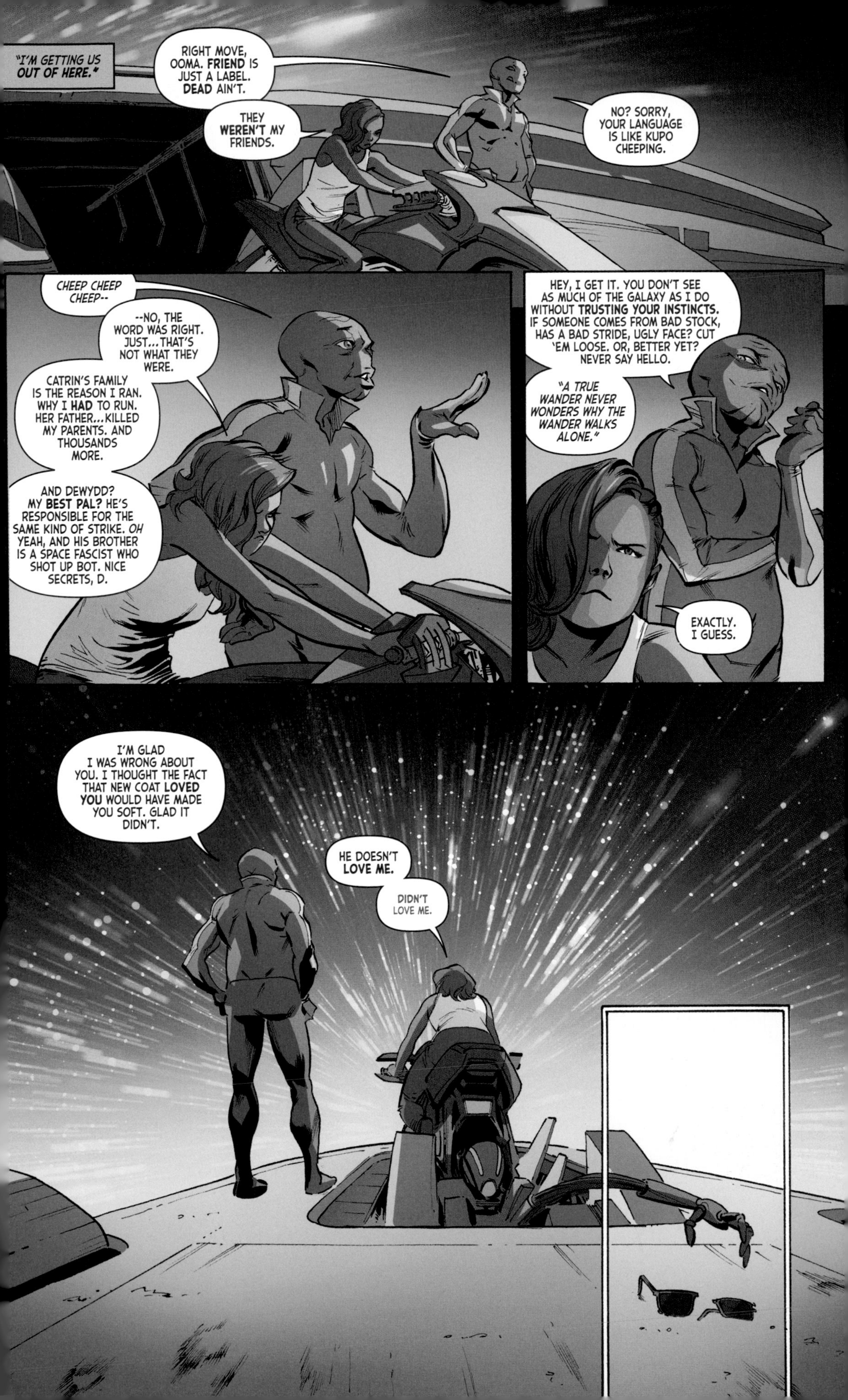
"I'M GETTING US OUT OF HERE."
RIGHT MOVE, OOMA. FRIEND IS JUST A LABEL. DEAD AIN'T.
THEY WEREN'T MY FRIENDS.
NO? SORRY, YOUR LANGUAGE IS LIKE KUPO CHEEPING.
CHEEP CHEEP CHEEP--
--NO, THE WORD WAS RIGHT. JUST...THAT'S NOT WHAT THEY WERE.
CATRIN'S FAMILY IS THE REASON I RAN. WHY I HAD TO RUN. HER FATHER...KILLED MY PARENTS. AND THOUSANDS MORE.
AND DEWYDD? MY BEST PAL? HE'S RESPONSIBLE FOR THE SAME KIND OF STRIKE. OH YEAH, AND HIS BROTHER IS A SPACE FASCIST WHO SHOT UP BOT. NICE SECRETS, D.
HEY, I GET IT. YOU DON'T SEE AS MUCH OF THE GALAXY AS I DO WITHOUT TRUSTING YOUR INSTINCTS. IF SOMEONE COMES FROM BAD STOCK, HAS A BAD STRIDE, UGLY FACE? CUT 'EM LOOSE. OR, BETTER YET? NEVER SAY HELLO.
"A TRUE WANDER NEVER WONDERS WHY THE WANDER WALKS ALONE."
EXACTLY. I GUESS.
I'M GLAD I WAS WRONG ABOUT YOU. I THOUGHT THE FACT THAT NEW COAT LOVED YOU WOULD HAVE MADE YOU SOFT. GLAD IT DIDN'T.
HE DOESN'T LOVE ME.
DIDN'T LOVE ME.

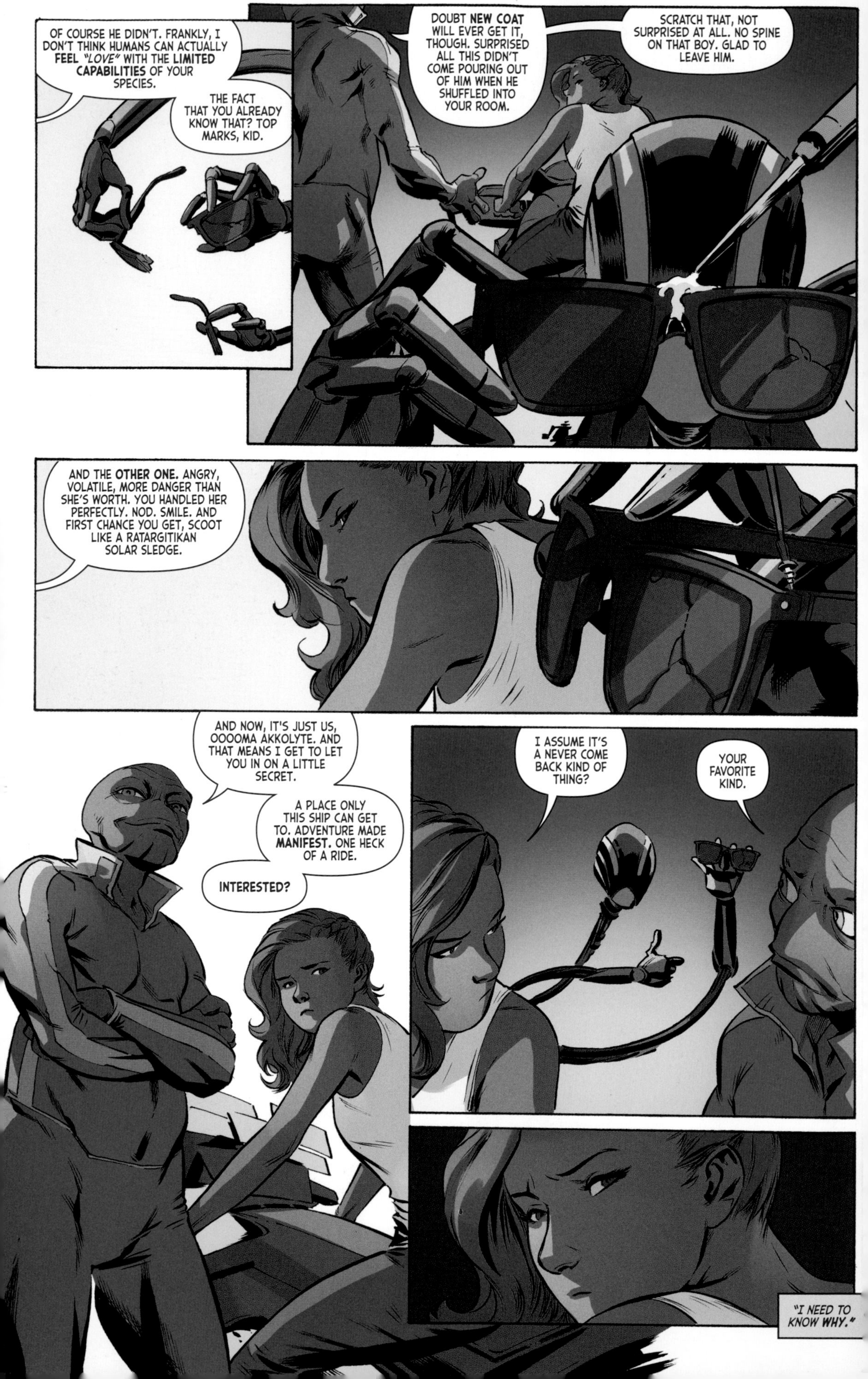
OF COURSE HE DIDN'T. FRANKLY, I DON'T THINK HUMANS CAN ACTUALLY **FEEL** *"LOVE"* WITH THE **LIMITED CAPABILITIES** OF YOUR SPECIES.
THE FACT THAT YOU ALREADY KNOW THAT? TOP MARKS, KID.
DOUBT **NEW COAT** WILL EVER GET IT, THOUGH. SURPRISED ALL THIS DIDN'T COME POURING OUT OF HIM WHEN HE SHUFFLED INTO YOUR ROOM.
SCRATCH THAT, NOT SURPRISED AT ALL. NO SPINE ON THAT BOY. GLAD TO LEAVE HIM.
AND THE **OTHER ONE.** ANGRY, VOLATILE, MORE DANGER THAN SHE'S WORTH. YOU HANDLED HER PERFECTLY. NOD. SMILE. AND FIRST CHANCE YOU GET, SCOOT LIKE A RATARGITIKAN SOLAR SLEDGE.
AND NOW, IT'S JUST US, OOOOMA AKKOLYTE. AND THAT MEANS I GET TO LET YOU IN ON A LITTLE SECRET.
A PLACE ONLY THIS SHIP CAN GET TO. ADVENTURE MADE **MANIFEST.** ONE HECK OF A RIDE.
INTERESTED?
I ASSUME IT'S A NEVER COME BACK KIND OF THING?
YOUR FAVORITE KIND.
"I NEED TO KNOW ***WHY.****"*

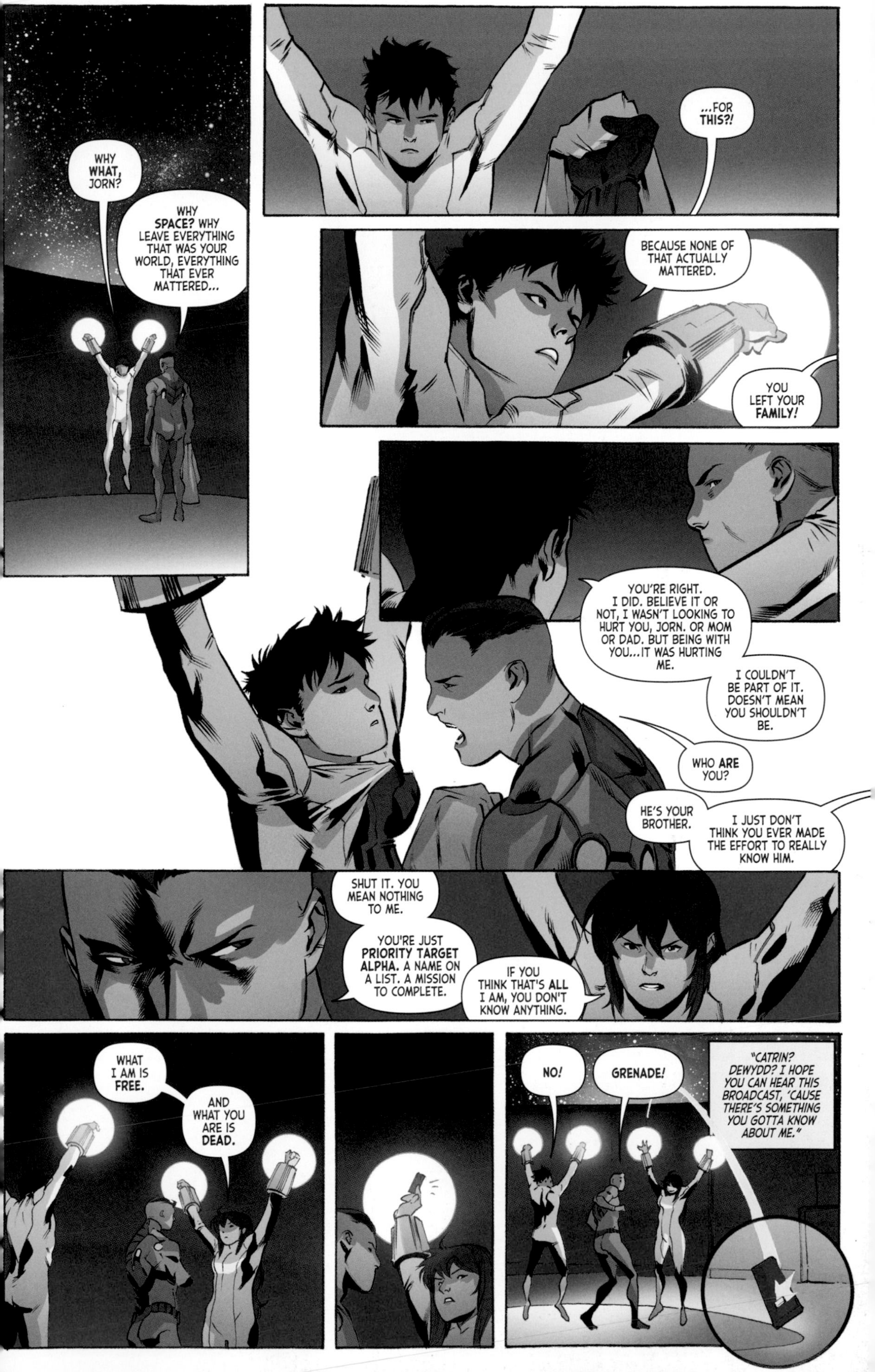
WHY WHAT, JORN?
WHY SPACE? WHY LEAVE EVERYTHING THAT WAS YOUR WORLD, EVERYTHING THAT EVER MATTERED...
...FOR THIS?!
BECAUSE NONE OF THAT ACTUALLY MATTERED.
YOU LEFT YOUR FAMILY!
YOU'RE RIGHT. I DID. BELIEVE IT OR NOT, I WASN'T LOOKING TO HURT YOU, JORN. OR MOM OR DAD. BUT BEING WITH YOU...IT WAS HURTING ME.
I COULDN'T BE PART OF IT. DOESN'T MEAN YOU SHOULDN'T BE.
WHO ARE YOU?
HE'S YOUR BROTHER.
I JUST DON'T THINK YOU EVER MADE THE EFFORT TO REALLY KNOW HIM.
SHUT IT. YOU MEAN NOTHING TO ME.
YOU'RE JUST PRIORITY TARGET ALPHA. A NAME ON A LIST. A MISSION TO COMPLETE.
IF YOU THINK THAT'S ALL I AM, YOU DON'T KNOW ANYTHING.
WHAT I AM IS FREE.
AND WHAT YOU ARE IS DEAD.
NO!
GRENADE!
"CATRIN? DEWYDD? I HOPE YOU CAN HEAR THIS BROADCAST, 'CAUSE THERE'S SOMETHING YOU GOTTA KNOW ABOUT ME."

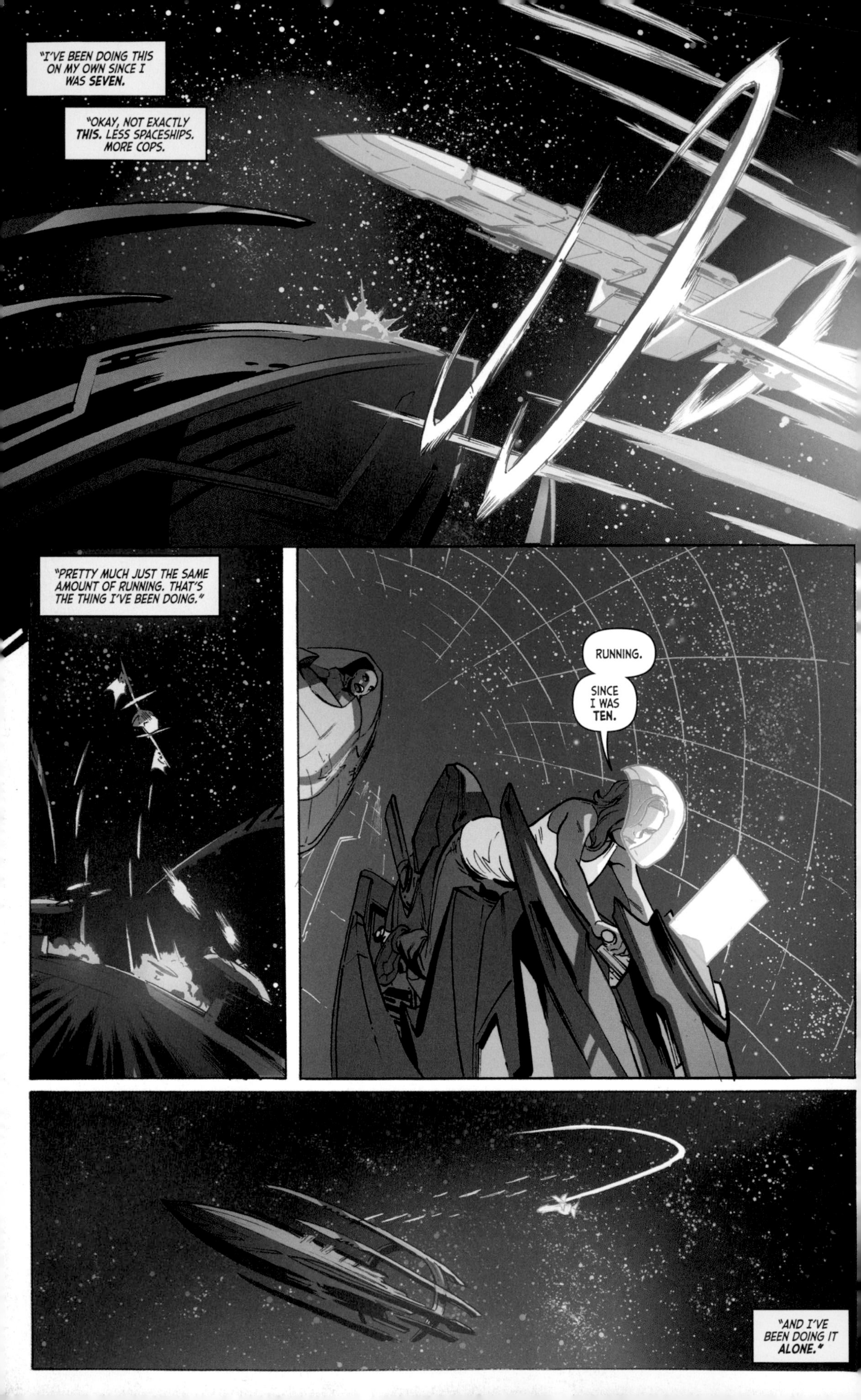
"I'VE BEEN DOING THIS ON MY OWN SINCE I WAS SEVEN.
"OKAY, NOT EXACTLY THIS. LESS SPACESHIPS. MORE COPS.
"PRETTY MUCH JUST THE SAME AMOUNT OF RUNNING. THAT'S THE THING I'VE BEEN DOING."
RUNNING.
SINCE I WAS TEN.
"AND I'VE BEEN DOING IT ALONE."

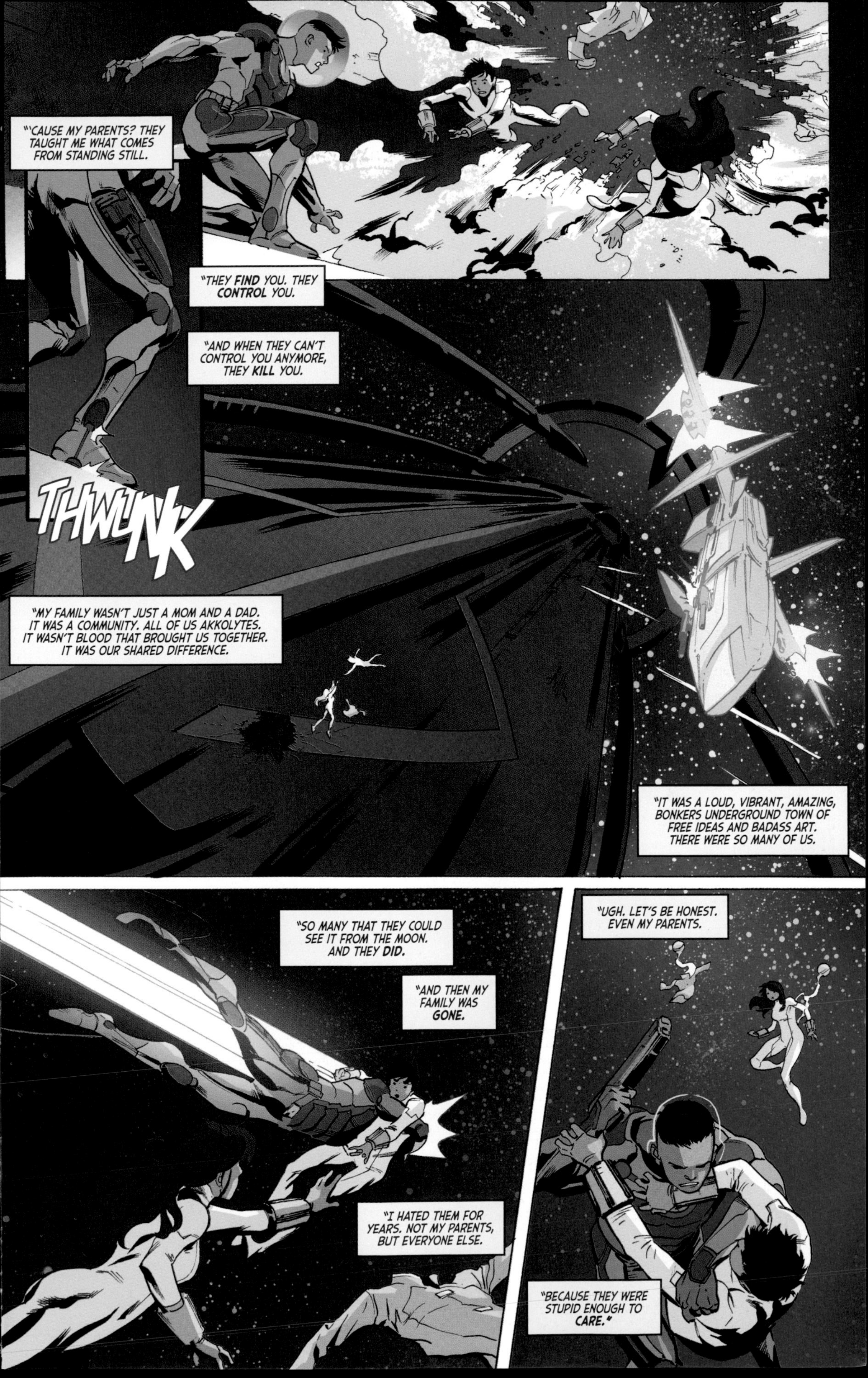
"'CAUSE MY PARENTS? THEY TAUGHT ME WHAT COMES FROM STANDING STILL.
"THEY FIND YOU. THEY CONTROL YOU.
"AND WHEN THEY CAN'T CONTROL YOU ANYMORE, THEY KILL YOU.
THWUNK
"MY FAMILY WASN'T JUST A MOM AND A DAD. IT WAS A COMMUNITY. ALL OF US AKKOLYTES. IT WASN'T BLOOD THAT BROUGHT US TOGETHER. IT WAS OUR SHARED DIFFERENCE.
"IT WAS A LOUD, VIBRANT, AMAZING, BONKERS UNDERGROUND TOWN OF FREE IDEAS AND BADASS ART. THERE WERE SO MANY OF US.
"SO MANY THAT THEY COULD SEE IT FROM THE MOON. AND THEY DID.
"AND THEN MY FAMILY WAS GONE.
"I HATED THEM FOR YEARS. NOT MY PARENTS, BUT EVERYONE ELSE.
"UGH. LET'S BE HONEST. EVEN MY PARENTS.
"BECAUSE THEY WERE STUPID ENOUGH TO CARE."

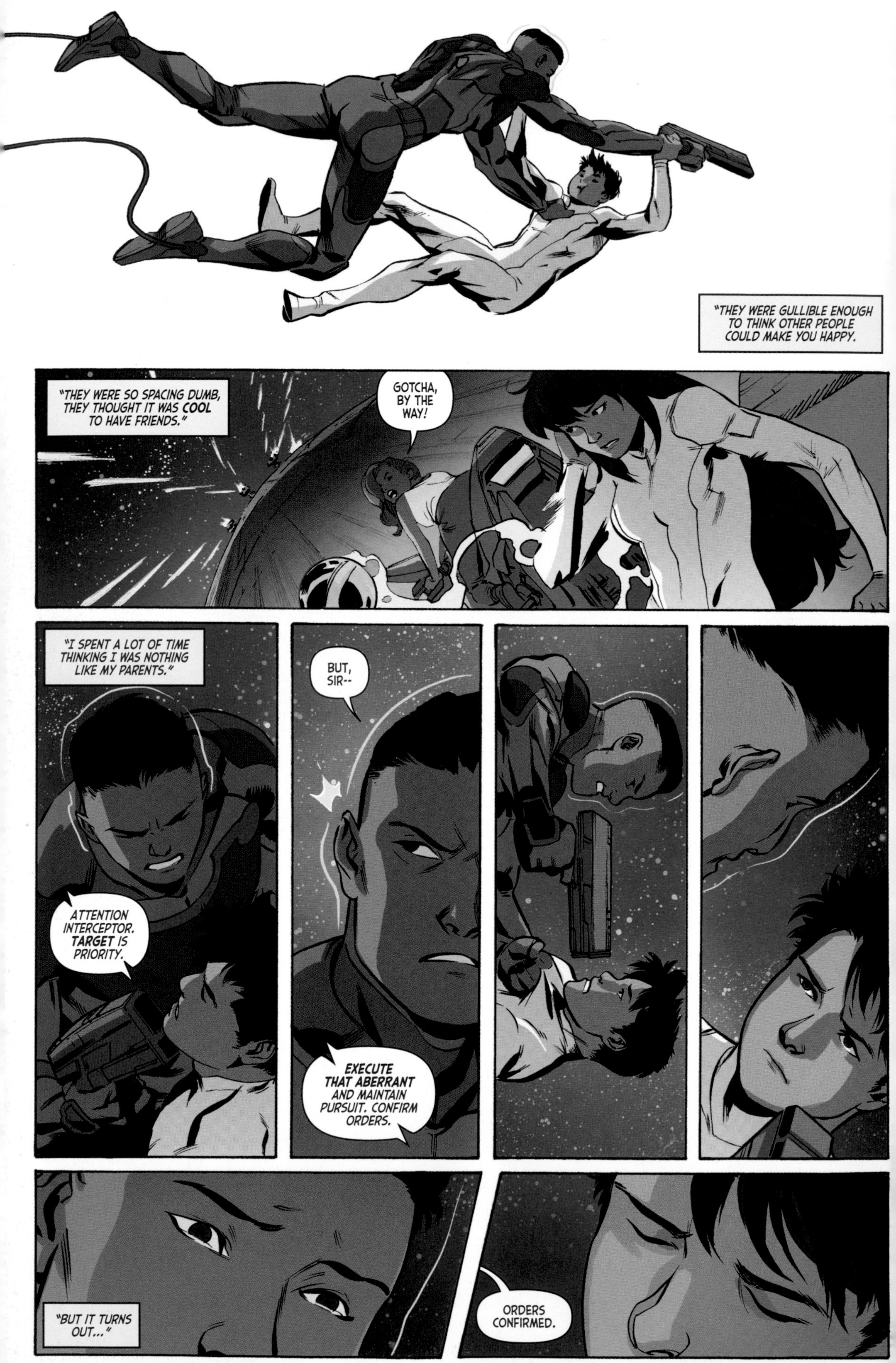
"THEY WERE GULLIBLE ENOUGH TO THINK OTHER PEOPLE COULD MAKE YOU HAPPY.
"THEY WERE SO SPACING DUMB, THEY THOUGHT IT WAS COOL TO HAVE FRIENDS."
GOTCHA, BY THE WAY!
"I SPENT A LOT OF TIME THINKING I WAS NOTHING LIKE MY PARENTS."
ATTENTION INTERCEPTOR. TARGET IS PRIORITY.
BUT, SIR--
EXECUTE THAT ABERRANT AND MAINTAIN PURSUIT. CONFIRM ORDERS.
"BUT IT TURNS OUT..."
ORDERS CONFIRMED.

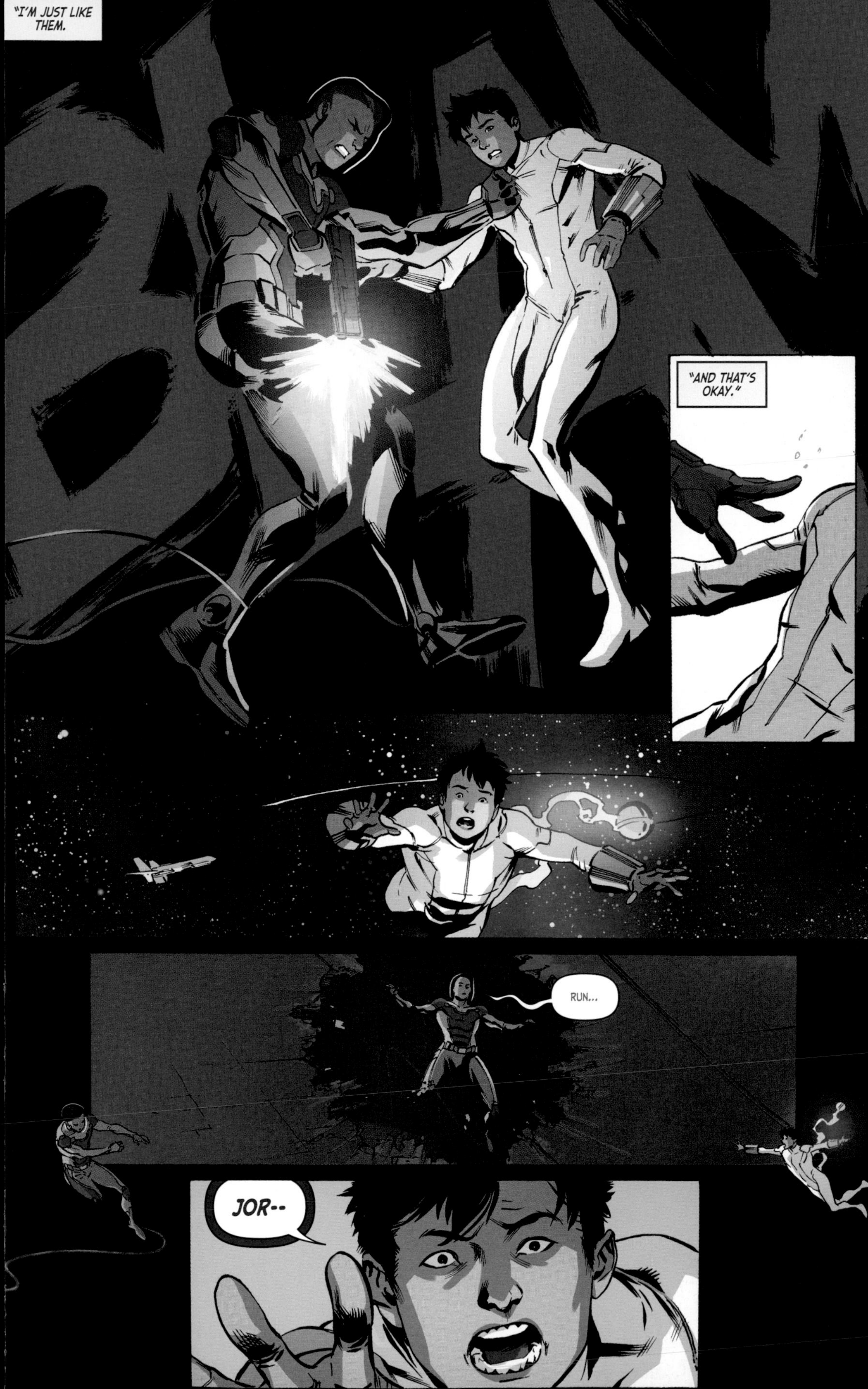
"I'M JUST LIKE THEM.
"AND THAT'S OKAY."
RUN...
JOR--

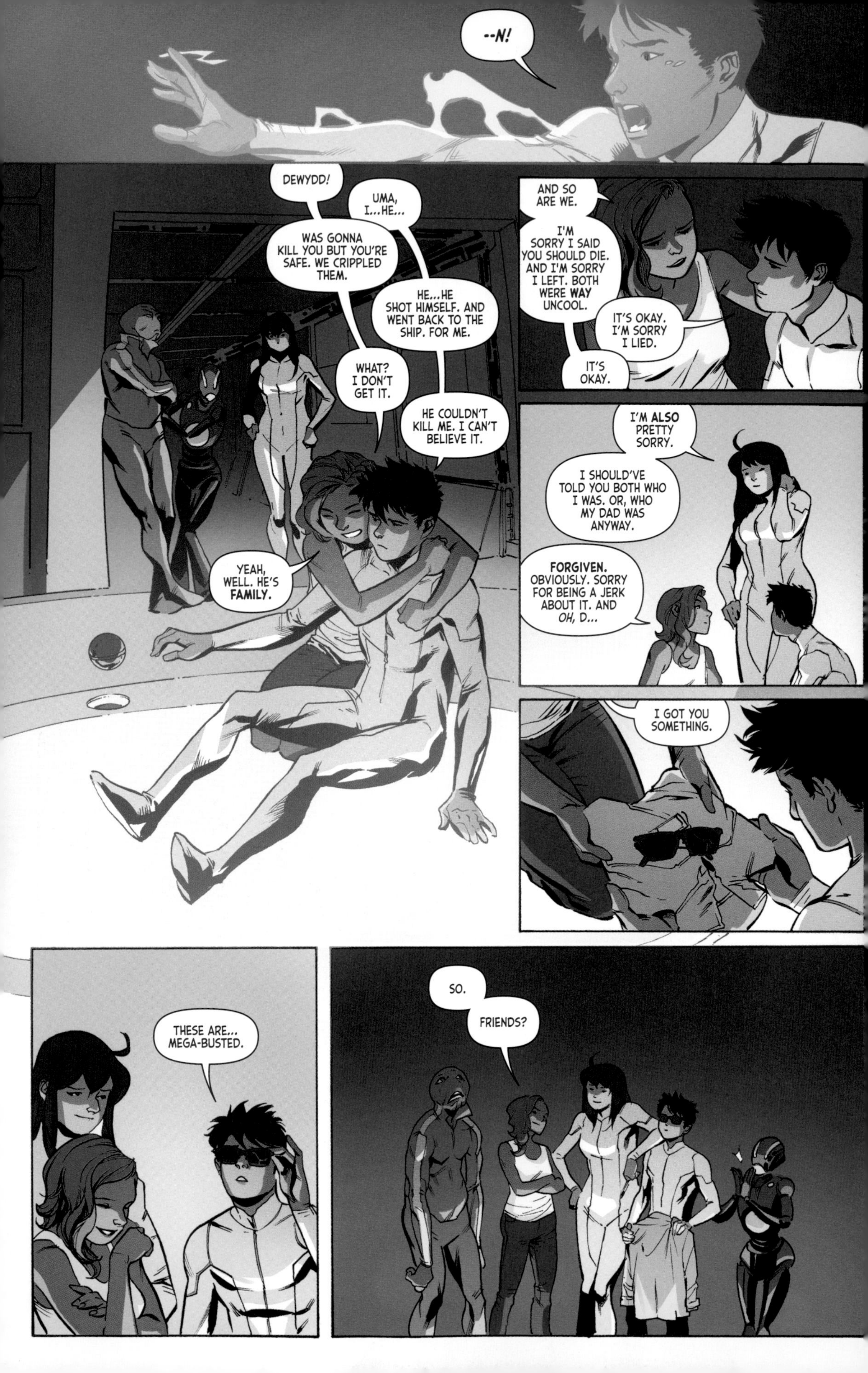
--N!
DEWYDD!
UMA, I...HE...
WAS GONNA KILL YOU BUT YOU'RE SAFE. WE CRIPPLED THEM.
HE...HE SHOT HIMSELF. AND WENT BACK TO THE SHIP. FOR ME.
WHAT? I DON'T GET IT.
HE COULDN'T KILL ME. I CAN'T BELIEVE IT.
YEAH, WELL. HE'S **FAMILY.**
AND SO ARE WE.
I'M SORRY I SAID YOU SHOULD DIE. AND I'M SORRY I LEFT. BOTH WERE **WAY** UNCOOL.
IT'S OKAY. I'M SORRY I LIED.
IT'S OKAY.
I'M **ALSO** PRETTY SORRY.
I SHOULD'VE TOLD YOU BOTH WHO I WAS. OR, WHO MY DAD WAS ANYWAY.
FORGIVEN. OBVIOUSLY. SORRY FOR BEING A JERK ABOUT IT. AND *OH,* D...
I GOT YOU SOMETHING.
THESE ARE... MEGA-BUSTED.
SO.
FRIENDS?

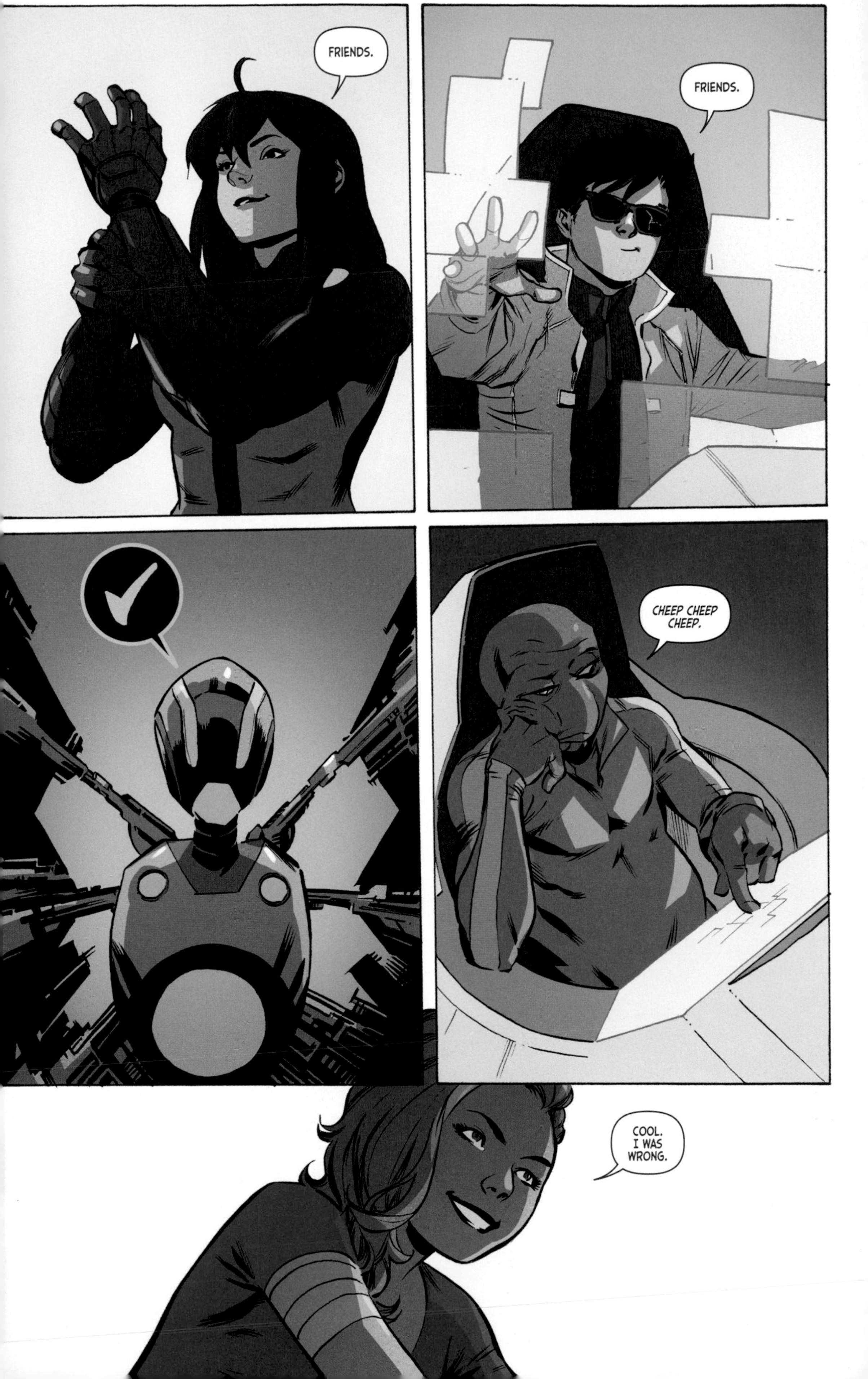
FRIENDS.
FRIENDS.
CHEEP CHEEP CHEEP.
COOL. I WAS WRONG.

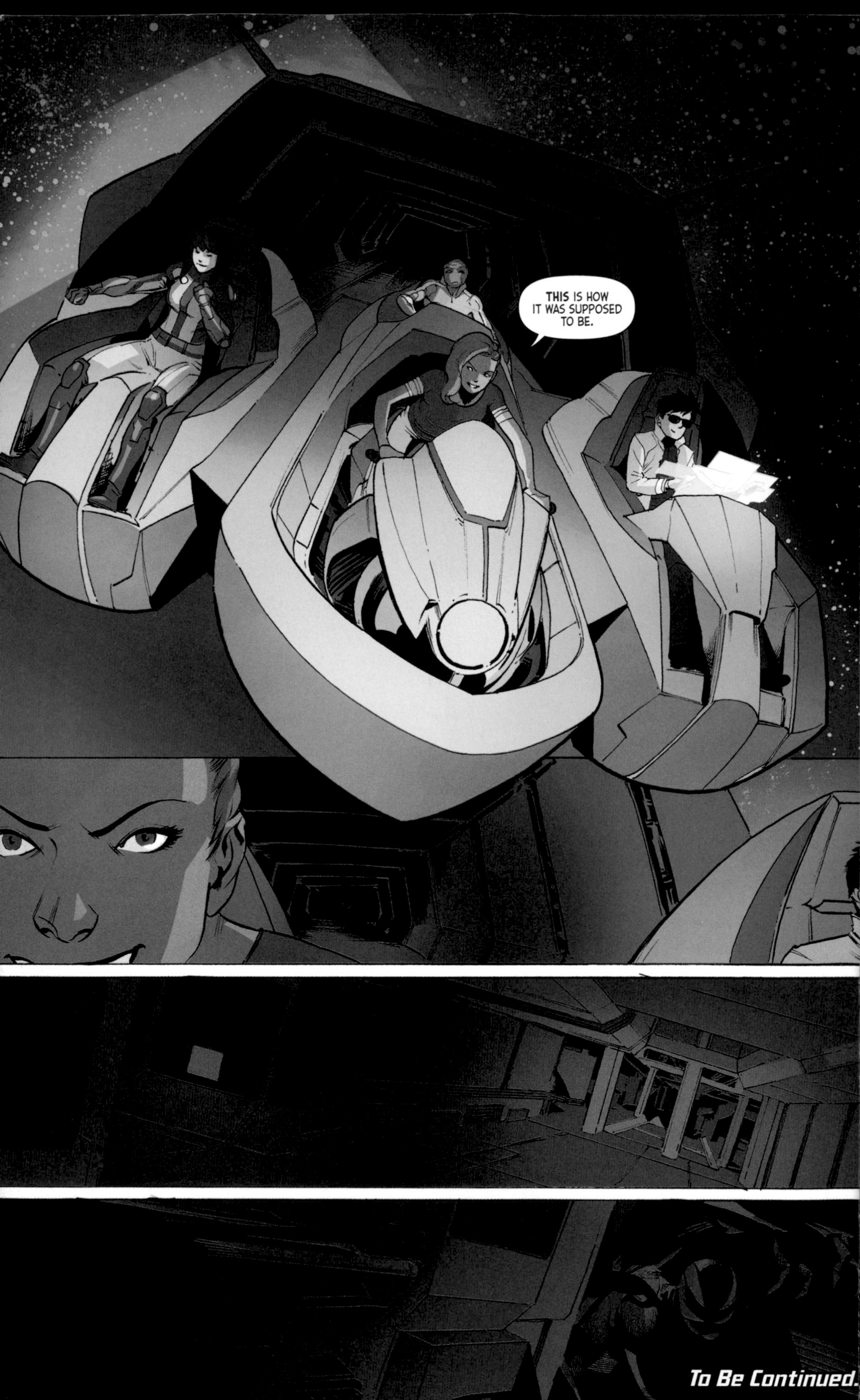
THIS IS HOW IT WAS SUPPOSED TO BE.
To Be Continued.

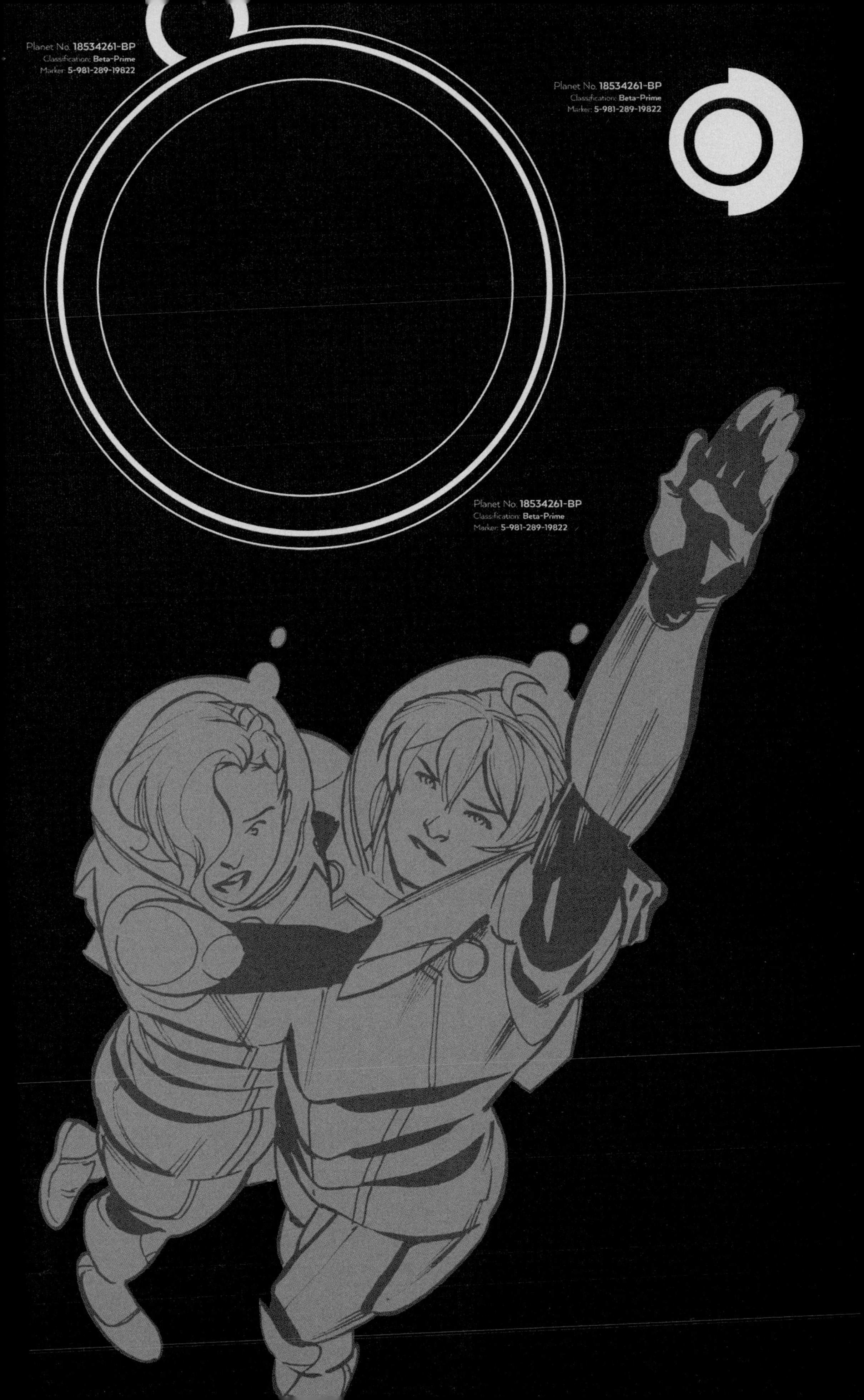
Planet No. 18534261-BP
Classification: Beta-Prime
Marker: 5-981-289-19822
Planet No. 18534261-BP
Classification: Beta-Prime
Marker: 5-981-289-19822
Planet No. 18534261-BP
Classification: Beta-Prime
Marker: 5-981-289-19822

ISSUE ONE COVER BY **MARCUS TO** WITH COLORS BY **IRMA KNIIVILA**

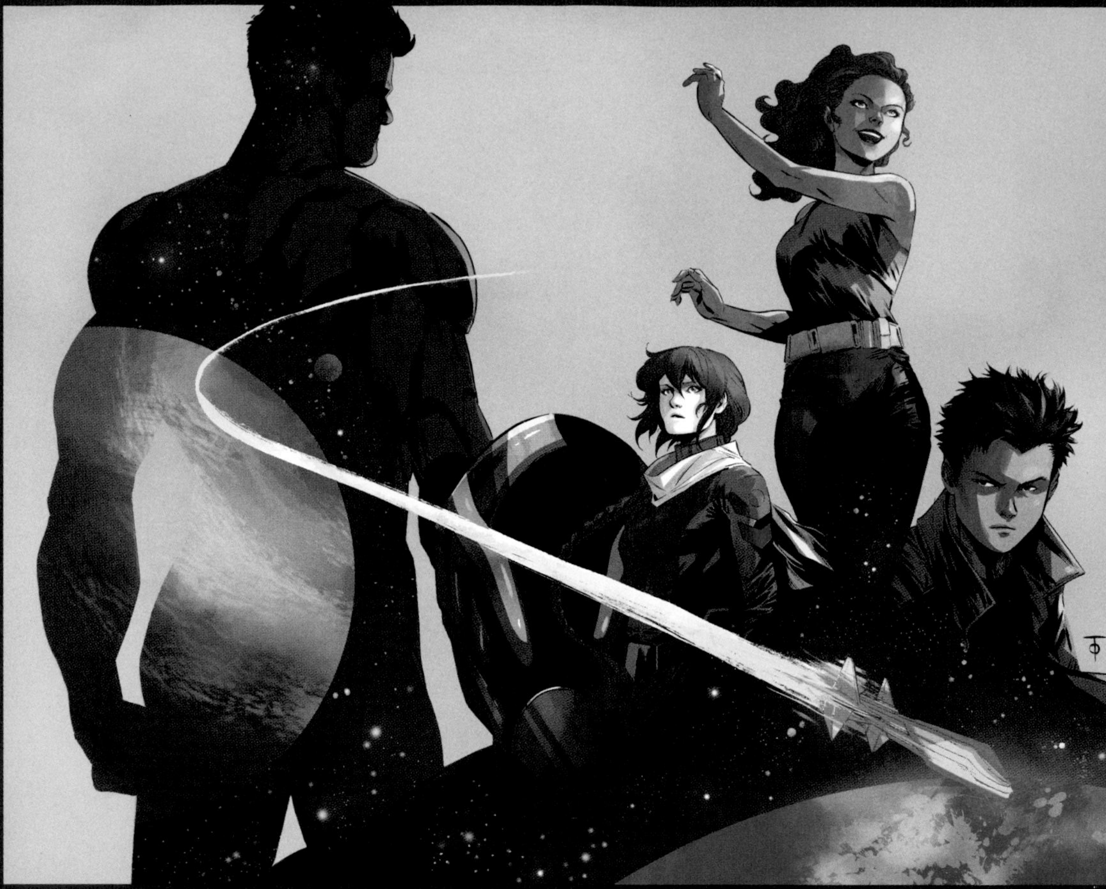

ISSUE TWO COVER BY **MARCUS TO** WITH COLORS BY **IRMA KNIIVILA**

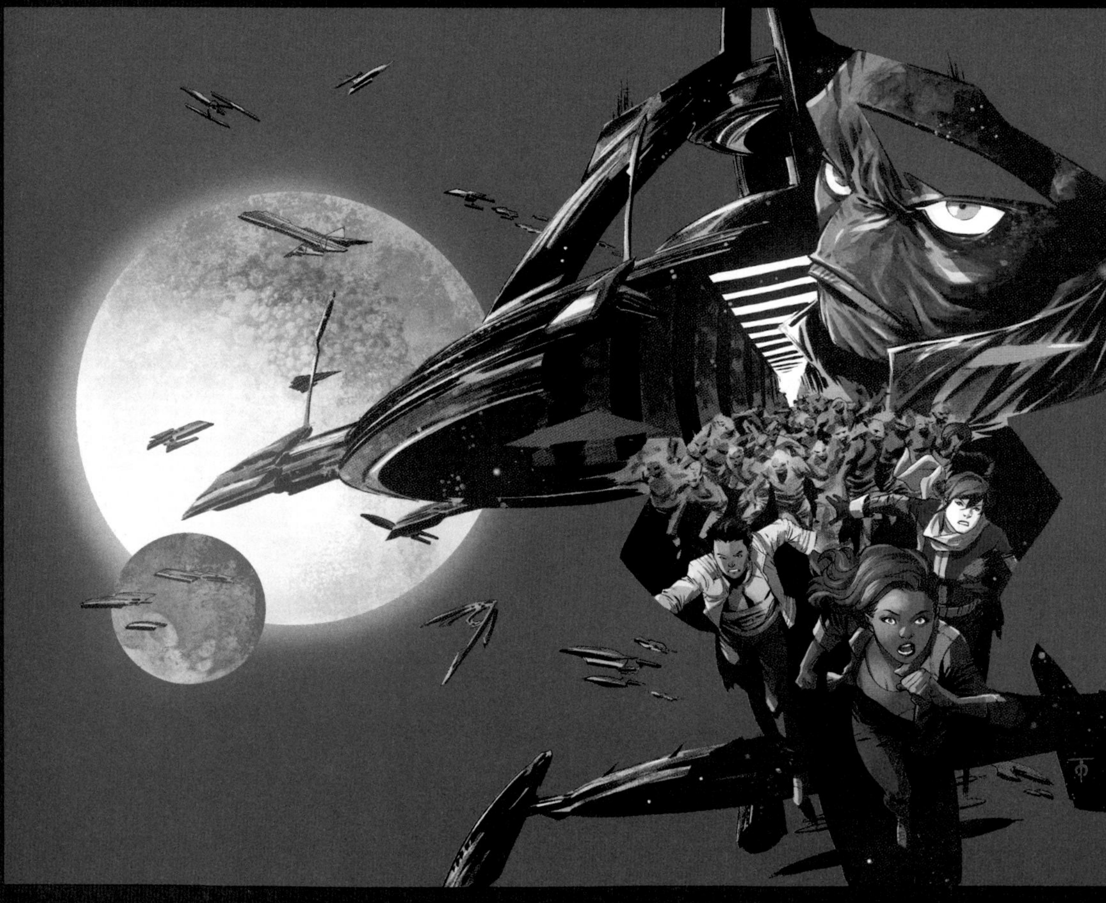

ISSUE THREE COVER BY **MARCUS TO** WITH COLORS BY **IRMA KNIIVILA**

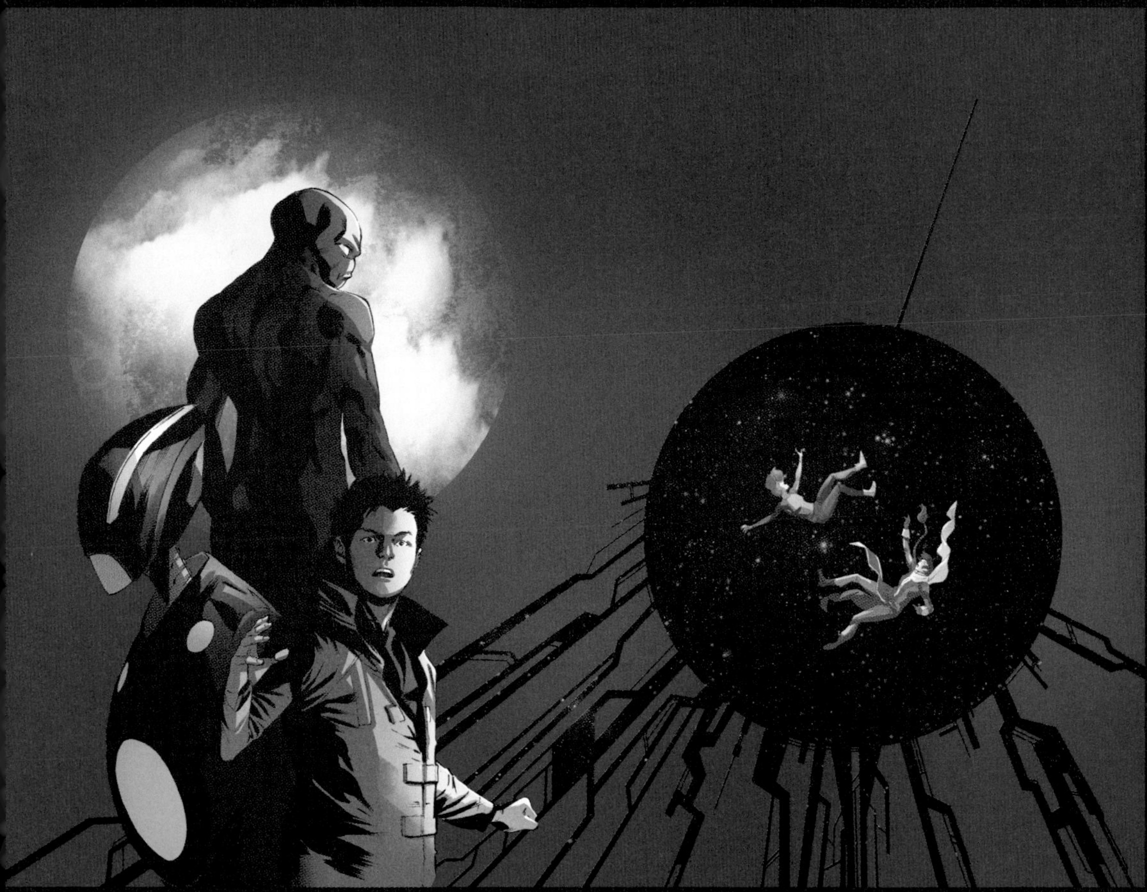

ISSUE FOUR COVER BY **MARCUS TO** WITH COLORS BY **IRMA KNIIVILA**

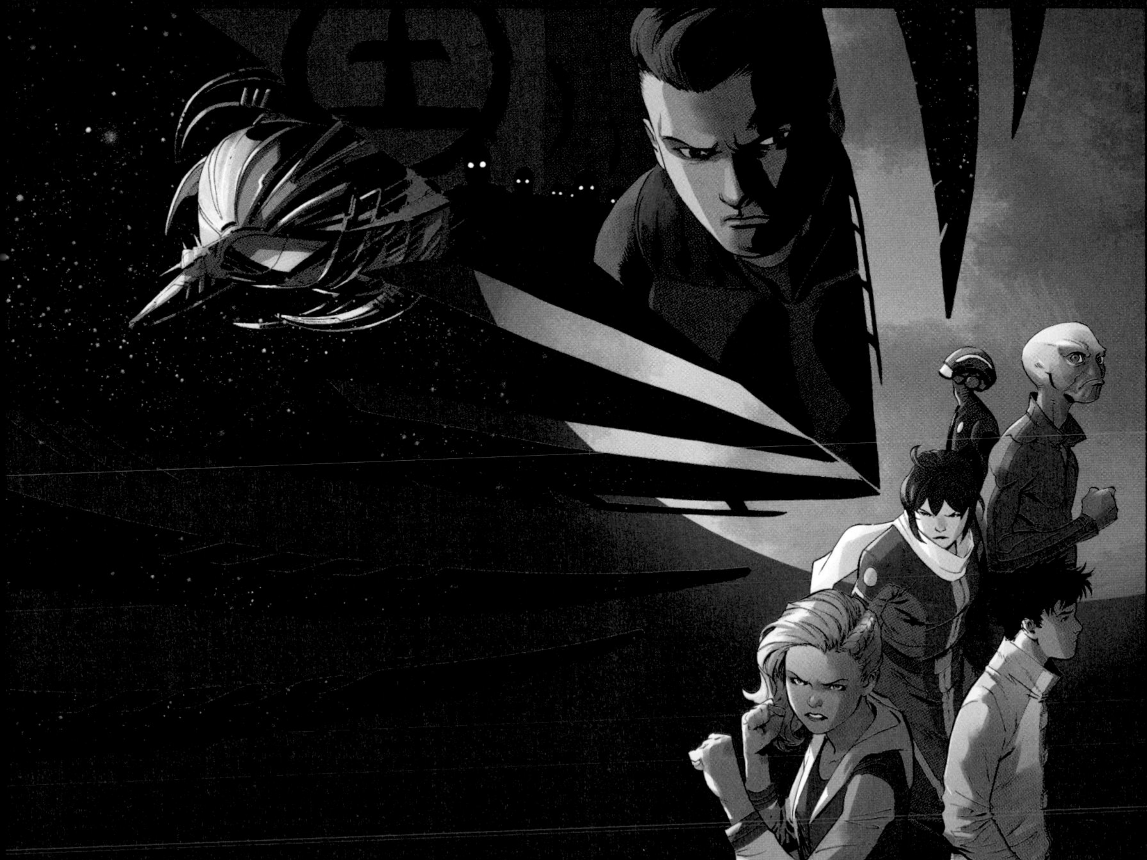

ISSUE ONE UNLOCKED RETAILER VARIANT COVER BY **NIMIT MALAVIA**

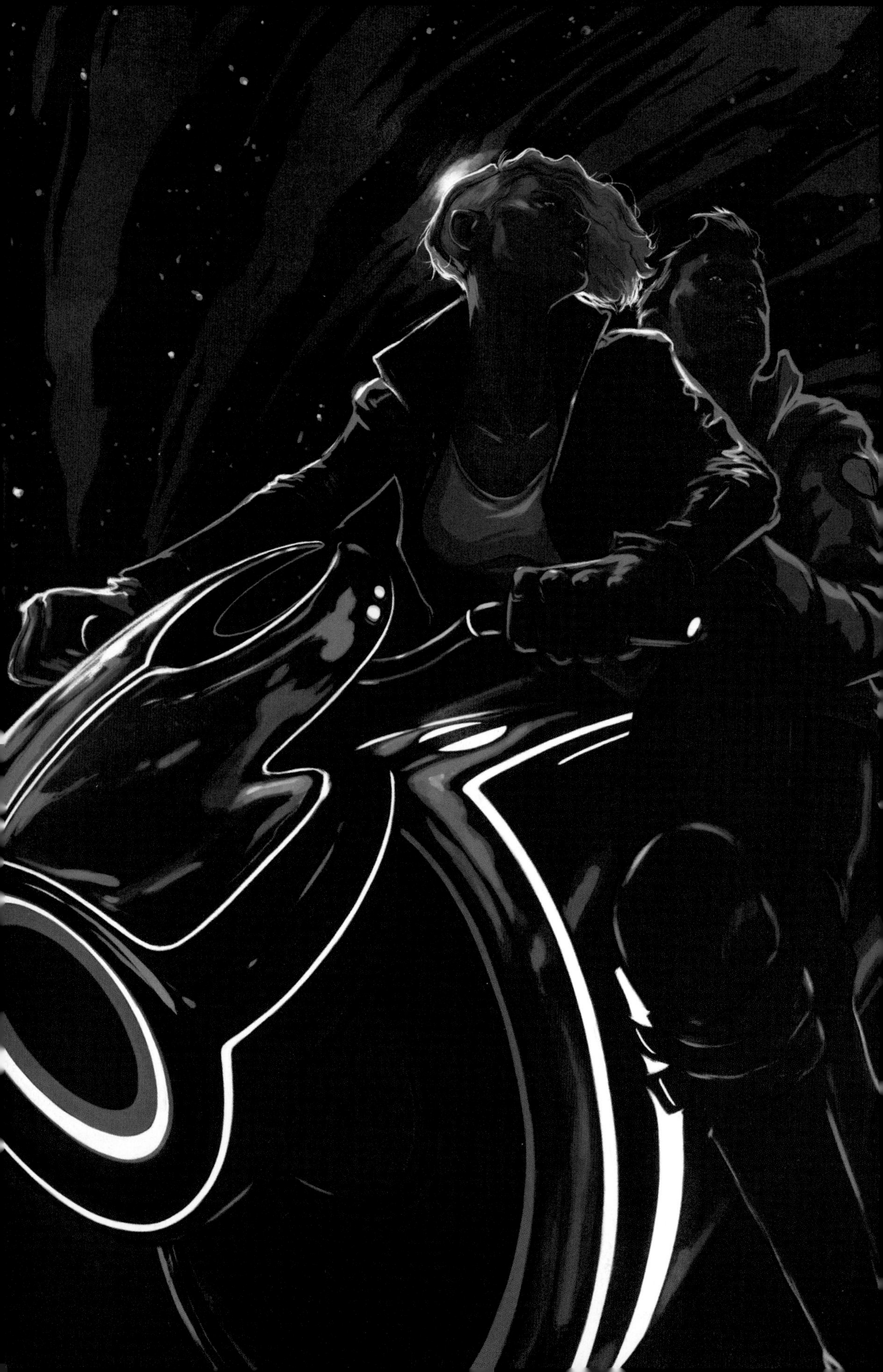

ISSUE ONE UNLOCKED RETAILER VARIANT COVER BY **TULA LOTAY**

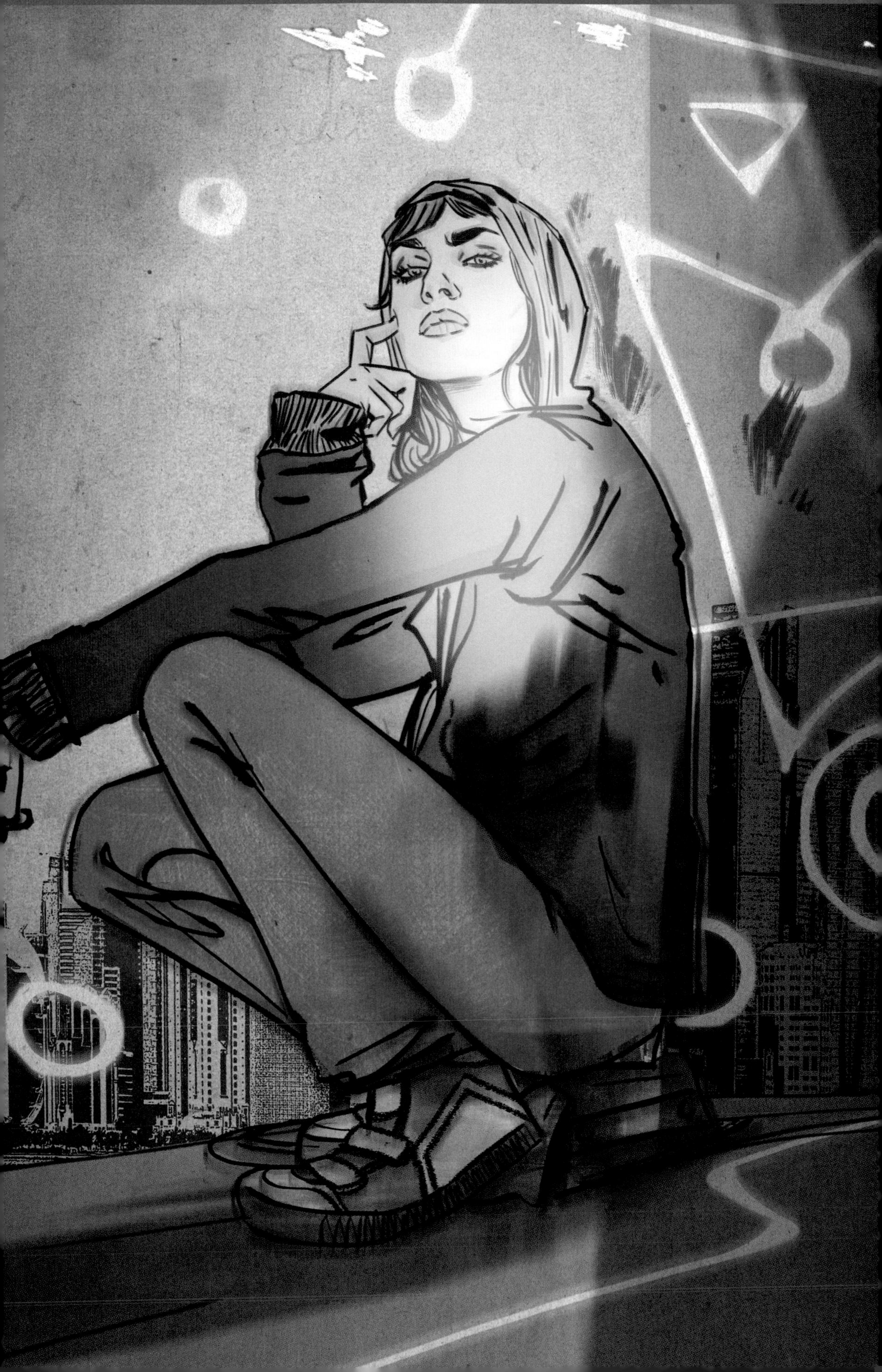

ISSUE ONE EMERALD CITY COMICON EXCLUSIVE COVER BY **JORGE CORONA** WITH COLORS BY **JEREMY LAWSON**

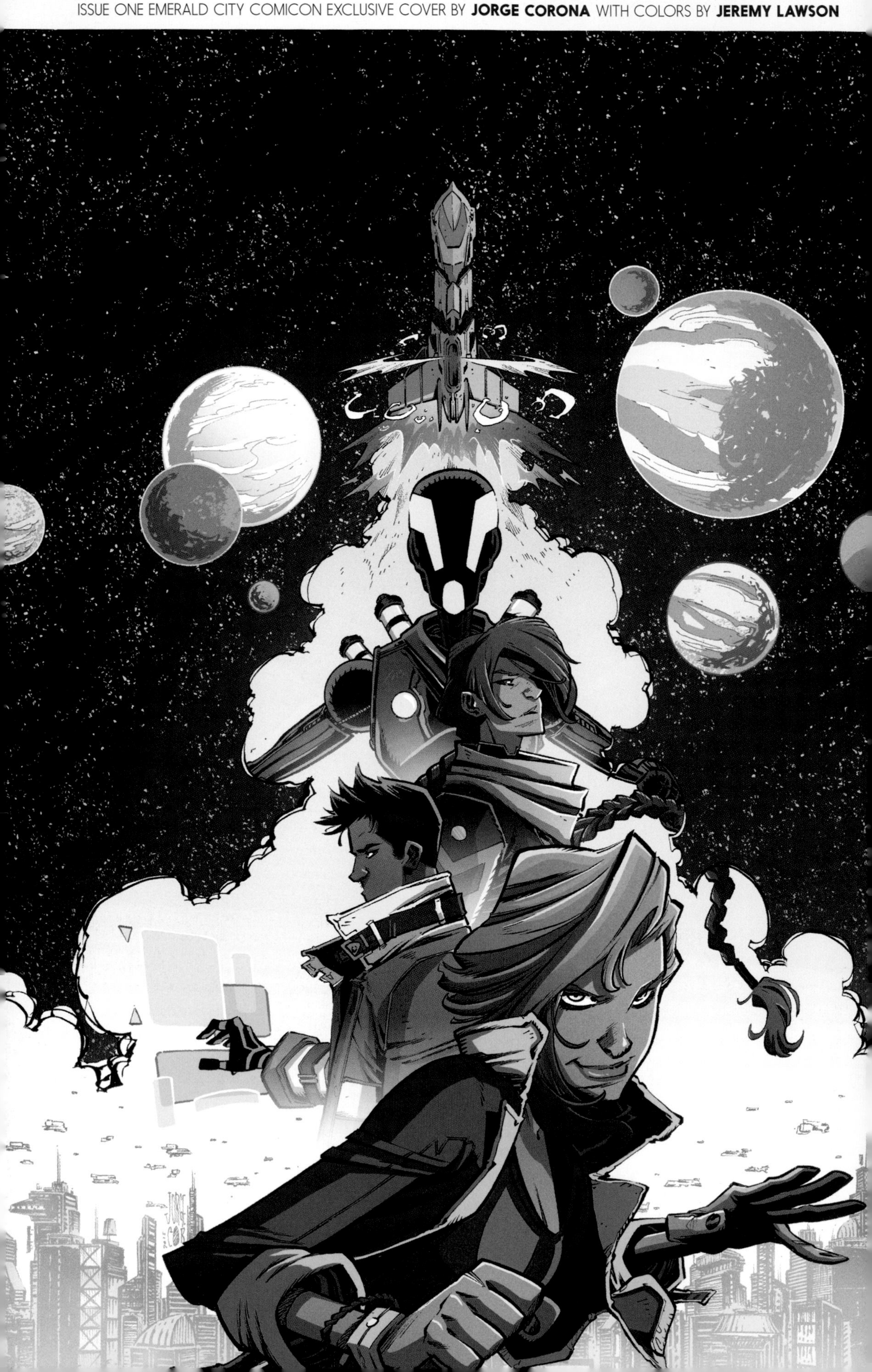

ISSUE ONE SECOND PRINT COVER BY **SCOTT HEPBURN** WITH COLORS BY **IRMA KNIIVILA**

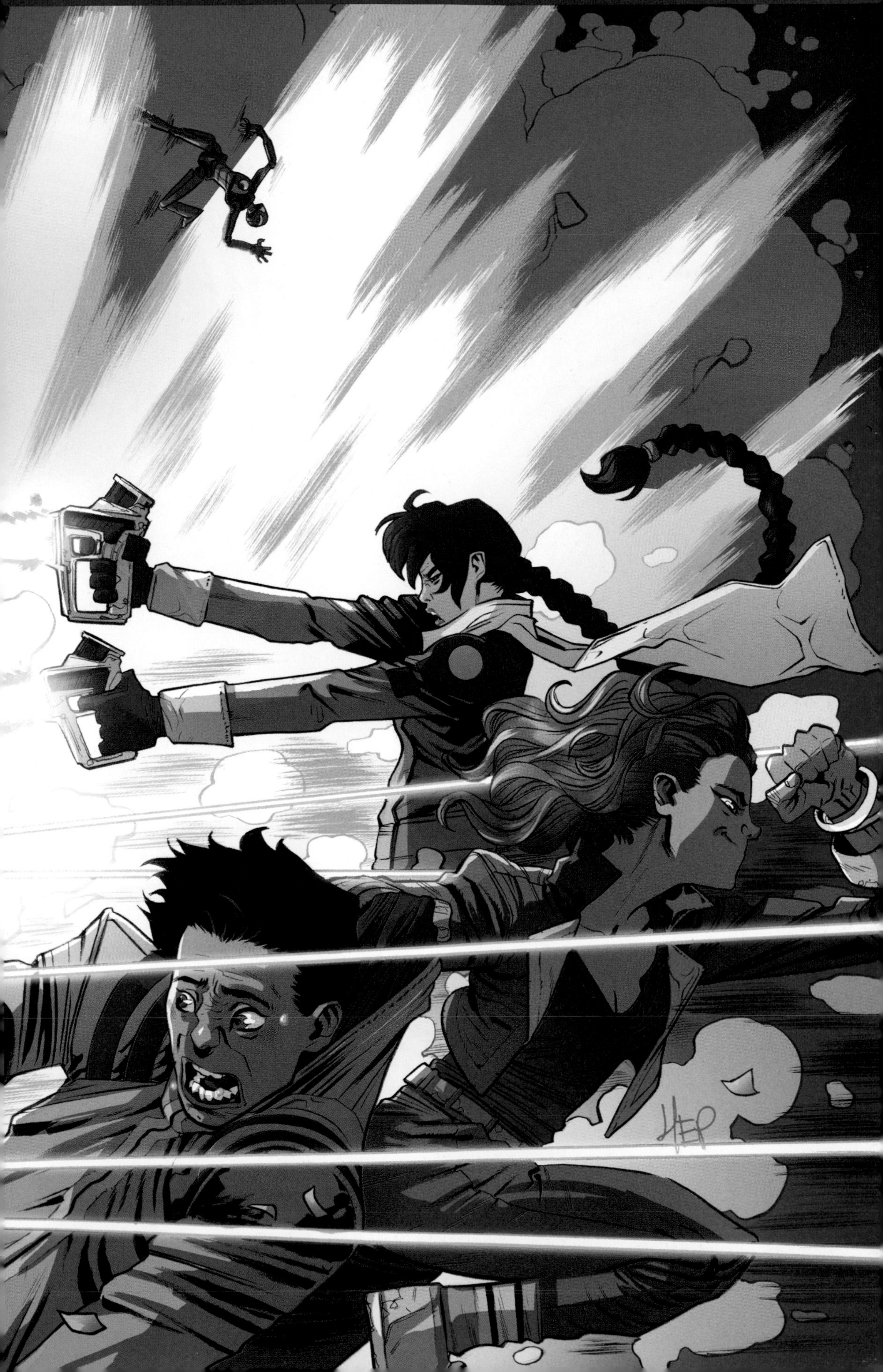

ISSUE ONE THIRD PRINT COVER BY **EMILY CHOI**

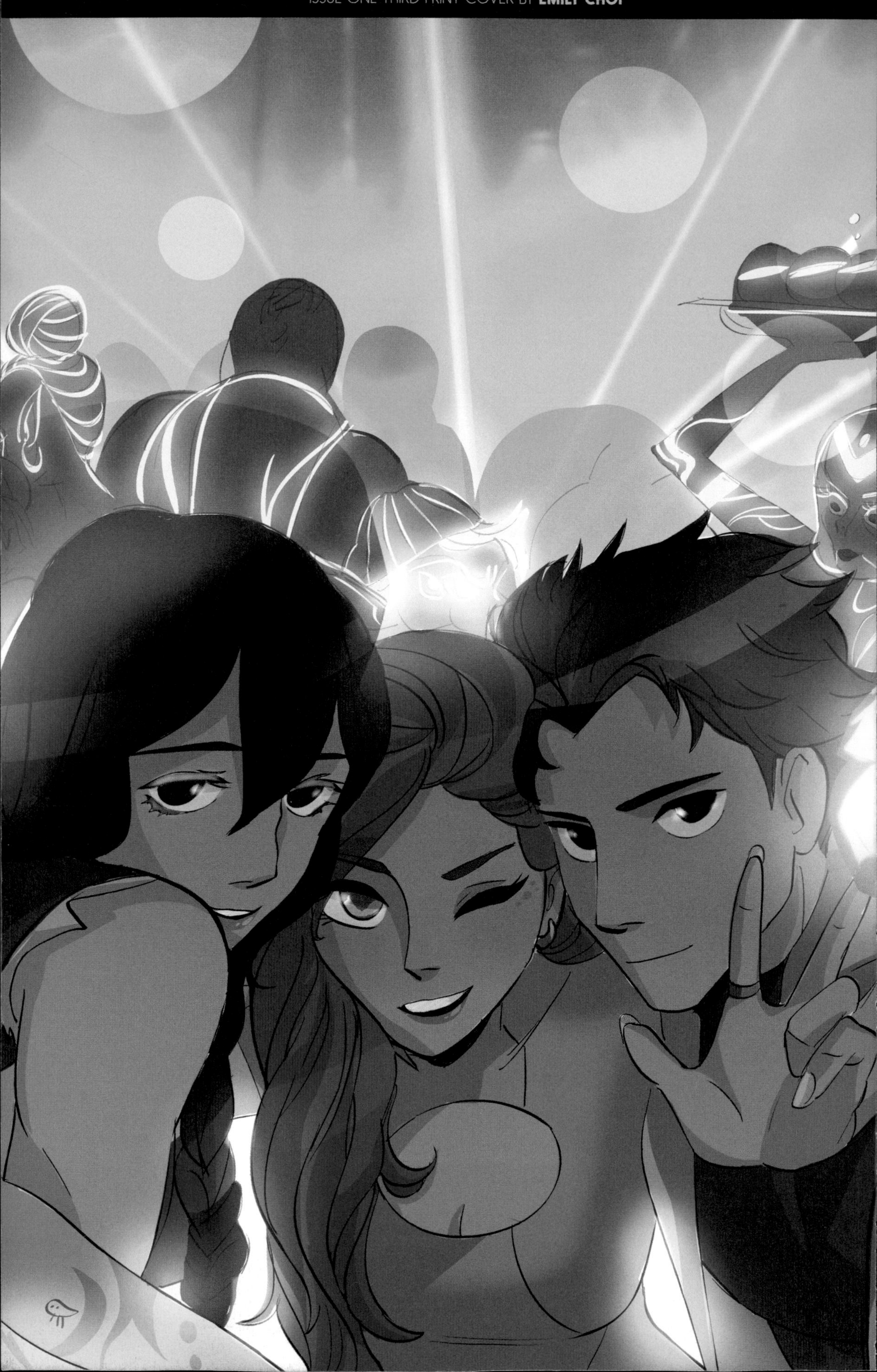

ISSUE TWO SECOND PRINT COVER BY **IAN HERRING**

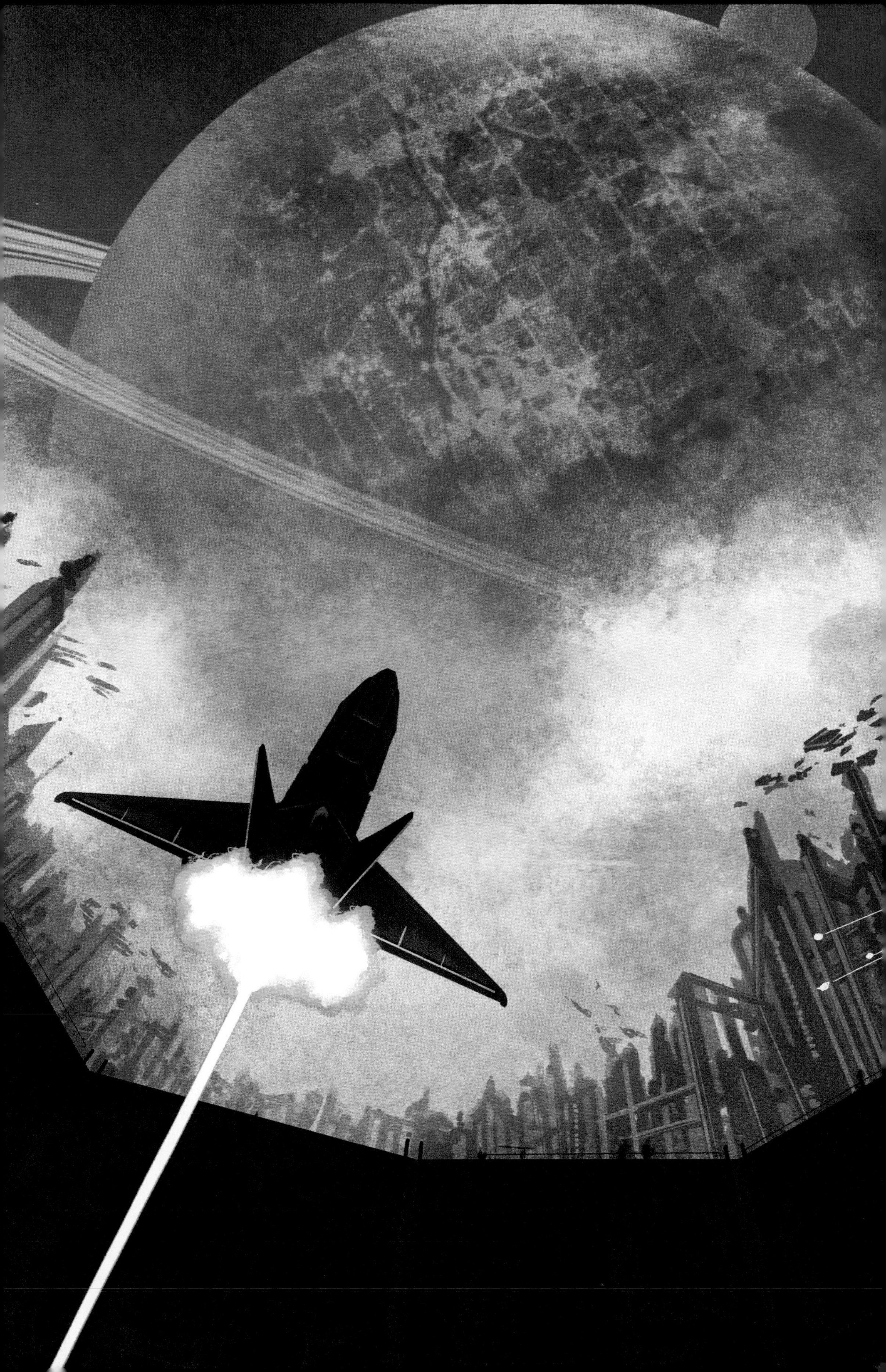

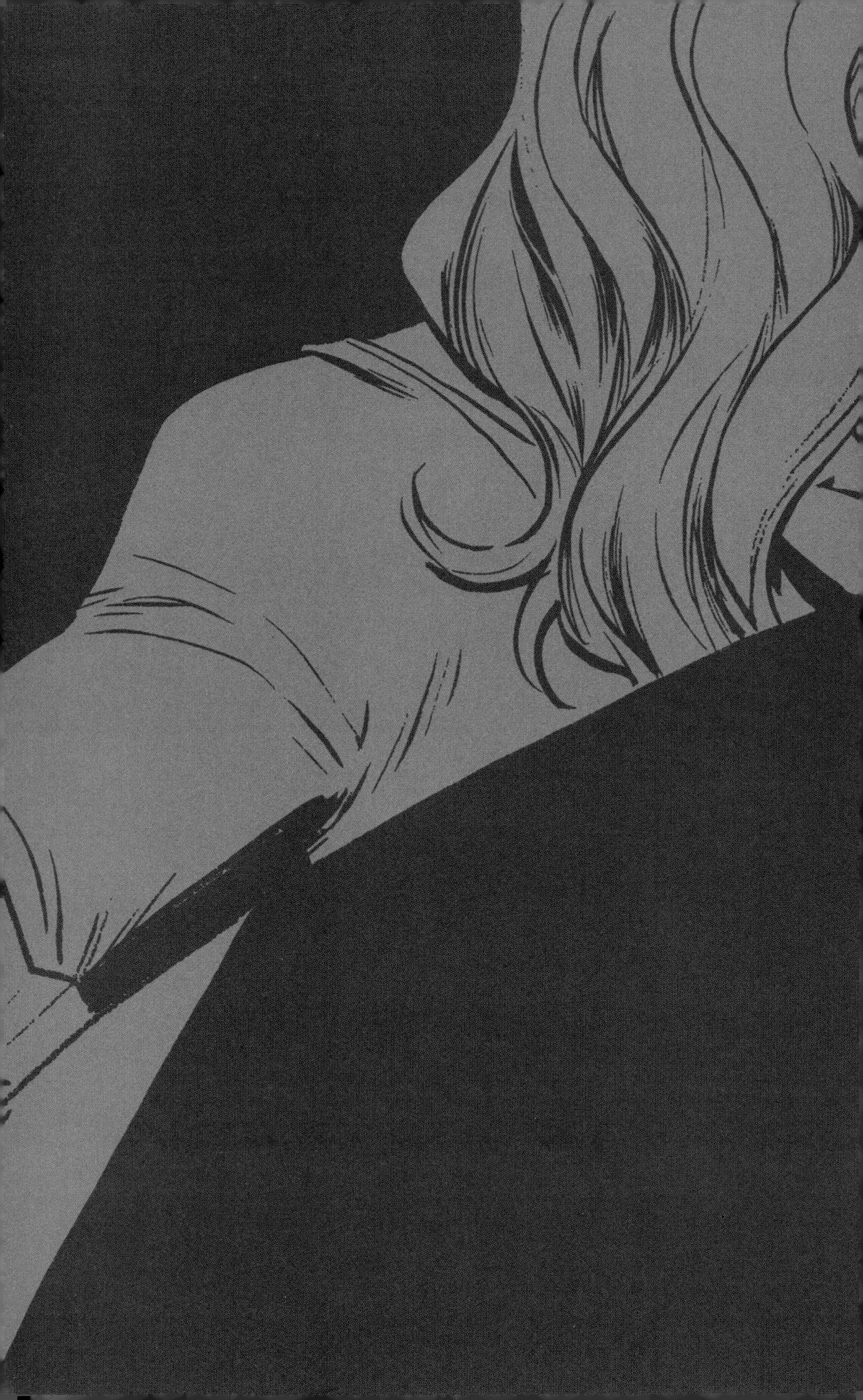

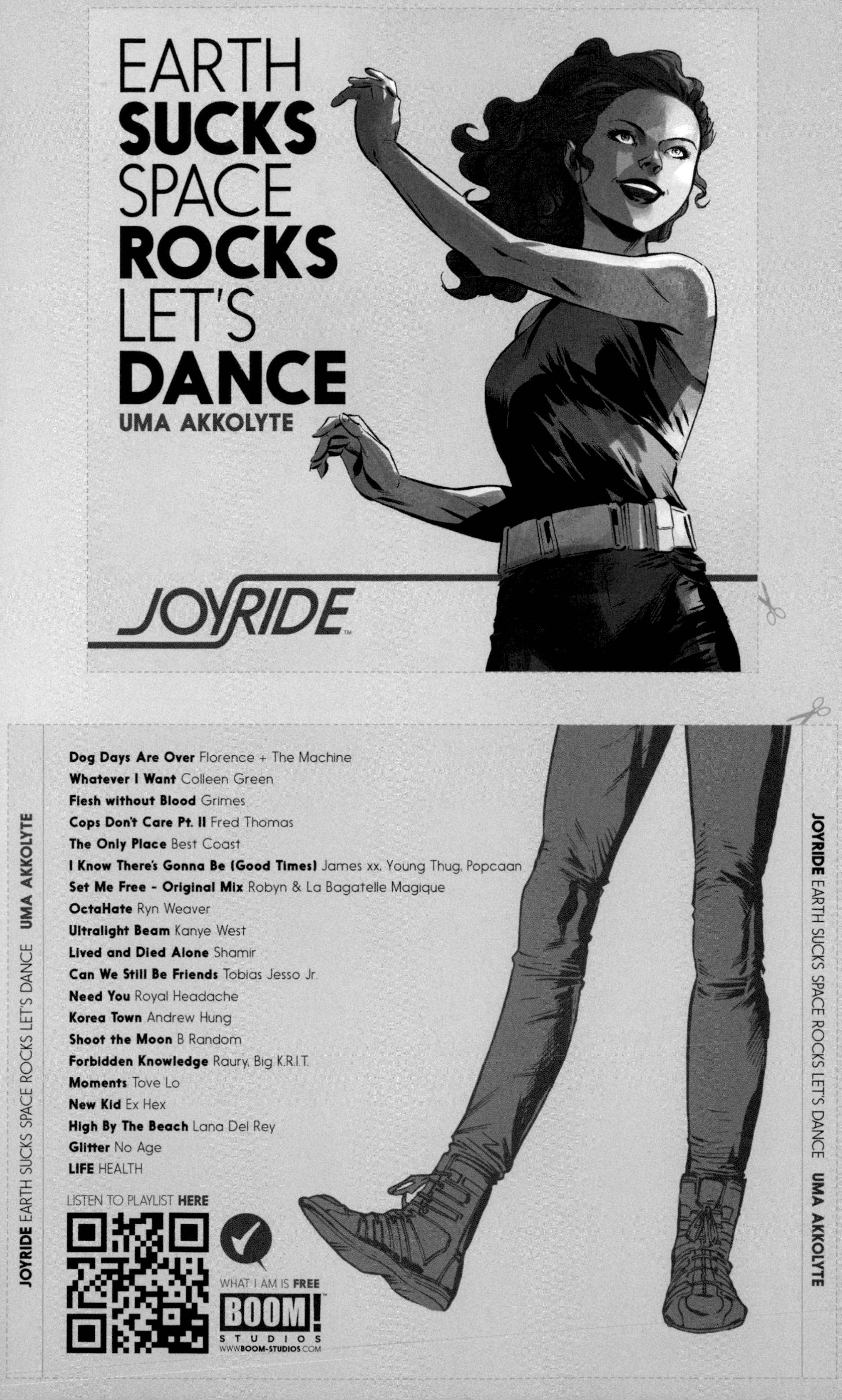
EARTH
SUCKS
SPACE
ROCKS
LET'S
DANCE
UMA AKKOLYTE
JOYRIDE™
Dog Days Are Over Florence + The Machine
Whatever I Want Colleen Green
Flesh without Blood Grimes
Cops Don't Care Pt. II Fred Thomas
The Only Place Best Coast
I Know There's Gonna Be (Good Times) James xx, Young Thug, Popcaan
Set Me Free - Original Mix Robyn & La Bagatelle Magique
OctaHate Ryn Weaver
Ultralight Beam Kanye West
Lived and Died Alone Shamir
Can We Still Be Friends Tobias Jesso Jr.
Need You Royal Headache
Korea Town Andrew Hung
Shoot the Moon B Random
Forbidden Knowledge Raury, Big K.R.I.T.
Moments Tove Lo
New Kid Ex Hex
High By The Beach Lana Del Rey
Glitter No Age
LIFE HEALTH
LISTEN TO PLAYLIST HERE
WHAT I AM IS FREE
BOOM! STUDIOS
WWW.BOOM-STUDIOS.COM
JOYRIDE EARTH SUCKS SPACE ROCKS LET'S DANCE UMA AKKOLYTE
JOYRIDE EARTH SUCKS SPACE ROCKS LET'S DANCE UMA AKKOLYTE

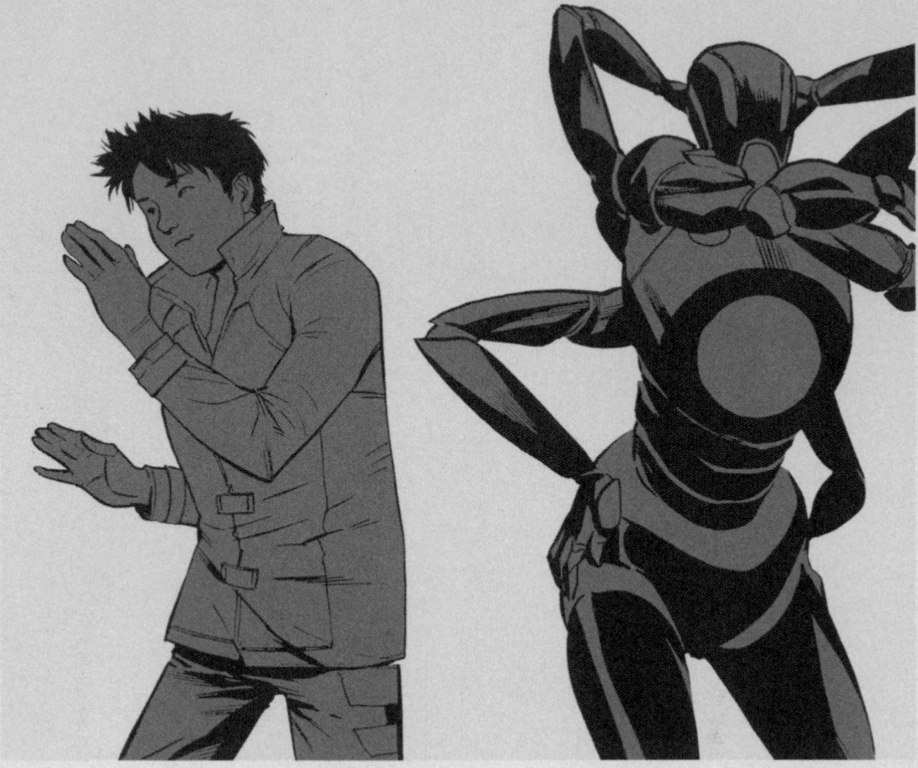

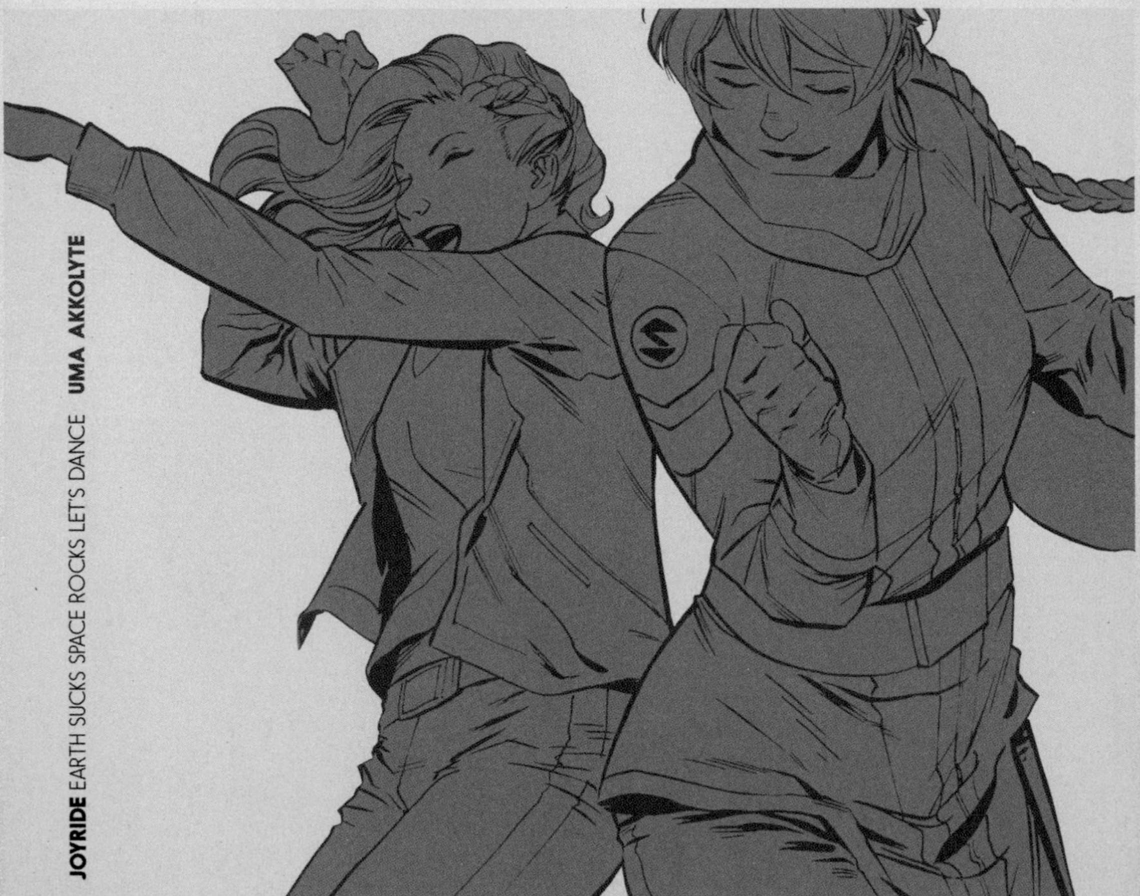

JOYRIDE EARTH SUCKS SPACE ROCKS LET'S DANCE **UMA AKKOLYTE**